No
2003
10-2006

D0651862

More Praise for *Why the Bottom Line Isn't!*

Dave Ulrich and Norm Smallwood lend great insights about what creates value. Executives should find it an enormous help in developing their organizations and their leadership styles. It's also a terrific source of analytic tools and how-to advice.

> —Ed Lawler, professor of Management and Organization, the Marshall School of Business, USC, and a founding director of USC's Center for Effective Organizations

Why The Bottom Line Isn't! is inspirational for every executive, as increasingly intangibles are the drivers of sustainable value creation. Ulrich and Smallwood demystify the management of what we usually call the "soft stuff." They provide clear and practical ways for thinking through the issues around your company's intangibles, and help you find out how the firm is actually dealing with them and what you can do to improve your company's ability to generate value from them. A must read for aspiring and seasoned leaders in meeting their most important challenges.

> —Rolf Huppi, former CEO of Zurich Financial Services

Investors, employees, and customers have intertwined the worlds of investing and stock prices with the psychological world of expectation and confidence. More specifically, how the world judges the value of an organization's intangible qualities—its leadership, teamwork, ability to learn, innovate, and develop strategy—is key to a willingness to buy shares or make a commitment to any organization. In this masterful and groundbreaking work, Ulrich and Smallwood have made these critically important intangibles so specific that leaders can develop and use them to create ever increasing levels of success.

> —Judith Bardwick, author of *Seeking the Calm in the Storm: Managing Chaos in Your Business Life*

We tend to spend our time worrying about the financial statements when, in many cases, our best opportunity to improve results is working on the intangible value of our organization, such as improving distribution, brand, and talent. Anyone who wants to know about how the overall value of a business is derived should read this book from cover to cover. Many of the ideas and observations have already worked their way into my day-to-day business activities. I don't mind if you don't read and apply the concepts; I'll have that much more of a head start on you and your company.

—Jerry J. Carnahan, chief marketing officer, Farmers
Insurance Group, Inc.

658.4
ULR

Why the Bottom Line Isn't!

How to Build Value Through People and Organization

Dave Ulrich
Norm Smallwood

WILEY

John Wiley & Sons, Inc.

Copyright © 2003 by Dave Ulrich and Norman Smallwood. All rights reserved.

Published by John Wiley & Sons, Inc., Hoboken, New Jersey.
Published simultaneously in Canada.

No part of this publication may be reproduced, stored in a retrieval system, or transmitted in any form or by any means, electronic, mechanical, photocopying, recording, scanning, or otherwise, except as permitted under Section 107 or 108 of the 1976 United States Copyright Act, without either the prior written permission of the Publisher, or authorization through payment of the appropriate per-copy fee to the Copyright Clearance Center, Inc., 222 Rosewood Drive, Danvers, MA 01923, (978) 750-8400, fax (978) 750-4470, or on the web at www.copyright.com. Requests to the Publisher for permission should be addressed to the Permissions Department, John Wiley & Sons, Inc., 111 River Street, Hoboken, NJ 07030, (201) 748-6011, fax (201) 748-6008. E-mail: permcoordinator@wiley.com.

Limit of Liability/Disclaimer of Warranty: While the publisher and author have used their best efforts in preparing this book, they make no representations or warranties with respect to the accuracy or completeness of the contents of this book and specifically disclaim any implied warranties of merchantability or fitness for a particular purpose. No warranty may be created or extended by sales representatives or written sales materials. The advice and strategies contained herein may not be suitable for your situation. The publisher is not engaged in rendering professional services, and you should consult a professional where appropriate. Neither the publisher nor author shall be liable for any loss of profit or any other commercial damages, including but not limited to special, incidental, consequential, or other damages.

For general information on our other products and services please contact our Customer Care Department within the United States at (800) 762-2974, outside the United States at (317) 572-3993 or fax (317) 572-4002.

Wiley also publishes its books in a variety of electronic formats. Some content that appears in print may not be available in electronic books. For more information about Wiley products, visit our Web site at www.wiley.com.

Library of Congress Cataloging-in-Publication Data:

Ulrich, David, 1953–
  Why the bottom line isn't! : how to build value through people and organization / Dave Ulrich, Norman Smallwood.
    p. cm.
  ISBN 0-471-44510-X (cloth)
  1. Organizational effectiveness.   2. Value added.   3. Corporations—Valuation.   4. Business enterprises—Valuation.   5. Intangible property.   I. Smallwood, W. Norman.   II. Title.
HD58.9.U474 2003
658.4—dc21

2002156192

Printed in the United States of America.

10   9   8   7   6   5   4   3   2   1

For our wives—Wendy and Tricia

Preface

This book began in what now seems like another time and another place. We did much of the thinking and work for this book in the late 1990s and into the early 2000s. We were curious as to why one firm's stock prices went sky high and another's stayed unchanged in the same industry with the same earnings. Our simple assumption was that two firms in the same industry with the same earnings should have had the same market value. It was just not so. In the rising market, some firms' stock prices went crazy while others did not. We were seeking a more rational explanation of this phenomenon as we worked to define the intangible attributes (or qualities) that communicated value to an investment community. In this era, leaders of large, global companies were bigger than life and were trusted to continue doing what they were doing, reaping unheard of market value for themselves and their firms. Our initial work on intangibles showed that investor confidence in leadership, employees, and the firm's culture increased market value as much as or more than financial performance.

In this era of positive intangibles, we often heard how helpful our concepts were for understanding the bull market. We remember meeting with the leadership development staff at Cisco when their price-to-earnings multiple was 150+ while the average in their industry was in the high 30s. Clearly, Cisco had built a reputation for knowing how to build market value by moving fast and learning how to do acquisitions the right way. It didn't hurt them that John Chambers,

Cisco's popular CEO, was regularly on the cover of many high circulation business magazines.

We also remember a meeting in Switzerland when an executive in the insurance industry asked us how AOL possibly could have purchased Time Warner. "Wasn't AOL a lot smaller than Time Warner?" We were able to show him the differences among revenues, earnings, and market value, and it made what seemed like an aberration understandable.

But by the time we started putting our ideas into final form in 2002, the business world had totally changed—terrorist attacks in New York City and the rest of the world, a longer than expected recession, ongoing news about dishonest earnings, corporate executives facing jail time, stock market declines, the collapse of several global companies with household names. This world was the era of negative intangibles. We originally worried that our ideas conceived in a different time would not matter anymore. We were wrong. Interestingly, our concepts about building intangibles have been equally useful in helping people understand the bear (down) market.

In bull markets, some companies get more market value than others. In bear markets, some company's market value falls more than others. This book helps to explain why. The bear market also underscores our point that the first level for building intangible value—keeping promises—is the key to improvement. Employees, customers, and investors must trust that a company will do what it promises to do before giving the company greater levels of intangible value. So, the concept of intangibles works during both up and down markets and provides some predictability about what might happen to a particular company depending on the strength of its intangibles. The ideas we derived in an up market now apply even more robustly in a down market.

As we have done our work on intangibles, we want to be clear about our unique contribution. Others (notably Baruch Lev and his colleagues) have recognized the importance of intangibles and especially the importance of measuring them. Our unique focus has been in trying to define how leaders build intangible value in their organizations. We have outlined some practical ideas for what actions leaders can take to build intangible value. Because it is so easy to focus on measurement and to find out about things that are easy to measure, we fear that some may fall into the trap of measuring too much, too often, and miss the point. We can measure a firm's R&D investment from public data, but we don't believe that leaders should spend all their time figuring out what percentage of revenues they should spend on R&D to affect intangibles. We wanted to make intangibles tangible for leaders and to communicate our ideas to leaders who can use the ideas day-to-day. We wanted leaders to be able to figure out how their daily decisions increase or protect the intangible value of their company.

Each chapter presents an intangible as a conceptual idea, with examples of how it has been used, and with tools for how leaders can deliver intangibles. As such, our unique contribution is not a clarion call for that specific intangible, nor a rigorous way to measure them, but a focus on what leaders can and should do to build intangible value.

With this more practical focus, we have tried to shift the responsibility of generating positive intangibles away from either the financial professionals or from senior managers who set strategic direction. Rather, the tools provided here are accessible to leaders of all functions and at all levels of an organization, and value *must* be created at all levels for maximum effect.

We should also note that our work lays out where human resource professionals can and should focus their attention. With an increasing scrutiny of ideas and programs, HR professionals must ensure that their work adds value. They can do so when their concepts, tools, and advice help build or protect market value. The outcome of leadership training is not just happier leaders, leaders with more skills, or leaders able to implement projects through action learning, but also leaders who build confidence in customers and investors and who deliver more shareholder value as a result.

We have also learned that this work applies to organizations of all types. We began the work with a focus on business organizations. As we have begun to pay more attention to other types of organizations (e.g., churches, schools, government agencies), we have found that the ideas from business quickly and easily translate to all types of organizations. Churches, for example, may have positive or negative intangibles or reputations, some of which are within their control and others outside their control. Building intangible value for a church involves working on the factors that are in the control of church leaders. This could include community relations, quality and capability of leadership, responsiveness to various community stakeholders, membership involvement in service projects, and so on. These intangibles impact the responsiveness of present and potential believers and charitable donations. Public agencies, school systems, and service organizations may have positive or negative intangibles often called goodwill. In these organizations, leaders may also act to help or hinder the creation of such intangibles.

We have worked very hard to ensure that this book is relevant for an up and down economy; that it has plenty of ideas based on sound theory but with a focus on implementation; that it is widely applicable from senior to lower management in both large and small firms as well as publicly traded and privately held companies.

We know our work is not definitive. Much more can be done to fill in the outline that we have sketched. We plan to continue in this work and we hope that others will collaborate with us. For more information about our work, visit our Web site at rbl.net.

DAVE ULRICH   NORM SMALLWOOD
Montreal, Canada   *Provo, Utah*

Acknowledgments

We cannot and will not take all the credit for producing this book. Two thoughtful and creative editors put their hearts and souls into helping us—Hilary Powers and Maryanne Koschier. Paula Sinnott and Larry Alexander at Wiley provided guidance that was invaluable.

Our Results-Based Leadership partners, Rich Lynch and Jim Dowling, provided helpful feedback throughout the writing. Special thanks go to Ginger Bitter and Kaylene Allsop for their indefatigable research and administrative support at every step.

We have drawn on ideas from many people. Baruch Lev has paved the way for the intangible work from a financial and accounting point of view. Ray Reilly corrected many of our misconceptions about this work. Wayne Brockbank and Dick Beatty have been important colleagues who have shaped our thinking and teaching at the university and in many other clients. We are especially indebted to Steve Kerr whose ideas and nudging ensures that we are on track and dealing with the right issues around measurement, accountability, leadership, and culture. We have drawn on work by Ed Lawler, Jac Fitzenz, Mark Huselid, Brian Becker, Warren Wilhelm, and Ron Bendersky to help link intangibles into the HR mainstream. From the strategy field, we have consistently drawn on work by C. K. Prahalad, Gordon Hewitt, Ram Charan, Gary Hamel, and Jim Collins.

Jack Zenger; Jon Younger; Joe Folkman; Victor Agruso; Jim Intagliata; Josh, Brittney, Ashley, and Zariah Quai; Ken LeBaron;

Betty Wardlaw; Doreen Hussey; and Elizabeth and Ted Hunter provided critical input and support and reviewed manuscripts. Greg Madsen and Dave Jacobs helped us make several of the more academic ideas accessible. Lynn Carnes tracked down hard-to-find information. Our agents, Rich Hill and Greg Link, were willing to give us information we sometimes could not hear from others. Murray Heibert has a knack for coming up with chapter titles and providing critical guidance.

Several colleagues and friends read and often reread drafts and offered feedback—Pete Sorenson, Buzz Nielsen, Dixon Thayer, Larry Harper, Scott Harper, and Judy Seegmiller. Others such as Bonner Ritchie, Lynda Gratton, Bob Kaplan, Marshall Goldsmith, Ron Ashkenas, Dale Lake, Jeffrey Pfeffer, and David Aaker continue to challenge us by their ideas and shape our thinking.

Many client-friends offered invaluable advice, including, but not limited to: Susan Curtis from StorageTek; John Nelson from Emmis; Jack Mastrianni, Paul Butler, Charlie Delacroce from Gillette; Laura Abioudon from Brady; Michael Volkema from Herman Miller; Katy Barclay from General Motors; Jens Maier from Zurich Financial; Ralph Christensen formerly from Hallmark; John and Pat Lawton from Scotia Bank; Paul McKinnon from Dell; Tony Rucci from Cardinal Health; Jim Madden and Bruce Ferguson from Exult.

We are indebted to the late Gene Dalton for his contributions.

D. U.

N. S.

Contents

1

Tangling with Intangibles: Knowing the New Game

The bottom line means business. It is about hard numbers that tell it like it is. It is *the* way to measure success. It focuses attention. It stops arguments. It is the scorecard. It is clear, precise, and understood. It is what all leaders aspire to and what organizations are evaluated by. It is the way it is. When any leader utters this sacred phrase—the bottom line—employees should put their heads down and get to work. In fact, the bottom line isn't what business is all about. It isn't the clear and precise numbers managers have been led to believe. It isn't the right scorecard for business success. It isn't the measure managers should go after while ignoring all other things. It isn't the way it is anymore. This book explores a new bottom line that creates real market value. In this new bottom line, the soft stuff is as important as the hard stuff because it builds customer, investor, and employee confidence about the future. Because leaders want to build confidence about the future, they need to discover a new bottom line, one focused on creating value through people and organization. When they do so, they will find that remarkable things happen. Employees are more committed, customers more satisfied, and investors are more confident.

The goal of this book is simple. *Why the Bottom Line Isn't* helps leaders at all levels create sustainable shareholder value and enables communication of this value to all interested parties, namely, the shareholders, the investment community, the regulators, the customers, and the employees of the organization. Accomplishing this purpose requires an integration of ideas from a number of different disciplines. It involves an understanding of the new role that intangibles play in company valuations and new shifts in thinking about organizational theory. It invites leaders in human resources, accounting, finance, and information technology to consider new dimensions to their roles. Ultimately, it challenges the reader to become a new breed of leader who is an architect of intangibles for his or her company.

Why the Bottom Line Isn't is based on our consulting experience with a wide range of companies, as well as research of leaders in the fields of organization behavior, finance, and accounting. It is based on the premise that there has been a change in the components of market valuation. The traditional viewpoint is that when a firm earns more money, its value goes up. The more it earns, the more investors value it. In recent years, however, that logic has begun to twist. Firms in the same industry and with similar earnings may have vastly different market values. This is based on the intangible value-components of a company.

Intangibles Make the Difference in Market Valuation

We visited with a CEO of a high-tech firm a few years ago and asked him, "What keeps you awake at night? What are you most worried about?" He replied that he worried about his firm's price/earnings ratio because it was half that of his largest competitor. This meant that investors valued his earnings at half of the earnings of his competitor. If both firms earned $100, his firm's price earnings (P/E) ratio of 20 meant the market value of his $100 was $2,000; his competitors' P/E of 40 meant that their $100 was worth $4,000. He said that he could cut costs 10 percent or increase revenue 10 percent but still significantly trail in the market value game. Earnings did not correlate with market value. He wondered how he could improve market value and sustain that value over time.

Another large global firm had a new CEO who wanted to transform the company—to change its culture and help it become more responsive to customers. He was having trouble getting his senior team to support this initiative and invited us to talk to them. At the beginning of the talk, we presented a chart showing this firm's P/E ratio for the last decade compared to the P/E ratio of its largest competitor. While the lines varied at times, the pattern over the decade was that this firm's P/E was consistently about 20 percent below that of its largest competitor. We pointed out that the chart showed that the market consistently valued this firm's earnings lower than those of the competitor. In trying to make sense of this difference, we suggested that the senior management team look into how their leadership actions may have contributed to the lessening of their market value.

Success makes its own story. Jack Welch has been described as a global business icon—and the description is well deserved. Table 1.1 shows some of Welch's financial results at General Electric (GE) from the period 1980 through the year 2000. The figures tell the story. During Welch's twenty years as CEO, GE's revenues grew dramatically (five times) through mergers, acquisitions, and internal business growth. Even more impressive, earnings rose almost 8.5 times. The growth in revenues increased the net earnings percentage by 70 percent. However, the most impressive number is market capitalization,

Table 1.1   Welch's Skyrocket

	1980	2000	Change (Multiple)
Revenue	$25.5 billion	$129.9 billion	5.09
Earnings	$1.5 billion	$12.7 billion	8.47
Market value	$61.25/share 228 million shares	$47.94/share 9.9 billion shares	
	$13.97 billion	$476.6 billion	34.1

which grew 34 times. Welch was not just masterful at growing revenue, reducing costs, and producing earnings, he found a way to communicate to the investment community the increased market value of those earnings.

What do these three stories have in common? They share variations in market value. Firms that earn the same profits may have vastly different market valuations even within the same industry. This information is important for leaders who desire to create market value, as well as for the employees who make the thousands of decisions that may increase or decrease a firm's market value. Although shareholder value is not the only outcome of interest to leaders, it ultimately drives and underlies most leadership choices and decisions. Without sustainable financial performance as measured in market value, firms don't have resources to provide for employees and customers. Increased shareholder value makes employees more committed and affects customers' ability to get new products. Figuring out how day-to-day decisions affect shareholder value becomes a primary goal of leaders, employees, and investors.

Determining the sources of market value becomes increasingly complex. The historical and simple answer is that when earnings go up, market value goes up. Firms that make more money should have more value to investors. However, as indicated in the first two cases, in the real world, firms with the same earnings may have vastly different market valuations.

Leadership Impacts Intangibles

Recent events at Enron, Worldcom, Tyco International, Rite Aid, Imclone Systems, and elsewhere are examples of the negative impact that intangibles have on market value. Leaders in these companies have destroyed billions of dollars of tangible and intangible market value for their own companies and have eroded the public's perception of the entire market. The public mood is currently one of confusion and distrust about the stock market because of the dishonest actions of a few. Only recently, the perception of corporate executives was completely different and the markets were infused with very positive intangible value. During the bull market, when everyone was making money, many executives attained celebrity status. These executives were seen as business geniuses who deserved high pay and perks. Ten years ago, in one of the first big windfalls, Roberto C. Goizueta, the chief executive of Coca-Cola received $80 million in pay and prepared to explain it at the annual meeting. Shareholders did not need convincing. During his speech, he was applauded four times, and no one criticized his pay. Everyone believed that leaders played an integral role in driving positive intangible market value.

You might conclude from recent events that intangible value is a function of the economic cycle. We disagree. When the dot-com bubble burst, the recession set in and stories of dishonesty grew, some firms' market value fell more than others. Firms that survived the market credibility crisis did so because their leaders made the intangibles tangible. These leaders met financial goals, had a strategy for growth, created core competencies aligned with strategy, and ensured organization capabilities. Intangibles often exist *within* an industry, not across industries. The patterns of P/E ratios of firms within an industry offer evidence of leadership intangibles in both up and down markets.

The concept of intangibles has a history outside business. Successful sports teams are often characterized by intangibles: the drive among teammates, the quality of coaching, the ability to win, and the like. Leaders of sports franchises build intangible value by promising and then delivering on successful seasons. They invest in public relations and often make key players larger than life—modern-day heroes and heroines. They sell memorabilia that further solidifies their fans' identification with their team. They work hard at selecting the best coaching and player talent possible and then invest even more in building a team culture for winning. Players and coaches are held accountable for performance. High performance results in big salaries and longer tenure. Poor performance leads to trades with other teams or getting cut.

In business settings, understanding and being able to leverage intangibles is of enormous interest to leaders. When intangibles are defined, leaders may make choices that affect not only what happens inside their firm, but also how investors value those decisions. Contrary to other more precise financial definitions of intangibles,[1] we define intangibles as the *value of a company not accounted for by current earnings.* Companies with high intangible value have higher P/E multiples than their competitors, and like coaches of successful teams, their leaders have earned the perception that they can be trusted to deliver on their promises about the future.

Three Streams of Thinking Lay the Foundation for the Architecture for Intangibles

Three streams of thinking further expand an understanding of business intangibles. They are in the areas of accounting, valuation measures, and organizational theory. For the remainder of this chapter, we look at accounting principles and recent studies regarding market valuations of intangibles. We examine the evolution of the balanced scorecard that has been used by many companies as a tool for strategic mapping and as a way to build organizational value. We explore the shift from a focus on organizational structure to organizational capabilities as a way to enhance market value. With these final foundation pieces, we then present our architecture for building intangible value in your firm.

First, Traditional Accounting Rules Are under Attack

Accountants try to figure out the true value of a firm's assets, but the value of the firm itself will almost always differ substantially from the number they come up with. What investors are willing to pay for a firm's assets—that is, its *market value* (stock price times shares outstanding)—provides a primary indicator of overall firm value. Investors seek information that helps them determine a firm's value.

Unfortunately, in recent years, the financial data publicly reported by firms do not reflect the accurate value of a firm. For example, *BusinessWeek* reports that earnings reported in a variety of forms (net income; operating earnings; core earnings; pro forma earnings; earnings before interest, taxes, depreciation, and amortization [EBITDA]; and adjusted earnings) have become increasingly suspect.[2] At Enron, executives used one derivative to hedge another derivative and allegedly used off-the-book transactions to hide $1 billion in debt and to inflate profits. As a result of concerns about publicly reported earnings, accountants have looked for more robust and accurate representations of a firm's market value, and this search has led to the study of intangibles.

Intangibles show up in business by boosting—or undercutting—investors' confidence in a firm's performance. Baruch Lev, an accounting professor at New York University and the thought leader on intangibles, has shown the importance of intangibles as indicated through the market-to-book value (the ratio of capital market value of companies compared to their net asset value) of the S&P 500 from 1977 to 2001, which has risen from 1 to over 6 in the past 25 years—suggesting that for every $6 of market value, only $1 occurs on the balance sheet.[3] This data shows that the value of many firms comes as much from perceived value as from hard assets. Firms like Coca-Cola and Merck have high market value from brands and patents. Technology-based firms like Amazon and Exult have high market value with relatively little in the way of either hard assets or patents. Even traditional companies like General Motors and 3M are increasing market value by focusing on brands, leveraging the Web, and restructuring.

Lev has defined intangibles from a financial perspective as a claim to future benefits that does not have a physical or financial (stock or bond) embodiment. He further identified sources of intangibles as discovery, organization, and human resources. *Discovery intangibles* include patents, trademarks, R&D programs, royalties, and innovations. Firms able to innovate through discovery have a higher market value than firms that do not. *Organization intangibles* include technology, brands, and customer costs. When leaders know how to manage these organization factors, they build more future value from present earnings. *Human resource intangibles* focus on training, culture, and leadership. Lev further suggests that the human resource domain of intangibles requires more work.

He argues that more accurate accounting systems should reflect the entire value of the firm, including both tangible and intangible assets. Tangible assets may be reliably measured and tracked and predictably valued, but intangible ones pose a more difficult problem—reflected in the way tangible assets are accounted for as assets and intangibles as expenses. The future value of tangible investments is relatively easy to specify (say, the depreciation of a building or plant). The future value of intangibles is more difficult to account for because the probability of a successful investment is less likely (i.e., it is harder to predict that an innovative idea will lead to shareholder return). He advocates creating a *value-chain scorecard* to track intangibles and forming an accounting policy-making body with input from the SEC to standardize and track intangible information.

With a similar viewpoint, Harvard professor Robert Eccles and his colleagues at PricewaterhouseCoopers (PwC) call for a "value reporting revolution" by changing financial reports to include more intangible information.[4] They find that only 19 percent of investors and 27 percent of analysts "found financial reports very useful in communicating the true value of companies." They argue for changing the performance measurement game to better allocate capital and assess the true value of firms. In identifying better measures of firm performance, they focus on "key performance measures—both financial and nonfinancial, and how they relate to each other, that they are measured and reported on, and that they create real value."

The rationale for their work comes from many studies, one of which (by PwC) asked CFOs, heads of investor relations, and other executives to evaluate 37 performance indicators. They found three clusters of performance indicators that mattered most:

1. *Customers:* Sales and marketing costs, distribution channels, brand equity, and customer turnover rates
2. *Employees:* Intellectual capital, employee retention, and revenue per employee
3. *Innovation:* Revenues from new products, new product success rate, R&D expenditures, and product development cycle

By focusing on these intangibles, investors can better determine the true value of a firm. Given that analysts and investors seldom access this intangible information, that companies don't provide it, and that it is somewhat random, the value revolution Eccles and his colleagues advocate seems a long way off, however much it may be desired. The Fair Disclosure (FD) regulation issued by the SEC in October 2000 encourages more open information to avoid insider-trading abuses, but the substance of that information is still vague.

Ernst & Young's Center for Business Innovation also attempted to find out how investors use nonfinancial information in valuing firms. They interviewed and surveyed investors on both the buy and sell sides of equity transactions to assess the importance of nonfinancial intangible issues in decision making. They found that nonfinancial measures do matter to corporate executives, and that investors consider these measures when valuing companies.[5] In the conclusion of their study, they find that nonfinancial criteria constitute, on average, 35 percent of the investor's decision. Sell-side analysts use nonfinancial data when evaluating companies and making buy/sell decisions, and the more nonfinancial measures analysts use, the more accurate their earnings forecasts prove to be.

Eight measures matter most:

1. *Execution of corporate strategy:* Management's ability to leverage skills and expertise, gain employee commitment, and align with shareholders
2. *Quality of strategy:* Vision for the future, making tough decisions, allocating resources
3. *Ability to innovate:* R&D pipeline, adapt to technologies
4. *Ability to attract talented people:* Hire, reward, develop, and keep the best
5. *Market share:* Current and future
6. *Quality of executive compensation:* Pay tied to strategic goals
7. *Quality of major processes:* Managing operations, ability to change
8. *Research leadership:* Creating and using knowledge

These findings and factors indicate that nonfinancial measures matter; they influence investor decisions and thus affect shareholder value. That is, total value creation comes from the creation of value to shareholders from customers, employees, suppliers, and communities.

In the accounting world, these intangibles have implications for reporting the accurate value of a firm's assets. Accountants struggle to measure and make tangible the intangibles, so as to reflect the more accurate value of a firm's total asset base. In this book, rather than debate current accounting systems, we explore how to make future probabilities of intangible investments more predictable. We focus less on how to measure intangibles and more on how leaders at all levels create intangibles. By showing how leaders make choices and decisions that affect intangibles, we can help them reduce intangible variability. Moving into the domain of leadership behavior also responds to Lev's call for more rigor about the human resource elements of intangible value and the Eccles group's call for a value reporting revolution by focusing on organization intangibles.

Second, a Balanced Scorecard Broadens the Definition of Important Measures

Balanced Scorecards have been used by leaders to measure the broad set of indicators that provide information about whether strategy implementation is on track. The balanced scorecard builds on the simple assumption that any organization has multiple stakeholders who must be served. In their foundation work, Robert Kaplan and David Norton discuss four elements of an organization that must be balanced: financial results, customer results, organization processes, and learning and growth.[6] Leaders are successful when they make choices and investments that balance across the four domains. Measurement or control systems succeed when they include measures of each domain.

Kaplan summarizes tangible assets in accounting terms: accounts receivable, land, cash, inventories, property, and equipment. He argues that intangible assets such as reputation, R&D, patents, and other organization elements have become increasingly important to a firm's market value. Table 1.2 shows the percent of market value related to intangible and tangible assets.

Other researchers have also found a link between intangibles and market value. Mark Huselid and Brian Becker, two researchers who link a firm's HR practices to shareholder value, found that an improvement

Table 1.2 Growing Importance of Intangibles

	Intangible (%)	Tangible (%)
1982	38	62
1992	62	38[a]
2000	85	15[b]

[a] Brookings Institute.
[b] Baruch Lev.

in their human capital index (a measure of a firm's investment in innovative HR practices) related to a firm's market value.[7] They, along with Dave Ulrich, have created logic for an HR scorecard that shows how HR practices align with business results. For example, they draw on Sears data showing that a 5 percent increase in employee commitment leads to a 1.8 percent increase in customer commitment and a 0.5 percent increase in financial results.[8] GTE, for example, created an employee engagement index based on seven questions from an employee survey and found that a 1 percent increase in this employee index resulted in a 0.5 percent increase in customer satisfaction.

As Kaplan and Norton acknowledge, the organization or human resource issues (defined as internal processes or learning and growth), are often leading indicators of future customer and investor results. Their work offers many examples of the steps to follow in building a strategy-focused organization through balanced scorecard work. They also acknowledge that designing a perfect scorecard doesn't guarantee success, and that implementation failures are usually the result of poor organization processes rather than poor scorecard design. However, the value that we see in the balanced scorecard is that it moves attention to those areas of the business that affect the intangible assets. These factors, if measured with as much discipline as that given to the financials, tell a story about future financial performance and future value.

Third, Increasing Organization Capabilities Is Key to Future Value

The accounting work demonstrates that intangibles matter; the balanced scorecard work shows that leaders should focus on leading indicators of future success. The missing elements in both domains are the insights into leadership choices and actions that can actually create sustainable intangibles. In other words, how leaders create market value through people and organizational capabilities is key to an increase in their company's valuation.

Leaders bring together people and resources to accomplish work. Traditionally, organizations were characterized by their visible hierarchy or structure or by the processes that were used to accomplish work. Leaders worked either to change the structure (remove people and levels) or to fix the processes through reengineering. Recently, however, work in the study of organizations has been shifting its focus from structure to capabilities.[9]

Capabilities represent the ability of an organization to use resources, get things done, and behave in ways that lead to accomplishment.[10] They form the identity or personality of the firm, govern the way work gets done, and help executives create an organization that succeeds. Rather than defining organizations through their morphology, researchers who observe large numbers of organizations are beginning to see them as bundles of capabilities. When we ask people to identify firms they admire, their replies tend to include firms like Microsoft, General Electric, Nordstrom, or Starbucks. We then ask them how many layers of management are in these firms. No one knows, or even cares. But, when we ask them why they admire the firm, they quickly pinpoint the capabilities of the firm such as the ability to innovate, serve customers, or deliver high-quality customer experiences. Their responses capture the transition from focusing on rules, procedures, policies, levels of management, and other hierarchical mechanisms to a focus on core competencies, processes, and culture. An effective organization is not defined by the number of layers of management, systems in place, or head count but by ability to respond to business demands. The age-old adage "structure follows strategy" is being replaced with "strategy follows from capabilities." Many theorists have picked up on this concept as a way to redefine the nature of organizations.

Capabilities are the skills, abilities, and expertise of the organization—how the people think and what they are able to do. As individual competencies are widely shared throughout the firm, they grow into organizational capabilities when they stop being tied to any one individual or any one program. Such organizational capabilities complement the technical core competencies that are resident in an organization. Organizational capabilities may then be characterized as the internal and external identity of the organization.

We believe that capabilities become the intangibles of a firm that are at the foundation or beginning of strategic maps and that fill in the gap between market and book value. This book focuses on how leaders turn capabilities within a firm into intangible value for a firm.

Architecture for Intangibles: A Blueprint for How Leaders Build Value

Intangibles can become tangible when they are understood and managed, allowing specific leadership actions and choices to define and deliver them on demand. When this is done, employees are more committed, customers feel more intimacy, and investors increase confidence.

This book outlines a way to build your own organization's intangibles. Based on the studies we have just reviewed and our experience as successful (and sometimes unsuccessful) change agents to leaders of global business over the last 20 years, we have formulated an Architecture for Intangibles in Figure 1.1.

This architecture defines four layers of intangibles in which leaders make choices that have impact. In our consulting work, we have seen leaders use the ideas with great impact. The CEO of a large insurance company explained his e-business growth strategy to investors using the framework. The next day, analysts wrote up the presentation in the trade journals using phrases such as, "At last, XYZ Company is putting its money where its mouth is" and "XYZ has a significant insight into how to build these new distribution channels." The financial impact: $1.7 billion dollar increase in market value! (Unfortunately, XYZ did not invest in building real capability and within a few months had lost the entire gain.)

Others have told us that this framework helps them understand Welch's behavior at General Electric. He became a master of building

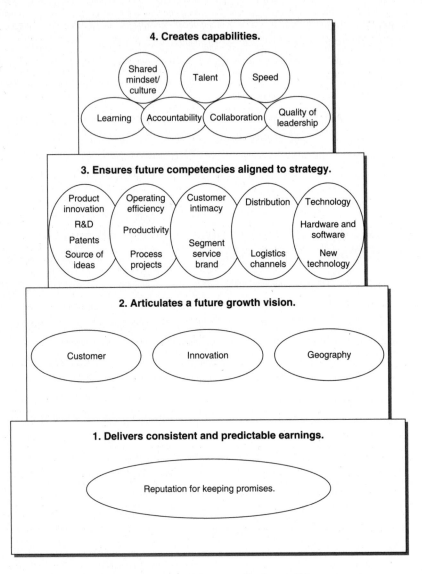

Figure 1.1 Architecture for intangibles.

intangible value. His secret? He developed credibility and the market trusted him to keep his promises. He told customers, investors, and employees exactly what he planned to do and then he worked very hard to ensure that real capability was put in place to deliver it. Earnings were delivered as promised. There were no excuses. In addition, GE leaders at every level spent the past 20 years building strong capabilities for speed and accountability that outpaced competitors. Over time, GE leaders earned a brand identity for developing leaders who deliver on promises. In fact, when Jeffrey Immeldt succeeded Welch and two senior GE leaders left for Home Depot and 3M last year, the stock of Home Depot and 3M increased at a much faster rate than the rest of the market due to raised expectations about future success for these companies.

A human resources (HR) executive in Paris with Boston Scientific is using the Architecture for Intangibles to redefine the role of HR at his company. Bob Hargadon has partnered with line executives to understand the firm's strategy. Based on this understanding, he has made HR responsible for delivering on the two organization capabilities most critical to implementation of the strategy. This includes coordinating with other staff organizations in a much closer way and deploying global centers of excellence led by HR. Within these centers of excellence, HR professionals provide education, coaching, tools, and consulting aimed at increasing impact and value.

With the Architecture for Intangibles, leaders can hype their company and get a temporary blip in value or they can use the Architecture for Intangibles to communicate to all leaders in their company how they can contribute to build a stronger organization that is differentiated from others in their industry.

What This Book Includes

The subsequent chapters discuss each level in turn. Level 1, "Delivers Consistent and Predictable Earnings," is the most critical of all levels to achieve. Without it, there can be no success in building intangible value at any other level. You must begin there, then evaluate where you are most likely to experience success. We have worked with companies that have built Level 1 and then skipped to Level 4, "Creating Capabilities" in their organization, achieving their desired goal of increased intangible value.

Chapter 2 addresses Intangible Level 1, which focuses on meeting current earnings projections. Leaders who fail to deliver on their promises lose credibility and the investment community loses confidence in them. Regularly meeting financial expectations implies that the leaders know their business, have made wise investments, and have the will to make difficult and innovative decisions to accomplish goals.

Chapter 3 takes up Intangible Level 2, which deals with having a strategy for future growth. Once leaders meet current numbers, they are expected to have a clear strategy for growing the business in the future, in terms of both revenue and cost. The chapter reviews elements of creating a strategy for growth and shows how leaders can install growth strategies for future earnings. When investors have confidence that a leader's strategy will produce a stream of future earnings, the current earnings are valued higher.

Chapter 4 explores Intangible Level 3, which deals with core competencies of the organization. Core competencies in this case refer to the technical or functional requirements for a business to succeed. Core competencies must be tied to specific strategies. The chapter summarizes many of the core competencies required for firms to succeed. When investors perceive that leaders have created core competencies, they have more confidence in future and current earnings.

Chapter 5 begins the discussion of Intangible Level 4, the capabilities of the organization, which continues through next six chapters as well. It focuses on talent. Talent represents the ability of an organization to attract, motivate, and retain the employees it needs for peak performance. Talent implies that the organization with the best, brightest, and most diligent staff will be the one most likely to succeed over time.

Chapter 6 highlights the importance of a shared mindset that establishes the culture or identity of a firm. When a firm has a common identity or culture, customers identify the firm as a brand and employees know what is expected of them. As an intangible, a shared mindset increases customer value by establishing confidence in the firm brand

and increases employee productivity and commitment by reinforcing behavior in accordance with customer expectations.

Chapter 7 discusses the intangible of speed. When executives can build agility, flexibility, or speed into their organizations, good things happen. Being right is not enough when being first is critical. Speed not only allows for first mover advantage into new markets and products, it excites and engages employees.

Chapter 8 highlights the importance of learning or knowledge management. Learning becomes critical to an organization when it attempts to generate and generalize ideas with impact. Leaders who build learning organizations encourage creativity and innovation of ideas within an organization unit, and then build disciplined processes for sharing those ideas across organization units. Learning capacity is an intangible value when organizations have the ability to move ideas across vertical, horizontal, external, and global boundaries.

Chapter 9 emphasizes the intangible of accountability. When organizations have individuals who are accountable for their behavior and outcomes, they have the ability to execute and deliver what they propose. Leaders build organizations with accountability by setting clear goals and having consequences for meeting or missing goals. This chapter defines principles and tools for shaping accountability that leads to execution.

Chapter 10 discusses collaboration as an intangible. Collaboration occurs when the whole is greater than the sum of the parts. Collaboration is required for companies that grow through merger and acquisition, for global companies, and for companies implementing shared services. This chapter explains the principles of collaboration and applies them to each of these settings.

Chapter 11 illustrates how leaders at all levels of the firm become an intangible asset. Effective leaders demonstrate competencies (knowledge, behaviors, and motives) and deliver results. The chapter explores how a leadership brand may be established and integrated into a firm. Investors who perceive a higher quality of leadership will have more confidence in a firm's future earnings opportunities.

Chapter 12, the conclusion, offers prescriptions for building intangibles for senior executives, leaders at all levels, and HR professionals. Creating intangibles is a shared responsibility and leaders throughout a firm must focus on building intangible value. We conclude with prescriptions for creating intangible outcomes via tangible leadership behaviors.

Throughout this book, we offer videoclips, assessments, and tools we have used with our clients. You can complete these assessments and tools right in the book or you can go online and complete them. The benefit of completing the online version is that the materials will be improved and updated over time and your results can be tabulated immediately. The Web site of our firm, Results-Based Leadership, Inc., is www.rbl.net/whythebottomlineisnt.html.

Figure 1.2 is a good place to start trying out these assessments. Once you have completed this form, you will have a good idea about which chapters are of most interest to you based on your assessment of your organization's needs.

Directions:
1. Rate your company for each of the 20 items on the audit.
2. Follow directions for scoring in the far right column.
3. Write down your scores for each of the five areas. Note chapters that correspond to areas with lowest scores:

Score	Related Chapters
Earnings	1, 2
Strategy	3
Core competencies	4
Organization capabilities	5–10
Leadership capabilities	11–12

To What Extent	Assessment 1 = Low; 10 = High	Scoring
1. Has our company delivered consistent and predictable earnings (results) over the past 3 years?		a. Add scores for 1 + 2 = b. Divide by 2 = c. This is your earnings score.
2. Do we have a reputation with our stakeholders that they can depend on what we promise?		

Figure 1.2   Intangibles audit.

To What Extent	Assessment 1 = Low; 10 = High	Scoring
3. Have we communicated a growth strategy to our investors and to our employees?		a. Add scores for 3 + 4 + 5 + 6 + 7 = b. Divide by 5 = c. This is your strategy score
4. Have our businesses articulated how they will be different from competitors?		
5. Have each of our businesses communicated a clear customer value proposition that appeals to their target customers?		
6. Have we developed balanced measures to track results for employees, customers, investors, and the organization?		
7. Does our structure and process for resource allocation match our strategic intent?		
8. Have we built core competencies (technology, operations, marketing and so on) that enable us to deliver what we have promised in our strategies?		a. Add scores for 8 + 9 + 10 = b. Divide by 3 = c. This is your core competency score
9. Have we invested to build certain core competencies at a higher level while maintaining industry parity in others?		
10. Do our leaders understand and support the different levels of investment for these choices?		
11. Have we built capability to ensure that we have the best talent possible?		a. Add scores for 11 + 12 + 13 + 14 + 15 + 16 + 17 = b. Divide by 7 = c. This is your organization capabilities score.
12. Do we rigorously take out costs to ensure overall efficiencies?		

(continued)

Figure 1.2 *Continued*

To What Extent	Assessment 1 = Low; 10 = High	Scoring
13. Do we collaborate effectively to leverage best practices across organization boundaries?		
14. Have we created the conditions where our best customers are treated the way we want them to be whenever and wherever we touch them?		
15. Do we have a learning organization where individuals, teams, and businesses are able to generate new ideas and then transfer them to where they will have most impact?		
16. Have we created the conditions where accountability is valued and high performance makes a difference?		
17. Are we able to move quickly to make necessary changes?		
18. Do leaders at every level know what they should deliver to make needed contributions to company success?		a. Add 18 + 19 + 20 = b. Divide by 3 = c. This is your leadership capability score.
19. Have we articulated what leaders stand for at this company—not only what results we need but how they should be delivered?		
20. Have we created a shared language and common tools for leaders at every level to help implement key organization capabilities?		

Scoring Interpretation

8–10: Excellent. Keep up the good work.

5–7: Needs Work. Get busy.

Less than 5: Important and urgent work needs to be done in this area.

Figure 1.2 *Continued*

Leadership Implications

The premise that intangibles can be built rests on some key assumptions:

- Intangibles determine an increasingly sizable portion of a firm's market value.
- Intangibles are not random; they can and should be managed.
- Intangibles are the responsibility of leadership at all levels of an organization. A CEO worries about intangibles as they affect an entire firm; a vice president focuses on intangibles within a more limited domain of influence; a first-line supervisor emphasizes the intangibles within the work team.
- Intangibles can be increased by applying a set of management tools and disciplines.
- Intangibles occur at hierarchical levels. Without the higher-level intangibles in place, the underlying intangibles will not add value.

The following suggestions will help you decide what to do to begin working on intangibles:

1. Compare your P/E ratio to that of your top competitors for the past 5 and 10 years. How are you doing?
2. Audit your leadership intangibles. The survey in Figure 1.2 provides some basic questions to use.
3. Find ways to present your leadership intangibles to your investors.
4. Find ways to present the intangibles to employees and invite them to find actions they can take to improve them.
5. Create a map that shows probable chains of causation from intangibles to financial results in your company.

2

Do or Die: Anteing Up the Table Stakes

What we have learned in working with organizations and watching the fluctuation of market value over many years is that a company's ability to keep its promises and deliver consistent and predictable earnings creates credibility in the marketplace, and this credibility translates into positive intangibles for the firm.

When an athlete or coach predicts a winning game or a championship season and then delivers, we are impressed with their confidence and we are also impressed by their capability to deliver. Other predictions they make about future success seem plausible. This is what happened in a recent World Cup of soccer. The Brazilian team has a highly successful track record for winning big games, especially the World Cup. Prior to the World Cup competition, several Brazilian players predicted they would win another World Cup. They delivered on their promise to their fans. If they predict that they will win the World Cup the next time, it is easier to believe them. The reverse is also true. If an athlete or a coach predicts a win and then loses, they are seen as braggarts and lose credibility because the promises do not match the results. When they make predictions about future successes, we are unlikely to believe them because they don't have a track record

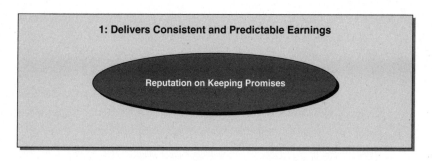

Figure 2.1   Focus on delivering intangibles.

for keeping their promises. Business leaders who consistently deliver on expectations earn credibility; those who do not deliver on expectations erode credibility. Meeting expectations is a starting point for building positive intangibles. Consistently delivering on expectations is what it takes to stay in the positive intangibles game and earns firms the right to increase other intangible levels in the Architecture for Intangibles. Examples abound.

Carly Fiorina, CEO of Hewlett-Packard, publicly targeted goals of revenue increase of 12 percent to 15 percent and equal or higher earnings. She offered guidance to investors and expressed continued confidence. On November 13, 2000, she told the investment community that HP's earnings for the fourth quarter were not going to meet expectations and would miss by a few cents. The company lost $23 billion in market value in the next few days. It didn't matter that even with the fourth-quarter miss, the annual earnings per share total for 2000 was 16 percent higher than 1999. The quarterly shortfall still caused enormous concern. The HP case is, unfortunately, not unique. When leaders lose credibility by making and missing promises, they put at risk not only their personal goodwill but also the intangible value of their firm as seen by investors. Just in the last couple of years, several CEOs were removed before their time:

- *Jacques Nasser at Ford:* Lost the confidence of the Ford family for his handling of Bridgestone/Firestone problems with Explorer tires.

- *Rick Thoman at Xerox:* Promised a return to the good times and then failed in several reorganizations contributing to earnings decline, flat revenues, and a 60 percent decline in the stock.
- *James Goodwin at UAL:* Goodwin resigned under pressure of unions who campaigned to oust him after he announced potential bankruptcy of United just days prior to union contract reviews.
- *Jill Barad at Mattel:* Received a $50 million severance package after leading Mattel into financial disarray.
- *Richard McGuinn at Lucent:* Promised a turnaround and did not deliver.
- *Durk Jager at Procter & Gamble:* Promised high growth and failed to deliver, then preannounced lower than expected Q3 earnings dropping the stock 30 percent in one day.

In many of these cases, the executives were removed because they lost the goodwill of their employees, customers, and investors. Some of this loss was due to making and not delivering on promises. As Ram Charan, a leading business consultant, states:

> Wall Street's unquenchable thirst for higher and higher quarterly earnings has put incredible pressure on CEOs. When expectations are not met, the effects are devastating. As the stock price drops suddenly and steeply, the CEO's credibility and leadership come into question. The value of stock options sinks, and employee morale with it. Any change initiative loses momentum. The CEO is distracted, to say the least, and people in the company begin to gossip. You can feel the energy draining away.[1]

When Good Planning Is Not Enough

Plans for earnings count but delivering earnings counts more. However, the reality is that even good companies with competent leaders can miss projections and lose earnings. Communication to all parties, especially to investors and internal stakeholders, is key to maintaining credibility and trust when this occurs. An example of the importance of communication follows.

Jacques Nasser was fired from Ford Motor Company after profits at Ford fell in the wake of the company's bitter fights with Bridgestone/Firestone over faulty Ford Explorer tires, followed by a series of other embarrassing product recalls. It is easy to speculate about what might have gone on in the corridors of power at Ford. Nasser was a forceful CEO but not a great communicator or relationship builder. His lack of communication prowess ultimately cost him the confidence of the Ford family, particularly Bill Ford. Mud was publicly thrown back and forth between Ford and Bridgestone, causing anger and resentment, particularly given the relationships between the Ford and Firestone families. Many people speculated that if this had been handled more discreetly, it might have had a better outcome. At any rate, shrinking profits, missed earnings, and loss of trust combined to oust Nasser from Ford.

Setting and keeping promises as a form of intangible value is not exclusive to executives in firms. No matter where they work, leaders must meet expectations: a sales manager sets high expectations for sales within her region and must now work to deliver those numbers; a manager of a government agency must meet budget requirements. IT managers earn credibility with their business partners by delivering systems and technology that meet the business units goals and objectives. They cannot make promises and then not meet them. Just think what would happen if human resources managers did not pay bonuses or stock options for performance as outlined in performance programs. Leaders throughout an organization must set and keep promises to earn credibility.

We have laid out the risks of missing expectations, of not having consistent and predictable earnings. Lost earnings erode credibility and eventually market value. However, the positive side of consistent and predictable earnings comes as leaders meet expectations by following some of the guidelines presented in this chapter.

Six Guidelines for Delivering Consistent and Predictable Earnings

Guideline 1: Set Realistic Expectations

When Eastman Kodak produced about $12 billion in revenue, its new CEO articulated his aspiration of becoming a $20 billion company in the next few years. This statement was intended to capture the attention and imagination of employees and point them toward a positive future state. But internal strategies also gain investor attention and expectations. Investors may at first be skeptical of such aggressive growth strategies, but they allow new CEOs to state their desired course. However, rather than see the ambition as aspiration, they interpret it as a promise that must be delivered.

Many of us have experienced the bold new leader who plans to change the past and create the future. With great enthusiasm, the supervisor stops old ways of doing things and invents new ways that have only newness to recommend them and promptly fall afoul of reality. When bold aspirational strategies fail to come to fruition, a cycle of cynicism may follow. Investors interpret failed strategy as a broken promise; employees may become suspicious of endless rounds of strategy statements that don't happen; and a vicious cycle of high hopes with lower outcomes reduces leadership credibility and erodes investor confidence. As evidenced in the Enron case, such erosion can quickly eat away a firm's whole value as missed expectations and lost credibility feed on one another.

On the other hand, executives who fail to lay out bold, aggressive strategies fail to capture hearts and minds of employees or investors. New executives who adopt a "me too" strategy have only moderate expectations, and build extensions rather than innovations that excite neither employees nor investors. Leaders who offer no hope for a better future don't go forward. With this framework in mind, we recommend that you find the balance between stretch and attainable goals and focus goals on a few key priorities.

When expectations are too high, they may lead to cynicism; when too low, they create apathy. Realistic expectations build hope and instill confidence by setting stretch but attainable goals or lowering expectations and then meeting them. Finding the balance between stretch goals that excite and energize but may create cynicism and lackluster goals that are attainable but not exciting may come from learning to set realistic expectations. These expectations ensure predictability of results. They come from being able to manage the paradox of ambition and action, future hope and daily behavior.

Fannie Mae is America's largest supplier of conventional home mortgage funds and the nation's second largest corporation in terms of assets. The company's recent history well illustrates how to set realistic expectations. Fannie Mae's previous CEO Jim Johnson and current CEO Frank Raines have done a superb job of setting and delivering on expectations for more than 15 years. They have achieved this through a series of clear initiatives focused on delivering earnings.

In 1991, Johnson outlined the "Opening Doors to Affordable Housing Initiative." By 1993, Fannie Mae successfully achieved the "Opening Doors" goal of producing $10 billion in purchases for low- and moderate-income and other special housing needs—and it did so more than 16 months ahead of schedule. Given this success, Johnson launched the "Trillion Dollar Commitment" in 1994, pledging $1 trillion in targeted housing finance that would serve 10 million low- to moderate-income families.

In 1998, Johnson retired and Raines became the new CEO. In 1999, Fannie Mae achieved the $1 trillion goal of mortgage loans outstanding, eight months early.

In the successful tradition of stretch goals, Raines announced the American Dream Commitment in early 2000, an initiative to provide $2 trillion in financing to serve 18 million targeted families by the end of the decade. Raines also announced the 646 initiative toward the end of 1999. In 1999, the earnings per share at Fannie Mae were $3.23. The goal of the 646 initiative is to double earnings per share to $6.46 in 2003, continuing the Fannie Mae tradition of delivering double-digit earnings growth. This will be quite a challenge to continue over the long haul—but the goal of $6.46 in 2004 looks very attainable in 2002.

In these and other cases, both imagining the future and enacting the present set expectations. Under the age-old adage, "promise less and deliver more," executives who set realistic expectations that lead to predictability focus goals on a few key priorities; they don't try to be all things to all people. Focusing on a few goals and delivering on them builds more credibility than promising many goals and delivering only a few.

StorageTek is an example of a company that is now getting it right. Based in Broomfield, Colorado, StorageTek, a data storage solutions provider, spent most of the last several years waffling about future direction. At one point, the company was put up for sale but did not find a buyer. High performers departed in droves. It couldn't meet its earnings promises. Its stock tanked.

Pat Martin, a former Xerox executive, took over as CEO of StorageTek in 2000. Martin immediately focused on a back-to-basics approach called Horizon One. He began to talk about accountability and delivering on promises—and he had a performance management system developed and implemented to put teeth in the talk. Leaders were fired. New leaders were hired from inside and outside the industry. The back-to-basics strategy was rolled out to every employee through learning maps—pictures of where the company had been and where it wanted to go in the near future. The new executive team formed and stormed. Almost 200 executives gathered for a leadership conference in the summer of 2001 where—among other more traditional activities—they learned how to play primitive musical instruments to the beat of a large drum that Martin was pounding to represent their direction. Those leaders who did not play an instrument chanted "one vision, one voice," representing their unity of direction in meeting customer expectations and delivering financial results.

In early February 2002, StorageTek met its earnings targets for the fourth consecutive quarter. In late February 2002, *Fortune* magazine named StorageTek as the No. 1 "Most Admired" company in the computer peripherals segment.

Guideline 2: Build Credibility by Degrees

Leaders who want to build consistent and predictable earnings need to act and act quickly. Recent research on change suggests that a *tipping point*[2] occurs when many little changes add up to substantive change. This research suggests that change does not occur all at once or in a linear way. Instead, it builds on itself. Tipping point research explains fashion. Early adopters of fashion may be seen as doing something a bit bizarre (wearing square-toed, high-heeled shoes that look funny compared to the general run of footwear). But the cumulative effect of increasing numbers' adopting the fashion shifts it from aberration to approval. Over time as more and more people start wearing these shoes, they become accepted. In particular, when the mavens and connectors (thought leaders) adopt the new fashion, others want to follow. A tipping point occurs when enough people adopt a style and it becomes fashionable.

In business, tipping points occur when enough activities add up to a shared effect. Leaders should follow the Hallmark logic of "think big but act small" or do something related to the consistent and predictable earnings. Leadership credibility comes from doing many little things that add up to a big impact. Trust, or credibility, is not all or nothing; it is generally built on predictability, dependability, accessibility, availability, and candor.

Research on tipping points as a path to credibility also has been reinforced in Jim Collins's recent work, *Good to Great*.[3] In his research, Collins found what he calls a "flywheel" effect, where leaders who had sustained change started with small successes that kept things moving. Once the momentum toward a change started, it could not easily be stopped or slowed.

Small actions build credibility. Successful leaders consistently inform their investors about progress on their work. Harry Kramer, CEO of Baxter Healthcare, sends a monthly letter to employees and investors about his month's activities. This personal newsletter not only informs everyone of key issues for the firm, it alerts them to what he is worried about personally. He also encourages employees to leave him voice messages (his favorite medium for connecting to employees). He may personally review and respond to 70 or 80 voice messages a day as a way to keep tabs on what employees are feeling and to share his concerns with employees. Another executive started a two-hour online chat session once a month where he invited employees, and later investors, to ask him any question they wanted. Fannie Mae's CEO, Raines, posts a weekly letter to all employees that is carefully drafted to communicate his views and build consistency.

All these ideas are ways to build credibility by degrees. Doing little things that lead to large results helps ensure predictability and consistency of results.

Guideline 3: Communicate Frequently and Publicly

Communication research indicates that the receiver of information needs to hear something 10 times for every unit of understanding. Consistent, redundant messages have more impact than bold, loud, infrequent blasts. Leaders attempting to build consistent and predictable results need to find ways to communicate frequently to investors.

As noted earlier, leaders may determine *what* to share, but they are required to share that information with all those interested in the firm, not just targeted investors.

Here are some hints about sharing information to build credibility effectively:

1. *Share frequently and regularly.* Investors don't want to be surprised with large information dumps; they want to know what to expect through frequent contact.

2. *Present the logic behind the guidance you offer.* Sharing the anticipated results is not sufficient; investors need to know the thinking and logic behind the projections. When people understand the why, they accept the what.

3. *Tell people quickly when circumstances change.* Unexpected events can change how business is run, and good communicators frequently share problems and concerns as well as solutions. The September 11 attacks dramatically changed some business conditions. Successful leaders shared the impact of these attacks on their business; less successful ones felt they could work their way out of the problem before sharing with investors.

4. *Build in feedback loops.* One-way communication comes when leaders talk and investors or employees listen. The danger of this communication trap is that leaders may be answering questions their audience doesn't want to ask. Two-way communication occurs when leaders know the questions that investors have and deal with them directly.

5. *Offer honest answers.* It's tempting to try to bluff when asked questions that don't have answers, but it's much better to candidly acknowledge the lack of information, then make a

commitment to find the answer to the question and offer a process for doing so.

With frequent and public communication, leaders can build credibility through the consistency and predictability of results. Risk is reduced because investors have access to the same information as executives. Investors begin to trust leaders because they share the same pool of information and know how the leaders turn that information into action. Communication builds confidence in the thought process and helps investors believe in the means as well as the end—in the way decisions are made as well as in the decisions that result.

In difficult times, leaders at the frontline often have to make hard decisions. In a paper mill, as the market declined, the first-line supervisor had to terminate 20 percent of his employees. This is a difficult task for any leader, made more poignant for this leader because of the small town and close personal relationships with employees and their families. Rather than act capriciously and autocratically, the leader shared information with all employees about the industry downturn, plant orders, and line operations. He then held meetings to talk about what the information meant. Employees soon realized that layoffs were inevitable. Then, as the supervisor crafted criteria for the layoffs and shared those criteria, employees understood why he did what he had to do. This does not make the inevitable easier, but it does build leadership credibility.

Guideline 4: Access Data Frequently— Know the Numbers—Look for Early Indicators

Too often the emperor really is naked—leaders are apt to be the last to find out what is wrong with the numbers. In a culture where those who share negative news are punished, unwelcome information goes underground and no one shares. Building consistency and predictability requires early indicators of problems or concerns so action can be taken. A culture of openness and candor occurs when employees who have relevant information about business results feel comfortable enough to share that data without worrying about punishment. *Balanced Scorecards* help leaders spot problems early in two ways. First, they recognize that lead measures around employee, organization, and customer results are the independent variables that drive financial results. Second, they give a heads up by getting the right level of data at the right time to the person or team accountable for action. For example, as measures cascade down the organization, the reporting period becomes more frequent and teams on the frontline address problems before they become bigger issues.

Leaders can build forums for upward communication, perhaps through the financial or accounting function. For example, Cisco has found a way to close its books daily. This information offers early alerts to the leadership team, highlighting areas where customers, products, or services may be having problems. With this information, the leadership team can anticipate problems and act on them before they turn into crises.

Communication forums can also be established at customer contact points. Leaders may be encouraged to visit customers and determine their needs. In one case, an executive arranged to follow the flow of his product through a customer's process. First, he visited purchasing and asked those who chose his product over another what they considered in making the decision. He then visited the shipping dock to find out how his product arrived and whether or not it was easy to work with. He then went to assembly and manufacturing to find out how easily his product fit into the firm's output. Then he went to marketing and sales to determine if his product helped market their product. Finally, at the end of the day, he met with the customer's CEO for an informed talk about how his product did or did not meet the customer's needs.

These forums can be with employees: in town hall meetings and suggestion systems, via e-mail or voice mail, in socials, informal events, training programs, or other forms of feedback and contact. Leaders need a sounding board where they come in contact with employees at all levels of the company. These sounding boards enable leaders to hear and sense what employees who have the most information are seeing and feeling. Forums where employees access information promote *open-book management:* Employees know as much about what is going on as their managers do, and they begin to develop economic literacy. They learn to use financial information to tell which indicators are hitting or missing the mark, and they can adapt their behavior to improve results long before management perceives a problem or develops a solution.

Early indicators may come from employees who are informal leaders and who might tell the formal leader about unrest or concerns among employees. Leaders who identify such informal leaders and offer to listen to them often learn in advance what might happen. For example, the mill supervisor shared his bleak news on downsizing with some of the informal leaders, inviting them to hone and prepare his message with employees. With customers, early indicators may come from target customers who are generally lead users within the industry. Again, knowing and working with targeted customers offers early warnings about what might happen.

Guideline 5: Make Bold Decisions When Necessary to Adjust

Consistency and predictability of results does not necessarily mean that what is promised can always be delivered. As a leader, you know that it's impossible to ensure that everything will always go exactly as planned. At times, the cause for the miss may be external—customers, markets, and environments change. At other times, the cause may be internal—lack of focus or response to change. Regardless of the cause, adjusting plans in the face of unknown events requires leaders to adapt rapidly. Consistency and predictability of results means taking bold action to meet the overall projection if at all possible. It also means adjusting the projection as soon as it's clear you're going to miss it, rather than waiting and hoping for a last-minute reprieve.

In the late 1980s, General Electric Aerospace faced a major challenge. Much of its production was U.S. defense business. At the end of the cold war, these market opportunities shrank dramatically. Welch made a deal with the head of General Electric Aerospace that the business would produce $300 million cash flow per year for five years. He reasoned that in a declining market, if General Electric Aerospace could maintain this cash position, it would actually be taking share and winning contracts. He argued, "No more required, but no less accepted."

In November 1992, the Aerospace team realized that they would produce close to $270 million, not the $300 million they promised. They faxed this information to Welch one evening. Less than an hour later, the head of Aerospace received a return fax with Welch's hand-written note:

> I received your fax. We need to talk. It is not acceptable to tell me you are $30m short 6 weeks before the end of the year. My plane will be sent to pick up you and your team. You will be in my office tomorrow morning at 8:00 A.M. with a plan to find the $30m or I will find it.

In his office the next morning, Welch explained his logic. He said that he had made promises to the investment community. When Aerospace comes in $30 million under its promise, he had to find the money from other businesses, which would now have to deliver more than they promised. He said it is not an option to go to investors and report a missed result. As the reality of investor commitments became clear, the Aerospace leaders examined the numbers more closely and identified ways to save money in the near term.

Welch's concerns were twofold. First, learning in November about a major miss by the end of the year was far too late. Early indicators should have been shared so that he could adjust expectations with investors or with other business leaders who would be required to make up the short-fall. Second, the team did not have a methodology for thinking through mistakes. They could and even should have had a range of scenarios for reducing costs to meet changing business conditions. Each scenario could have identified decisions that could be made to reach the target for that scenario. As the business conditions worsened from one scenario to the next, the subsequent decisions could have been identified and thought through in advance, so that bold choices could be made to meet require-ments or adjust expectations.

When results are missed, it is critical to be candid and honest—and to learn from the experience. Then it is even more important to craft a plan for moving ahead, not looking back to blame or judge but looking forward to act and respond. Resilience or recovery is as important as making sound original plans. Resilience comes as misses are acknowl-edged, lessons are learned, and actions are taken to go forward. The Aerospace executives, in a spirit of resilience, should have anticipated their missed earnings much earlier in the year, acknowledged rather than hid from them, planned scenarios to help them respond, and then acted boldly when the failures actually occurred. It's a career-limiting move to bring up problems without offering solutions.

Guideline 6: Legally Level Earnings, If Possible

Leaders with variable earnings try to manage by reducing earnings risk. Risk may be measured on two dimensions: variability and probability. Variability occurs when earnings vary widely from quarter to quarter or year to year. Variance in quarter-to-quarter earnings creates havoc among investors, who vastly prefer consistent and predictable results and earnings that grow at an anticipated rate. Reducing variability comes from portfolio mix, smoothing, or reporting to normalize earnings.

Portfolio mix reduces variability by combining results from businesses that operate on different cycles. In an economic downturn, short-cycle businesses that depend on consumer buying will be more quickly affected. Firms heavily invested in consumer products and services (appliances, home electronics, and the like) face rapid earnings erosion when customers retrench. Other businesses have long-term contracts that customers can't drop easily: products with long lead times (plant and heavy equipment construction), recurring demand (operating fuel supplies), or ongoing services (third-party maintenance agreements). Leaders who build a business mix that includes both short and long cycles avoid earnings variability.

Smoothing occurs when earnings can be moved forward or backward, depending on the business requirements. An example is for seasonal businesses to offer discounts during their "off" season to improve revenue and then combine these lower financial results with higher peak season results. The best time for skiers to buy equipment is in the summer not the winter because most ski equipment companies offer discounts in the summer when they are not making as much money. Smoothing practices can go too far as regulators have discovered. One of these techniques is the "cookie jar" technique in which a company saves up reserves in good times and uses them in bad times. Another is not recognizing expenses in a timely manner, so that true performance indicators are disguised.

Leadership Implications

Meeting expectations is the first step toward building intangible value. Abraham Lincoln's point of view for leaders who want to increase intangible value might have been that you can fool some of the people some of the time but you can't fool all of the people all of the time. It is impossible to build a perception of value beyond earnings until there is a perception of trust through meeting promises. Meeting expectations begins with setting realistic goals, building in measurements and feedback loops, making bold adjustments to strategies when necessary, and communicating to both internal stakeholders and external shareholders. Collectively, consistent and predictable earnings increase leadership credibility and build intangible value.

Here are some questions to consider as you assess the implications of the quest for consistency:

1. How many quarters has our firm made the earning targets it offered as guidance?
2. How much information do we share with the investment community? What are the priorities we share with them?
3. Do we have mechanisms for two-way communication with investors?
4. Can we identify the target investors for our industry and firm?
5. What are the relationships we have with these targeted investors?
6. Do we have early warning indicators to suggest that we might miss expectations?
7. How have we responded when we missed expectations in the past? What could we do better?
8. Do we have scenarios for different market conditions?
9. What do we do to smooth or level earnings?
10. Do we systematically look for ways to unleash trapped profitability?

3

Growth: Setting
Your Own Odds

In Chapter 2, we discussed the first level for building intangible value—keeping promises by consistently and predictably delivering earnings. Now we discuss the second level of intangible building—describing how the firm will grow in the future. Firms whose future looks better than their present have higher market value than firms with little opportunity for future growth. Over the past 10 years, the average P/E ratios in growth industries (high-tech, biotechnology, and the like) are much higher than those in traditional industries. Within industries, firms with a credible growth strategy usually have higher market value than those with little hope for growth.

Growth rarely just happens, except to the extent that business currents give everyone in an industry the same boost. Outstanding

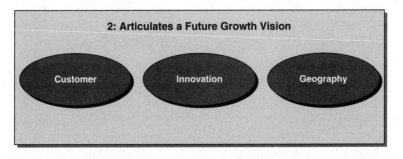

Figure 3.1 Focus on future growth.

growth—growth that represents intangible value and makes a difference to investors—comes from having a point of view about the future, from understanding how to invest today's resources for tomorrow's returns, and from building a vision of what *can be* that goes beyond *what is*. Few leaders attempt to maintain the status quo; most talk about growth and about their hopes for a better future. This chapter reviews the content and the process for designing a growth vision. Our intent is to summarize current thinking about growth and share our perspective and experience on what we believe is most important when getting input and crafting a growth vision.

Growth as an Intangible Value to All Stakeholders

Leaders who create a growth vision shape and capture the future. So much has been written about visions and values and their impact on both organizations and individuals that they have often become the snake oil of corporate life. Managers gather in exotic locations, craft lofty but vacuous pronouncements, and publish them widely, claiming to have done their job. Such simplistic notions have made vision and value statements a favorite target of cynics ranging from Scott Adams' "Dilbert" comic to academic literature.

On the other hand, visions focused on growth do engage employees. When employees feel that their day-to-day work connects clearly to a larger purpose, particularly one focused on growth, they direct both thoughts and behavior to that purpose. In addition, vision statements help investors see that present investments will result in future opportunities for sustained profitability, and they help customers have confidence in a firm's long-term viability and probability of success. Leaders who craft growth visions put concepts into the statement that describe what *can* be. We have found that meaningful growth visions focus on gaining share of opportunity rather than just market share in an industry. They spark innovation and creativity and instill hope for what can be done in the future. All this provides a competitive advantage over firms that rely on bureaucracy and tradition and replicate what has been done successfully in the past. Research has shown that the market value of firms varies depending on their growth strategy, as follows:[1]

Strategy Type	Compounded Annual Growth Rate (%)
Profitable growth	19
Cost cutting	12
Unprofitable growth	8
Shrinking	5

Companies with profitable growth strategies demonstrate a compounded annual growth rate (CAGR) of 19 percent whereas companies that primarily employ cost-cutting strategies demonstrate a much lower CAGR of 12 percent. Growth also affects employee morale. In another study, employees of growth firms reported 72 percent satisfaction; employees of shrinking firms reported 57 percent satisfaction.

Let's look at the vision statement of Merck, a pharmaceutical company with a well-articulated growth strategy and excellent market value. At Merck, the vision focuses on how research can "provide society with superior products and services that improve the quality of life and satisfy customer needs." The core and absolute value of Merck is: "We try never to forget that medicine is for the people. It is not for the profits. The profits will follow and if we have remembered that, they have never failed to appear."[2] This growth-centered vision communicates purpose to employees, products to customers, and sustained profits for investors. As a result, it represents intangible value.

How Do You Create a Future-Focused Growth Vision?

As many of you know, defining a future-focused growth vision comes when a leader examines what might happen in the future from a number of perspectives: What are future technology trends? Customer requirements? Competitor moves? Employee characteristics? Investor expectations? Through these lenses, the leader can envision how the firm is likely to grow in response to these future states. Sometimes, leaders can respond by acting on their own, seeing future opportunities, then privately crafting a response to them. Other times, leaders may use some form of focus groups or teams to define the future and a growth vision for it.

To illustrate, let's look at what happened when Allied Signal and Honeywell merged. The leadership team of the newly formed company focused on one question: How do we grow the new company? To answer it, they gathered feedback from several hundred employees from all over the world through Intranet and focus groups. The employees felt a tremendous interest in participating and helping shape the new growth vision. The result was an emphasis on growth not just through acquisitions but through innovation and the employment and constructive use of talented people. As this vision rolled out through "town hall" meetings, employees saw how they could make growth happen. More recently, Honeywell has continued to grow and stabilize its market value. Analysts are bullish about the strategy for future growth and the potential return on investment for investors.

Leaders at all levels of organizations have the obligation to build growth visions, to envision a future state that shapes how people in their organization think about themselves and their work unit, and how they act. Josh Quai is an engineering supervisor at Honeywell. He watched the corporate battles from a distance and as an interested observer. Rather than get seduced into endless debates about what Honeywell should do or who should run Honeywell, he kept his attention focused on his unit. He periodically gathered his team together to keep reminding them to focus on what was within *their* sphere of influence and not to spend energy on things they could not control. The team concentrated on creating a sense of purpose for their work, defining how they could grow and better serve their customers. By acknowledging the corporate issues, but not dwelling on them, Josh led his team to focus on their agenda for growth and to gain commitment to that agenda.

A well-crafted growth vision creates commitment by managing both the content of a growth vision (what it looks like) and the processes for building a growth vision (what to pay attention to when crafting a growth vision). By articulating a growth vision, leaders build intangible confidence in employees, customers, and investors. Let's look first at content, and then at the processes.

Content in a Growth Strategy: Three Avenues to Growth

Making a persuasive statement that you want to grow and actually figuring out how to grow are two different skills. The latter is more important. Strategic clarity exists when a growth vision is articulated in ways that communicate how growth will occur to those inside and outside the firm. Growth visions need to define alternatives for growth and then specify desired actions for each alternative. We have used the idea of a growth tripod to communicate three primary alternatives for growth (see Figure 3.2).

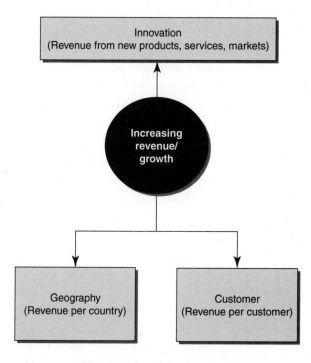

Figure 3.2 Growth tripod.

By clarifying how resources are allocated across the growth tripod, leaders craft a growth vision. On the *Customer* leg of the tripod, revenue growth comes from targeting customers, figuring out new channels to connect with them, building a brand that creates value, and ultimately gaining customer share of each targeted customer. Revenue growth that comes through *innovation* shows up in product or service extension or creation. *Geography* brings revenue growth from expanding business either within countries or in new countries.

The following steps help your executive team bring strategic clarity to your growth:

1. Go over the alternatives represented in the growth tripod and allocate a range of attention (from 0-low, to 10-high) to each dimension.
2. Ask each individual on an executive team to allocate 20 points across the three dimensions with the caveat that the points may not be divided equally and that one dimension must receive 10 points.
3. Share the individual scores to determine the team's current state, then engage in debate and dialogue to reach a consensus on growth strategy for future.
4. Identify specific actions the firm will take on growth using the proposed strategy.

The growth tripod can also serve as an icon for explaining to employees and investors where anticipated growth will occur. Each growth strategy involves its own direct action.

Growth Through Customers

Revenue growth through customers may occur through multiple mechanisms. It may mean a new distribution channel (Home Depot sells products over the Internet, allowing it to reach customers in their own homes), a strong brand that increases revenue (adding "by Marriott" increases the price of a room at Fairfield Inn and boosts the occupancy rate because guests are attracted by the Marriott brand), or customer relationship management (Royal Bank's wealth-management service works to get more revenue per customer by increasing each customer's personal return).

Customer growth visions begin with a *customer value proposition*. Value in any transaction comes from the receiver more than the giver. The receiver, or customer, of a firm must be at the heart of a vision statement. John Chambers, CEO at Cisco, talks about a customer vision:

> Customer satisfaction is the most important measure to me, and if you really believe that, then you've got to tie it to your reward system, to your management practices, and we do. . . . We measure customer satisfaction every way imaginable. We measure it on a scale of one to five, after every customer visit. We track every problem by how well we respond to it and I review how well we are doing with every critical account every night. The measurements are not only done in absolute terms, but relative to our key competitors as well. Once a year, we total all these results and we pay managers based on how well they score.[3]

At Marriott, the whole staff's primary focus is to take care of the customer. By serving customers through dedicated employees, Marriott maintains a high share of its targeted customer population. The exceptional employee service entices frequent travelers to return to Marriott whenever they can. Customer service occurs at the frontline, the point where customers interact with the hotel. At Marriott, customer contact points focus on the front desk, restaurant managers, and bell stand managers, who all come into direct contact with guests. When leaders of these operations and all employees understand customer service and implement it into employee behaviors, customer commitment grows.

Customer-centric growth visions establish the firm's identity in the minds of the best customers. This firm identity becomes a future-focused brand equity that distinguishes the firm for customers and focuses employee attention.

Publix Super Markets has a growth vision, "where shopping is a pleasure." This customer passion is instilled into all new associates, as they are encouraged to be friendly, service-oriented, and responsive to customers. Store managers reinforce this message through formal meetings with employees and by informal discussions about how to improve the customer shopping experience.

Eli Lilly focuses on "answers that matter" as shorthand for the ideal response the company hopes its pharmaceuticals and services will evoke from prescribing physicians and buying consumers. Finding answers permeates all levels of leadership action, with leaders encouraged to not just raise problems but propose alternatives.

A major airline was working to redefine its vision. Rather than start with traditional goal statements ("We want to make 12 percent return on investment"), its leaders crafted a growth vision by focusing on what they wanted to be known for among their best customers in the future. To do so, they formed a customer-centric growth strategy through four steps: (1) identify key customers, (2) define success in customer terms, (3) spell out value to customers, and (4) make sure the customers know and share the value proposition. The net result was that the airline built a customer-focused growth vision around the identity it desired to have with its best customers. The customer value proposition became a driver of employee commitment. Employees knew that their dedication and effort had an impact. They could see that as they worked to make the airline on time, easy to do business with, and friendly. Travelers who had a choice would choose them first. Such a growth vision becomes an intangible value when the anticipated revenue increase occurs and when investors and employees have confidence in the future growth based on the vision.

Growth Through Innovation

Innovation can also be a critical path for growth. There is no such thing as a mature business; every business must find ways to grow and expand its products, services, and reach. Innovation focuses on share of opportunity—on what can be more or better. Innovation focuses on creating the future rather than relying on past successes. Innovation matters because it fosters growth. It excites employees by focusing on what can be, anticipates customer requests, and delights customers with what they did not expect, and builds confidence with investors by creating intangible value.

Leaders who focus on innovation constantly ask: What's next? In all domains of their business, they recognize the ever-shorter half-life of many organizational products or processes. *Half-life* means that 50 percent of current products or work processes are obsolete because of new knowledge. For example, if an organization has a 10-month half-life, that would mean that every 10 months half of the products or work processes are obsolete because of new customer requirements, new technology, new process design, and so on.

Innovation occurs in many business domains. Innovative product offerings include revolutionary new products or product extensions (i.e., added features, performance, or functionality). Business strategy innovation changes how the enterprise makes money (as with the current emphasis on services), where the enterprise does business (opening up new geographies), how the enterprise goes to market (via new channels), how the customers experience the firm (its brand identity), or how the firm serves customers (as when eBay discovered it could grow by helping customers sell things to each other). Administrative innovation occurs when new processes are introduced in finance, information technology, marketing, human resources, manufacturing, or other staff systems.

Since innovation matters, has many facets, and depicts a firm's identity, leaders who institutionalize innovation need a protocol, as outlined in Table 3.1. Protocols identify decision points that leaders may follow to ensure success. Accountants follow accepted standards as a protocol to ensure accuracy and reliability in reporting financial data. Lawyers follow routines as protocol in preparing their legal briefs and arguments. Architects have accepted standards or protocols that they must adhere to in turning ideas into blueprints. Leaders may also follow a protocol in ensuring innovation. Innovation protocols ensure repeatable success by stipulating a definitive process that can be both learned and applied.

Innovation Protocols—Setting Standards for Growth

Innovation Protocol 1: Idea Generation.   Innovation originates with ideas: fresh ideas, different ideas, and streams of ongoing ideas. Leaders inspire new ideas by focusing on customers, encouraging risk takers, and forming alliances. Most product and strategy innovation comes from gaps or holes in existing customer expectations.

Table 3.1 Innovation Protocol

Dimension of Innovation	Concept and Question (How well does my unit. . . .)	Assessment for My Unit (0 = Low; 10 = High)
Idea generation	Look for new ideas; encourage creativity; seek iconoclasts; constantly probe for what could be; form alliances with sources of new ideas.	
Impact assessment	Filter ideas from concepts to viable products and services through a rigorous methodology.	
Incubation	Test ideas by running pilots, constantly learning about what works and what does not.	
Investment and commercialization	Allocate resources to successful products and services and turn them into commercial ventures with defined governance structure.	
Integration	Share learning from the innovation to the rest of the organization; allow cannibalization to occur.	
Improvement	Instill a process of continual learning about what works and what does not.	

Top-down innovation occurs when leaders define target customers and analyze their unmet needs in new ways. An example is General Samuel Woods, who identified the impact of freeways in the United States as a forerunner of suburbs where people could live apart from where they work. With this insight, he was able to develop Sears stores in suburbs where people lived rather than in the urban areas where they worked.

Customer-pulled innovation draws on customer panels where leaders use focus groups of current and future customers to determine unmet needs. For example, the high school students Motorola consulted made it clear that they wanted colored telephones and pagers to match their daily attire. Engineers who focused on the pager and cellular technology had no clue that customers might prefer a host of color-co-ordinated phone services.

Inside-out innovation capitalizes on the efforts of the iconoclasts that exist even in the most staid and traditional firms. These individuals don't accept the way work is done just because it has been done that way before; they are passionate about learning opportunities; and they often experiment with new approaches. Rolf Huppi, former CEO of Zurich Financial unleashed a series of innovations in the insurance business. Leaders from around the world came to Zurich, Switzerland, where they learned an innovation process. Part of the process was to identify new business opportunities and then to prioritize those that seem most promising. The best ideas were presented to senior executives who can fund them. This process led to new business opportunities. It has also encouraged leaders from different parts of the world to network around new ideas to help them cooperate in the future.

Outside-in innovation comes from alliances with sources of knowledge. Innovative leaders form alliances with places that generate ideas—universities, research centers, and research consortia. Passing the idea test through focusing on customers, encouraging iconoclasts, and forging alliances ensures a continuous flow of ideas. Eli Lilly has made agreements with hundreds of alliance partners in their search for new drugs and compounds. Managing these diverse alliances is a critical skill for future success.

Innovation Protocol 2: Impact. Not all ideas lead to successful innovation. *Creativity* means new ideas; *innovation* means new ideas that have impact. In the pharmaceutical industry, a four-stage process for innovation generally occurs: idea to compound to experiment to commercial product.[4] The rule of thumb is a $10:1$ ratio at each stage. That is, every 10 thousand ideas generate a thousand compounds that yield a hundred experimental trials that wind up with 10 commercial products.

More generically, moving from ideas to impact requires rigorous filtering, including the following elements:

- *Strategic fit:* Will the idea fit the existing strategy of the business?
- *Potential value:* Will the idea be commercial?

- *Opportunity size:* Will the idea be large enough to pursue?
- *Competition level:* Will the firm be able to distinguish itself from competitors with the product or service?
- *Employee passion:* Will the firm find employees who have both passion and competence to do the innovation?

Leaders may filter product, strategic, and administrative ideas through these screens with both objective and subjective data to turn ideas into impact. These assessments prioritize product, strategic, and administrative ideas worth pursuing.

Innovation Protocol 3: Incubate.   Ideas that pass the impact screen merit additional attention through incubation preserves where experiments pilot test and adapt ideas and turn them into innovations. Target customers can be invited to validate new products or services, and both customers and investors can help confirm strategic assumptions. On the administrative side, incubation preserves can ask groups of employees to help determine the viability of the administrative action. Incubation preserves thus provide proof of concept (whether the innovation makes sense to a customer, investor, or employee audience), technological feasibility (whether the firm has knowledge to create the innovation), and resource accessibility (whether the firm has resources to pursue the innovation).

Successfully passing through the incubation protocol encourages further investment. However, failures from pilots are equally important because they focus future investment. Incubation pilot programs should have as many failures as successes so that prioritized investments may be made.

Innovation Protocol 4: Invest and Commercialize.   Ideas that pass the incubation test deserve further investment. These ideas may then be field tested to assure commercial value. Launching a product innovation requires marketing, R&D, manufacturing, sales, and service resources. These resources allow products or services to be assessed with a large audience to determine breadth of market potential. To launch a strategic investment requires strategic clarity around product portfolios,

distribution channels, and geographic scope. Administrative investments require talent (people to do the job), finance (money to design
and deliver the innovative program), and technology (data sources to
monitor the innovation). As these resources are committed, innovation
reaches critical mass. Marshalling these resources comes as leaders build
governance mechanisms to assure focused investment.

Some innovations can be governed at a distance through alliances or
joint ventures. In these cases, the firm takes a financial or knowledge
equity position in the innovation but does not control it. Other innovations are governed via an internal venture capital group that sponsors
new ideas. These innovations become corporate experiments, supported
by corporate resources. Pockets of excellence within a business promote
innovation because they provide a source of new ideas that can be transferred to other parts of the company.

Innovation Protocol 5: Integrate.   Innovation requires integration of
new ideas into standardized ways of doing things. With product innovation, this means that new products or services both complement and
cannibalize the old. With strategic innovation, new business models become commonplace throughout an enterprise as they replace the status
quo. With administrative innovations, practices that worked in one division become integrated across an enterprise.

Leveraging innovation across an enterprise comes through
moving talented innovators across businesses or geographies so they
operate in a career mosaic throughout the enterprise. Leveraging innovation also comes when incentives encourage sharing of information and ideas. In one firm, 20 percent of the bonus pool was allocated
to individuals not within the leader's chain of command. This pool of
money allowed leaders to reward individuals outside their hierarchy
who shared information. Leveraging innovation comes when task
forces, training programs, and teams include people from multiple divisions and geographies so that information can be shared, thus avoiding a "not invented here" culture and encouraging those who both
share and borrow ideas.

The test of integration is the extent to which innovations flow
across business, division, function, and geographic boundaries.

Innovation Protocol 6: Improve. Innovation does not end, it evolves. It requires successive improvement where lessons learned are constantly codified, adapted, and implemented. Leaders committed to innovation improvement constantly monitor the innovation. Product innovations have life cycles. As the life cycle for a new product slows, it behooves leaders to encourage ideas for a new round of innovation. Strategic innovations also must evolve so that successful strategies in one time period or business evolve when new business conditions arise. Administrative innovations have a life cycle of their own where improvement in the administrative system must continually evolve.

Innovation leaders often build in ongoing monitoring processes—quarterly or semiannual reviews of product, strategic, or administrative innovations where questions about the rate of innovative change are evaluated.

Growth Through Geographic Expansion

Just as customer share replaces market share as a way to focus on target customers, country share can replace overall global revenue. Some firms track revenue from outside their home country to determine their overall global index. Just as not all customers are equal, not all countries are equal. Some countries deserve more investment and attention and some less. This rather obvious fact highlights how global revenue growth may occur, paralleling targeted customer revenue, in a three-step process: (1) select a target country, (2) develop a strategy to enter its markets, then (3) use experience in that country as a base for expansion either in the geographical region or among similar countries elsewhere in the world.

Step 1: Select Targeted Country

Leaders need to identify countries where their products or services would be in most demand. This assessment might include the following points:

- *Market maturation in the country.* For example, most of the growth in vehicle sales in automobiles will occur in emerging markets.
- *Consumer or customer demographics.* Countries that are emerging markets will have automotive buyers who buy smaller, less expensive cars for economic reasons.

■ *Risk assessment of doing business in the country.* Some firms in the oil exploration business know that unstable political situations create great risk that their investments may be taken over by the government.

■ *Cultural fit.* PricewaterhouseCoopers pulled out of Japan because Japanese businesses don't use consultants the way businesses in the United States or Europe do.

With these assessments, leaders can begin to array countries along a preference continuum from high to low likelihood of success. Targeted countries can then be measured by local market penetration rates.

Step 2: Form a Country Entry Strategy

A country entry strategy is built on two dimensions: (1) One dimension highlights tasks that will be done in the country, and (2) the other specifies how those tasks might be managed (see Figure 3.3 on page 52). The tasks represent the traditional business tasks in accomplishing work. At times, early country strategies start with a few tasks (i.e., distribution) that do not fully commit the company to the country, or with a focused task strategy (i.e., manufacturing) that commits the company to the country in a targeted way. How these tasks might be managed relates to *governance*. Governance may be arrayed along a continuum from low to high intensity. Lower intensity governance would be relationships where the firm commits fewer dedicated resources to the country (i.e., licensing); higher intensity governance requires greater resources (i.e., merger). A country entry strategy uses the grid in Figure 3.3 to plot an evolution of business within a country. At times, a company may choose to work in one column exclusively (i.e., manufacturing) and not have full presence in the country; or at other times, a firm may evolve over time to fill in the entire grid.

Step 3: Evolve Geographic Strategy

A geographic strategy evolves as a firm shifts from international (build it in home country and ship it) to multinational strategy (where the firm focuses on building business in targeted countries) to truly global strategy (where the firm has success in targeted countries that it multiplies in its operations across the world).[5] A truly global strategy for

How We Do It (Governance)	What We Do (Functional Focus)					
	Distribution	Sales	Marketing	R&D	Manufacturing	Service
Representatives						
Licensing						
Sharing of assets (leasing, joint ownership)						
Franchising						
Consortia						
Shared operational work						
Equity position in partner						
Merger						
Acquisition						
Expansion of existing business						

Figure 3.3   Geographic growth.

growth recognizes local requirements but builds global advantage in manufacturing, distribution, technology, marketing, and brand. It ensures that learning from one country is shared with other target countries. One large consumer product firm with products in over two hundred countries decided to rethink its global organization pattern. It started with regions—North America, Latin America, Europe, Asia-Pacific, Africa, and so on. Then it realized that this regional structure was based on geographic proximity rather than the opportunity to profit by moving ideas and knowledge from one country to another, which works best with countries that have similar profiles. For example, Australia is more like Canada than Vietnam in terms of market

Table 3.2   Growth Companies and Their Strategies

Company	Strategy
Amgen	*Innovation:* Focuses on a few product extensions and goes after them strongly.
Hewlett-Packard	*Innovation:* Develops new products superbly.
Nucor	*Innovation:* Created the mini-mill to produce a new product and continue to redefine the rules for low-cost steel production.
Coca-Cola	*Customer:* Focused on "share of stomach" as a rallying cry to ensure profitable growth globally.
Home Depot	*Customer:* Provides stores with everything for the do-it-yourself and contractor market.
USAA	*Customer:* Dedicates itself to customer franchise . . . serving its targeted customers (people in the military) better than anyone, through technology and personnel who make it easy for customers to do business with them. (Convenience is the customer value proposition.)
Wal-Mart	*Geography:* Focuses on distribution to achieve geographic concentration. Starting with small markets that permitted a geographic monopoly, the chain is now moving to more populous areas.
McDonald's	*Geography:* Worldwide duplication of its restaurant concept supports values of quality, value, service, and cost in every location.

maturity, market opportunities, consumer buying patterns, and the like. So the firm created five levels of market maturation as a global organization whereby knowledge and experience would be shared.[6] As these issues are dealt with, a global growth vision may follow.

The growth tripod, presented in Figure 3.2, lays out choices for a growth vision. These choices determine the content of the growth intangible. Table 3.2 offers some cases of firms that have successfully adopted growth strategies we advocate. With this growth strategy, these firms had intangibles that created value for investors and employees.

Using the growth tripod, Josh's engineering team at Honeywell discovered that they had relatively little impact on geographic growth, but they could make a difference to both product innovation and customer share. They began to adapt an innovation process for generating new products and services and they began to target key customers to define how they could offer value-added services. Again, even within a larger firm, leaders at all levels can shape growth opportunities.

Process

Content is not enough, however. It turns out that the process of the growth strategy must also be designed to ensure that it delivers value.

Refining Your Growth Vision: Focus on a Few Elements

A firm cannot be all things to all people.[7] Its growth vision must focus on a few priorities that endure over time. We once watched a large firm go through a prioritization effort that reduced 280 key issues to 71. Its managers felt they had made real progress. Unfortunately, few employees can cope with the complexity of that many key initiatives, so the reduction—dramatic as it was—made little difference in practice. Another firm, after months of working on an agenda for future firm positioning, ended up with a vision statement with four strategies, five parts of a mission, eight values, six priorities, eight key trends, and seven goals. In small enough type, all these items could be put on one page. Executives in this firm were excited about the strategic planning process and dramatic rollout of their "new future direction" with video, brochures, and employee meetings. Six months later, most employees had seen a video or read a brochure, but they hadn't changed their behavior. The firm faced the same challenges and senior management had lost credibility with investors and employees about creating and delivering on a growth strategy.

Growth strategies need to avoid *concept clutter*—the tangle that results when *all* good things squeeze themselves into the growth strategy. A useful strategy lists just the critical elements, the things most likely to bring about growth. Not everything worth doing is worth doing well.

Not everything that could be in a growth strategy should be. Leaders who use growth strategies for positive intangibles recognize that a few key messages repeated frequently have more impact than multiple messages shared loudly. As firms become more complex, the messages from the leadership need to be simpler to permeate the layers and multiple groups within a firm. At Continental Airlines, Gordon Bethune managed a turnaround emphasizing growth by focusing and refocusing on four themes: (1) being profitable, (2) becoming cash positive, (3) performing on time, and (4) building a corporate culture. All management actions needed to fall within one of these four categories. Similarly, during Elizabeth Dole's tenure as CEO of the Red Cross, she constantly focused on no more than five key issues at a time.

Communicating Your Growth Vision: Create Messages That Work

Crafting simple messages for complex businesses is not easy. We have illustrated this with the diamond shown in Figure 3.4. At the top, the question is easy: How do we compete to win? As leaders begin to answer this question, they do multiple analyses leading to the vision, mission, values, priorities, goals, and all the rest at the wide place in the diamond. Stopping at the widest part of the diamond results in concept clutter. The bottom half of the diamond focuses attention on key themes and messages. This focus makes the growth strategy memorable as repetition builds understanding and commitment. As noted earlier and in our experience with every organization that is trying to change something, a message needs to be repeated 10 times for every one unit of understanding. Simple messages, repeated constantly, become accepted and acted on. To move to the bottom half of the diamond, leaders can bundle or cluster ideas, put them in sequence, prioritize them, resist the appeal of ideas that don't fit the current initiative, and delegate work that interferes with the process.

Bundle or Cluster

Think of a menu at a restaurant. Restaurant managers bundle hundreds of items into simple categories such as drinks, appetizers, salads, main

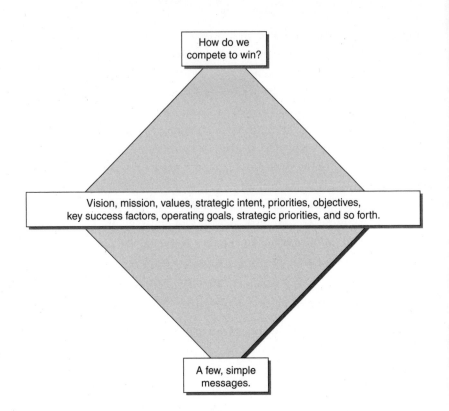

Figure 3.4   Simple messages for a complex business.

courses, and desserts so that diners can organize their selections. In a large manufacturing business, the bundle with a header called Six Sigma could incorporate process management, quality training, flowcharting, work inventory flow, and so on.

Sequence

Meals at good restaurants come one course at a time—salad, main course, dessert. In a business, the key to good sequence is to ensure that the relationships between initiatives build on one another over time, just like courses do at a restaurant. If this sequence is not clear, there is a perception of faddishness.

Prioritize

At your favorite restaurant, you might not always want to eat a three-course meal. Your eating preferences are important in your food selection. You may just want a salad or just a drink or dessert. For business leaders, setting priorities is the ongoing process of determining which initiatives will have the most impact and are most likely to get implemented. Focus on these. Just say no.

A good waiter will always come back to your table and tempt you to eat more than the salad. Sometimes, you have to just say no. Once priorities are set based on impact and implementability, it is critical for leaders to say no to existing and potentially new initiatives that do not meet these standards. Initiatives should not exist because they are popular or the pet project of a senior executive.

Delegate

Norm's wife, Tricia, is known for ordering more than she can eat and then insisting that others share her food. She is supremely confident that others will want to try eating her unusual (and large quantity) requests and we always do. Leaders who delegate must trust that their employees will deliver the work even if it is different from how they might approach it.

Leaders who use these ideas usually find that they can focus their time on what matters most; setting focused growth visions that engage employees. One firm created an index of return on time invested (ROTI) that tracked how leaders were spending their time. ROTI scores were highest when leaders focused their efforts in a targeted area where they could have highest impact. Take a look at your own calendar. What you're actually doing is your best measure of your current priorities. Once you've established the key issues for your own efforts, a periodic calendar check will help you keep your vision and time in synch.

Inspiring Others: Stretch the Present and Envision the Future. Growth visions need to establish stretch goals and demanding targets. They energize employees to grow to levels that once seemed out of reach and to accomplish things that seemed impossible. High aspirations come when the opportunity for growth exceeds a company's current resources. Companies that create new markets often establish aspirational visions that focus employee attention and energy on delivering this vision. Medtronics' vision for growth is to "restore people to full lives." This vision is constantly indoctrinated into employees through meetings with the CEO and COO, through customer visits where people share stories of how using Medtronic products enhances their well-being, and through conferences on ethics and morality at Aspen Institute.

When Southwest Airlines first opened for business, the standard for competitiveness in the airline industry was consolidation to national carriers who had a hub-and-spoke strategy. This strategy allowed large carriers to bring passengers together into one site, then move them to destinations near that site. American used Dallas, Chicago, and New York City as its hubs; United picked Denver and Chicago; Delta worked through Atlanta, Cincinnati, and Salt Lake City. Northwest had Minneapolis and Detroit. Airlines dominated these hubs, controlling most of the traffic in and out of them with the expectation that the mini-monopolies would encourage passenger loyalty, discourage competition, and lead to airline success, particularly among the higher paying business travelers. Then along came Southwest. Started as a regional carrier in Texas, the airline focused on point-to-point travel, not hubs, and offered low fares to target the nonbusiness traveler. Southwest's vision was to be a no-frills airline, with great service (on time arrival and departure), low cost, and a positive passenger experience. This vision ran counter to conventional wisdom. Using it as a calling card, Southwest employees were dedicated to new standards of service and performance. Employees were encouraged to use their creativity to serve customers through more entertaining announcements and relatively casual dress, to ensure productivity by loading and unloading the airplane quickly to reduce turnaround time and move customers quickly, and to maintain an enthusiasm and culture of fun.

An aspirational growth vision takes shape when leaders perceive a future others haven't seen—and describe that future in opportunity terms. Jeffrey Bezos conceived the potential power of the Internet as a business-to-consumer distribution channel before anyone else did. Although his Amazon.com began as a book distributor, his vision was to redefine retailing itself. He perceived a future opportunity space that others did not see; then he made his idea real to his employees and engaged their hearts and minds in making it happen. Many have watched Amazon blaze this new trail and criticized Amazon's business model as one that might never deliver a profit. However, Amazon has broadened into toys, electronics, and so on to capitalize on its distribution advantages and relationships with customers. It has recently delivered its first profits. Time will tell how successful Amazon can become. An aspirational vision needs to define what can be, not what is; to create a new definition of success rather than accepting the old; to encourage imagination of new alternatives more than analysis of existing choices; to inspire innovation more than replication. Crafting an aspirational vision comes when leaders ask:

- What's next?
- What has not been done that could be?
- What would be unique about this industry? Product? Firm?
- What might happen in 5 to 10 years if these new ideas come about?
- If I could work with a blank sheet, what would I do next?
- What are others in my industry doing and what could I do differently?

These questions help leaders define *what can be,* not *what is.* Then the resulting aspirations need to be turned into visions and values that paint a picture for employees of what can be.

The CEO of a hospital wanted to be known for outstanding patient care. He felt that exceptional patient care in administrative things (check-in, food service, housekeeping, and the like) and medical treatment (nurses and physicians) would be a differentiator for his hospital, thus encouraging physicians to send patients, thereby increasing revenues. To create an image of this vision, he contracted with a movie director to illustrate the changing emphasis within his hospital. The resulting short, humorous videos demonstrated the old and new expectations for patient care. Showing this video to employees and patients turned his vision into behavior and raised the standard for patient care.

Governing for Growth—Coordinate the Implementation.   Governance deals with how work is accomplished, and it can be adjusted to assure growth. Part of this job is organization design. In general, assigning growth work to subunits and giving them a free rein increases their probability of growth. Hewlett-Packard consistently shifts work to subunits to allow them to grow. Intel, as a large internal venture capitalist, funds new divisions where growth can occur. 3M has virtual startups where new ideas are incubated then let go with the originator moving the idea forward.

Governance can also deal with ways to coordinate a growth strategy. One firm formed a group it called the Growth Opportunity Council. This council was chartered with overseeing the growth strategy in the firm and ensuring revenue increases. The firm began by defining which leg of the growth tripod to focus on (in this case innovation), then investing and allocating resources to sponsor innovation (following a version of the innovation protocol in Table 3.1). The council played a number of roles in fostering growth. It set priorities for what should happen; it allocated resources (money, time, and the best talent); it protected the innovators even when things did not go as planned; it offered advice on ways to improve; and it ensured that the growth ideas were embedded in the firm.

Governance also deals with culture—the values and patterns of behavior of employees inside as perceived by customers and investors outside. The culture of growth includes risk taking, an outside perspective, challenge, candor, resilience, and resolve. As executives turn these cultural dimensions into behaviors and then weave them into human resource practices (who to hire, what to teach, how to pay), an organization is governed to grow.

Finally, governance requires leadership. Leadership for growth comes from leaders who, in Andy Grove's (Intel) terms, are "CEOs without a memory" who look forward, not backward; who clearly state a growth strategy

To get more ideas on growth, go to: www.rbl.net/whythebottomlineisnt.html.

and stick with it; who engage employees in the actions to deliver the strategy; and who see and create opportunities and accomplish them.

Leadership Implications

Having a legitimate strategy for growth may be one of the most critical intangibles. Leaders who build a growth agenda excite investors and employees. When leaders are able to turn that growth agenda into specific, concrete plans by using simple icons such as the growth tripod and when they follow the process tips, they build intangible value.

Growth visions become real and effective when employees see how their day-to-day behavior moves the company closer and closer to achieving its visions. Leaders who turn vision into commitment make sure that vision translates into employee behavior. Here are some of the questions that leaders might ask to make vision real:

1. How will this growth vision or value affect employee X (pick an employee two or three levels below the leadership team) next week, next month, next year? What will this employee spend more or less time doing? How will this employee feel about working here? What could this employee do that would show the vision is real?
2. What systems (staffing, promotion, compensation, training, communication, decision making, financial resource allocation) do we need to change to make the vision real to employees?
3. How would a customer or supplier working with our firm know we behaved in a different way? What would they see because we implement this vision?
4. If managers could do a time log of who they spend time with, what decisions they make, where they spend time, and what information they process, how would it be different with the new vision?

Leaders who answer these questions focus on the impact of the vision more than the vision itself. They want to make sure that a vision causes an employee to think and behave differently.

4

Writing the Playbook: Matching Strategy to Skill

Know-how builds intangible value. Once you have a growth vision, the next step in the architecture is to invest in technical know-how that is consistent with this direction. This involves assessing the major opportunities in your industry and market; designing your unique business strategy to realize your vision; and then aligning your organization's

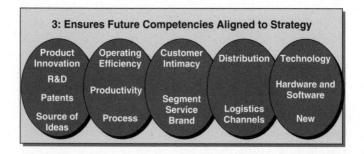

Figure 4.1 Focus on aligning future competencies to strategy.

core competencies, that is, technical know-how embedded in functional areas to this strategy. In the previous chapter, we discussed how to build a vision and choose from among growth strategies options. In this chapter, we look at the evolution of thought on the importance of core competencies in business, and we present guidelines on how to build core competencies in your organization, giving examples of companies who have done an exemplary job.

Core Competencies: Put Your Resources Where Your Strategy Is

The core competencies are the functional areas of expertise within an organization (as opposed to its social or cultural norms). Originally, the concept of competence focused on individual knowledge and behaviors. In the 1930s, the Hay group explored the competencies of individuals in three domains (know-how, problem solving, and accountability) as a way to determine the relative value of an individual's contribution. Hay points are calculated based on how much an individual employee accomplishes in each domain. This emphasis on the individual remained the focus of competence work until a landmark article by C. K. Prahalad and Gary Hamel.[1] This article, "The Core Competence of the Corporation," made two shifts in the competence logic: (1) from the individual to the organization as the unit of analysis and (2) from social and cultural issues to more technical ones.

The new argument led to a focus on technical competencies embedded within firms. For example, Honda has the ability to build efficient engines; NEC has the ability to miniaturize products and services; 3M has bonding and coating expertise; Amazon has distribution know-how. Leveraging this core competence or expertise enables firms to build growth strategies. Honda wants five engines in every garage (car, motorcycle, lawnmower, snow blower, leaf blower); NEC continually innovates new and smaller products; 3M has scores of products that use coating and bonding technology; and Amazon distributes more than books and CDs. Every organization has core competencies, or bundles of technical expertise, that enable it to deliver value to customers and investors.

Core competence varies by industry. In pharmaceuticals, firms better at building the competence of commercializing R&D into products build more market value than their less adept peers. In distribution (Federal Express, United Parcel Service, Airborne), logistics is a core competence. All of these firms must master the ability to collect, ship, and deliver packages in a timely way. The firms best in this competence are likely to gain more market value than those that are weaker in it. Each industry has a predominant set of core competencies required for success (lodging requires service, automobile production requires manufacturing quality, consulting requires client engagement, etc.).

Core competence also ties to the strategic focus of a firm. Within an industry, a firm may take a strategic focus as a way to differentiate itself from its competitors. In the process, leaders can pick one of five primary strategic foci:[2]

1. *Product innovation:* We compete through new products. (California Pizza tries to create new types of pizza.)
2. *Operating efficiency:* We compete through reduced cost and more efficient operations. (Little Caesar's sells pizza on price and volume.)
3. *Customer intimacy:* We compete through customer relationships. (Sbarro's provides a better dining experience by offering a variety of Italian foods as well as pizza.)
4. *Distribution:* We compete through multiple channels and get the product to the customer efficiently. (Domino's delivers pizzas quickly.)
5. *Technology:* We compete by taking advantage of a technology that is at the core of every product we sell. (Pizza Hearty—a hypothetical new company—sells pizza that reduces cholesterol as customers eat it because it includes psycillium grains.)

Each of these strategic foci has a unique set of core competencies required for it to be successful (see Table 4.1).

Leaders who invest in core competences that align to strategy build market value because investors come to believe that these organizations

Table 4.1 Core Competencies of Strategic Foci

Strategic Focus	Compete Through	Core Competencies Required
Product innovation	New products created; track percent of revenues created from products in last 3 years.	Invest in R&D. Win new patents. Create new sources of ideas.
Operating efficiency	Reduced costs through more efficient operations; track ratios of operational costs versus competitors.	Manage productivity. Improve processes. Make project choices.
Customer intimacy	Building customer bonds; track customer share from targeted customers.	Segment target customers. Service or connect with target customers. Build enduring brand.
Distribution	Alternative channels of going to market to customer; track revenue from each channel to customer.	Manage logistics. Create channels to customer.
Technology	Investments in new technology; track through access and application of new technology.	Develop unique technology. Apply hardware and software for success. Design product or service.

have the functional requirements to accomplish work. When investors perceive an organization as having a leadership position in a core competence area that is aligned with its strategy, they have more confidence that the firm will execute its strategy and deliver future earnings.

Aligning strategy to core competence occurs at any level of an organization where a strategy exists. For example, a floor supervisor at Wal-Mart worries about customer service and, thus, must pay attention to the core competencies to deliver an excellent customer experience. An IRS collection agent worries about alternative ways to connect with the taxpayer and might focus on distribution core competencies. A utility firm manager worries about cost and focuses on the core competencies related to efficiency and cost reduction. Leaders have the obligation to identify, source, and maintain core competencies tied to strategies. When they do so, intangible value follows.

Product Innovation: Research and Development and Patents

A product innovation strategy requires core competencies focused on creating new products. Innovation likely derives from research and development (R&D) investments. R&D has become a source of study for intangibles because of its strategic importance and because it is one of the few intangibles reported in traditional financial statements. Studies of the impact of R&D on firm performance have shown the following:[3]

- R&D expenditures have a return on investment of 20 percent to 35 percent annually; a major contributor to productivity within firms.
- R&D focused on science and technology that leads to new products has more impact than process R&D.
- Industry R&D has higher returns than government-sponsored R&D.
- R&D announcements that imply commercialization of products yield positive investor results.[4]
- Investors value R&D spent by large firms more than that of small firms.[5]

Leaders who desire to compete through product innovation must invest in R&D efforts that turn ideas into products. We proposed an innovation protocol in Chapter 3. The research we report in this chapter supports the importance of R&D investment as an indicator of commitment to innovation. In our work with clients, we have found these guidelines to be useful:

- *Allocate resources (money and talent) to R&D efforts.* In difficult economic times, it is tempting to cut costs by stopping R&D investment. Such short-term action impairs long-term value and impedes the flow of products.

- *Take bold risks to be the first mover into new markets.* First movers have the chance to gain dominant share and to define product standards. Sometimes leaders wait to see if market potential exists and miss share of opportunity in new markets. Our colleague, Tom Kinnear, a professor at Michigan Business School, reports that first movers gain 2.5 times as much market share as late entrants into new markets.[6]
- *Focus attention on the few critical products that will become commercial successes.* To repeat our refrain from Chapter 3, not all things worth doing are worth doing well. Leaders focused on innovation need to focus resources on the most likely successes, not on every potential product. This requires experimentation across a broad array of opportunities, but also focus on the innovations most likely to succeed.
- *Allocate leadership attention to R&D innovation.* Leaders send messages about what's important through the way they spend their personal time and energy. Continually visiting R&D sites, reviewing R&D progress in formal meetings, engaging in informal dialogues with R&D leaders, and publicly talking about R&D investments and success communicates a high level of leadership commitment that employees, customers, and investors alike will be quick to see and believe.
- *Track R&D successes.* This information can be derived from investment in R&D, patent applications and citations, new products being developed, new products commercialized, success rate of new products (e.g., percent of sales of products introduced in previous three years), and customer satisfaction and perception on innovation.
- *Build a disciplined innovation process rather than focusing on a single innovation.* The innovation protocol we propose in Chapter 3 suggests that innovation is an ongoing process, not a single event. Leaders may be enthused about a particular technology or commercial success, but should be more attentive to the process of a continued flow of product successes. Dave Evans, founder of Evans and Sutherland, loved the technology in the supercomputer division of his business and spent most of

his time there but the company made most of its money in building simulations.

■ *Spread the R&D message both inside and outside the firm.* Make sure people know about the R&D process, and provide empirical evidence of its success.

When declaring a product innovation strategy, leaders must follow suit with core competencies focused on R&D. They must invest leadership time, energy, and money on building the core competencies consistent with product innovation, such as R&D, sales, and marketing. When they do so, their firm's intangible value increases because investors develop greater confidence in the investments in infrastructure that produces sustainable innovation.

Operating Efficiency: Managing Costs

Firms can compete by having lower costs than competitors and then offering customers lower prices. In the airline industry, Southwest has lower prices for consumers; in the automotive industry, Hyundai cars are cheaper than their competitors; in office furniture, Hon attempts to offer lower prices; in retailing, TJ Maxx offers fashion for less. In each of these cases, leaders compete through offering lower prices to customers. To sustain lower prices, these leaders must build a core competence of managing costs. Leaders have three major options for how to reduce costs and deliver value: productivity, process, and projects (Figure 4.2).

Managing Costs Through Productivity

Productivity comes when leaders develop competence in how to do more with less. Two general approaches can be used to increase productivity. First, leaders can develop competence in finding new ways to do work. This can come when leaders include employees in work-out type initiatives intended to identify and remove unnecessary bureaucracy,[7] find different ways to do work (eliminate a task, do it less often,

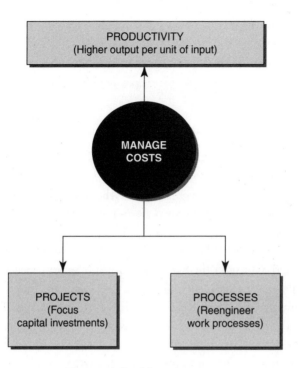

Figure 4.2   Managing costs.

do it less frequently, do it through technology), or organize resources to deliver work (through shared service organizations or outsourcing). Each of these efforts is a way to rethink and redo how to do work more efficiently. Employees enjoy being asked to reduce costs when there is a clear process such as work-out and a solid rationale for the reductions.

Second, productivity can come by reducing employee costs through headcount reduction. This option can be arrived at too quickly. Leaders who want to build a committed workforce should be very careful not to reduce headcount often. However, when headcount reduction is *necessary,* it should be done quickly, fairly, and boldly. Ideas for how to be fair include removing employees voluntarily (encouraging early retirement), reducing hiring (not replacing those who leave), or offering incentives for people to leave short of retirement age. At times, removing employees requires involuntary retrenchment through performance discipline or downsizing. When headcount is reduced and work is redesigned, productivity increases. Cost-conscious leaders continually commit to finding ways to maintain productivity and track it through measures of output per unit of employee input (revenue per employee, units produced per employee, profit per employee, etc.).

Managing Costs Through Process Improvement

A third option for improving productivity is process improvement. Process improvement comes from analyzing and reengineering work processes to remove steps required to do the work and save time in the process. Leaders committed to process improvement apply the disciplines of Six Sigma, quality, or reengineering key processes within their firm.

To become more efficient, each of these (and other) processes can be delineated. Consider the use of tools for process improvement such as process mapping, flow-charting, variance reduction, Pareto diagramming, root cause analysis, and statistical process control.[8] These tools can help you streamline operations, reduce waste, focus processes on customer value, and reduce costs. Ensure that the process improvement methodology does not become more important than the outcome. Process improvement is a means to an end, not an end in itself. Outside experts as well as employee proponents of process improvement methodologies often get a religious fervor about their work. When investing in these activities, keep in mind that the intended outcome is to reduce costs by improving workflow processes, not to have more process improvement infrastructure.

Managing Costs Through Project Improvements

Project improvements reduce costs by analyzing and prioritizing projects or investments. At times, to reduce costs, some capital investments may be delayed, modified, or cancelled. Delaying investments means deferring them to a future time frame when the firm has more money to perform the project. For example, following the terrorist attacks of September 11, 2001, airlines delayed equipment purchases based on new economic conditions. Companies postpone capital improvements in facilities or technology until they are economically viable. At times, large capital investments may be modified to reduce exposure or risks or even permanently cancelled.

As leaders make choices across the three domains for cost (productivity, process, project), they develop competencies in delivering low-cost goods and services. Southwest consistently has the highest productivity among the airlines;[9] Motorola, Honeywell, and General Electric claim hundreds of millions of dollars of savings through disciplined process improvement; and many firms have delayed, modified, or cancelled capital improvements to reduce costs. The outcome of these efforts can be tracked through operating costs as contrasted with competitors. On the balance sheet, this may show up as sales, general, and administrative (SG&A) costs or in some other measure of operating efficiency.

When a leader embarks on a strategy of operating efficiency, the subsequent competence in cost reduction becomes critical for investors to have confidence in the sustainability of the strategy. Leaders who focus on costs continually monitor their costs versus those of their competitors, seek productivity gains, encourage process improvements, and prioritize project investments. They make trade-offs among the three paths for operating efficiency, hold others accountable for delivering results, and build a cost culture into all decisions. By so doing, they meet financial projections and build intangible value.

Customer Intimacy: Building Relationships of Value

A customer strategy attempts to compete through building deep relationships with targeted, profitable customers by understanding and filling their needs better than competitors. For example, grocery stores with frequent user cards attempt to capture a higher share of targeted customers' budgets through increased intimacy. That is, they want as much as possible of their best customers' individual grocery expenditures. Behind customer intimacy are core competencies of segmentation, service, and branding. A good example of an organization that has incorporated these core competencies and built relationships of value with its customers is Harrah's, which is in the gaming industry.

The core competence of *segmentation* means that leaders know their target customers and focus attention on them. Harrah's competes in a tough industry. Gaming depends traditionally on the disposable income of people who choose gaming as a source of entertainment. When recession hits and disposable income drops, most gaming competitors lose dramatically. Harrah's developed a segmentation core competence that divides customers into categories based on their spending patterns and designates diamond, platinum, gold, and silver customers based on how much money they spent on gaming activities. With this initial information, Harrah's discovered that diamond and platinum customers are less affected by economic swings than other customers. As a result, company staffs work to learn all they can about this target group of customers— their preferred games, dining preferences, room preferences, and other inducements. In addition, the staff continually update reports on the demographics of these customers (mostly people in their fifties with high personal net worth) and their interactions with Harrah's. They then work to build connections with them.

Harrah's enhances their customer service by connecting with customers—creating a competence of *bonding with target customers*—in a variety of ways. They have dedicated employees who build long-term relationships with targeted customers and give them personalized concierge service and tailored products from the time they arrive in the casino until they leave. For example, when a diamond customer approaches any of Harrah's restaurants, the maitre d' notices the diamond lapel pin, moves the customer to the front of any waiting line, provides a preferred table, then uses the database to bring preferred drinks and meals as quickly and efficiently as possible. In addition, Harrah's sometimes involves targeted customers in staffing, training, compensation, and communication practices. The net result of these activities is customer intimacy and increased customer share.

Customer connectivity can also be enhanced when all employees have meaningful exposure to or *interaction with targeted customers*. Such exposure can occur in many ways. Ford has factory assembly workers visit with customers on showroom floors as part of the sales effort, which also allows them to learn firsthand about customers' opinions. Other firms have cross-sections of employees (instead of marketing departments or consultants) conduct telephone or in-office market research. Saturn regularly brings customers into its factories to bind customers and employees together. Medtronics involves patients and physicians in company celebrations; patients and physicians personally deliver the messages around as the celebrations unfold. One very personal example is that Medtronics built a video Web site featuring Norm's daughter, McKenna, before, during and after she underwent scoliosis surgery using an innovative procedure (www.iscoliosis.com). Unilever provides the well-orchestrated opportunity for employees to visit customers in their homes to learn of their product usage habits firsthand while exhibiting the company's commitment to employee involvement. Harley Davidson executives are expected to ride their own motorcycles to company-sponsored rallies and then interact with their customers. All of these activities result in information and mindset convergence between employees and customers.

When leaders segment and serve customers well, they build a firm brand that creates enduring value for the customer and investor.[10] A firm brand has life beyond any individual leader:

- It focuses less on a particular product or service and more on a pattern of customer experiences over time.
- It begins with and emphasizes a view of the firm from the customer in, from the outside in.
- It creates an identity and reputation for the firm, not just one leader or product from the firm.
- It focuses on the ways in which the firm creates a customer experience that goes beyond the use of one product or service.

As a result of strong firm brands, customers select products and are willing to pay a premium for the product of their choice (as with the higher price Bayer can charge for aspirin, compared to chemically similar generic drugs) and the intangible value of the company increases.

BusinessWeek estimated the world's most valuable brands by anticipating the future earnings of a firm based on its brand.[11] According to this study, Coca-Cola, Microsoft, IBM, and General Electric are the most valuable brands in the world.

Leaders committed to customer intimacy build core competencies around segmenting target customers who are most critical to a firm's success, building service connections with them to gain customer share, and creating a sustainable firm brand identity that goes beyond any single product or person. These leaders spend time asking about and learning who the target customers are, working to know details about customer buying patterns, and seeking ways to connect with those customers. They include customers in presentations, see their work through customer eyes, and constantly measure customer service as leading indicators of financial performance. Investors see consistency as an intangible that adds to the overall value of the firm.

Distribution: Logistics and Channels

A distribution strategy focuses attention on how to efficiently and effectively connect with target customers. With the advent of Web-based technology and the Internet, customers began to find multiple channels to interact with a firm. Through wise investments in logistics and channel competencies, leaders build relationships of value with customers and accomplish their distribution strategy.

Despite the dot-com boom and bust, the fundamental premise that the Internet offers customers an alternative channel is a new business reality. Compare Dell and Compaq. The two firms had roughly the same market value at the beginning of 1997, but five years later, Compaq's market value stayed flat—no appreciable increase or decrease. Meanwhile, Dell rose to 1400 percent of Compaq's market value, and then dropped in the market decline to about 700 percent. At the end of 2002, Compaq, a firm with the same revenues as Dell, had a market value of about $15 billion versus Dell's $73 billion. Compaq and HP have merged and Dell is likely to remain independent. Although a variety of issues might affect this intangible value, Dell's distribution strategy has often been cited as its key competitive strength. Dell has invested in core competencies that support this advantage.

Dell makes it easy for customers to connect with them. They offer direct sales through multiple channels. Customers can purchase a Dell computer through catalogues, Web sites, telephone representatives, or other direct customer contact. Dell customizes its computers to customer requests and has the unique logistical support needed to build computers to order. Compaq distributes many of its products through retail outlets, requiring inventory and marketing forecasts. Dell has mastered core competencies of customer interface, made-to-order products, logistics through the supplier network, and customer service through multiple channels.

Other well-known companies follow a distribution strategy and invest in core competencies that support it. Federal Express (FedEx) has created a package tracking system that allows customers to check on the location of their packages at any time using the Internet. The handheld computer system carried by each FedEx driver provides input to a complex computer network designed to ensure on-time delivery. Wal-Mart has implemented a technology-based ordering system whereby any product sold anywhere in the Wal-Mart chain is immediately registered with the supplier of that product. This makes for smoother inventory and accurate daily tracking of product flow. Baxter Healthcare has placed an order-entry for its hospital products at each nursing station. In the past, a hospital had to depend on purchasing department personnel to convey product demand to Baxter. With each nursing station connected to the Baxter network, Baxter knows at once when products are used and is able to provide a timely and continuous resupply without interruption or bureaucracy. Although television ads joke about the repairman knocking on the door of an unsuspecting homeowner and saying, "Your refrigerator needs repair; it just contacted me," such remote sensor technology exists. It enables firms to deploy a distribution strategy that builds intangible value.

Leaders committed to a distribution strategy invest in multiple channels to serve targeted customers and allow the customers to pick the channel that works best for them. Then the infrastructure behind the channel enables customer service as the customer defines it. They ensure that distribution technology focuses on logistical support for customers, that customers find the technology easily accessible and friendly, and that

customers can find a channel that works for them. These investments—
and their success—make a difference in the stock market as well.

Technology: Opportunities to Apply Know-How

A business that follows a technology strategy looks for new opportunities to apply their unique technological know-how. A business with a technology strategy is a solution looking for the right customer or the right problem to solve. A core competency for these firms is applications engineering, or the search for ways that new customers might use the core technology. This competence also looks for how the technology could be converted into new products.

Qualcomm (based in San Diego, California) has adopted this strategy. It develops, manufactures, markets, licenses, and operates advanced communications systems and products based on its proprietary digital wireless technologies. Qualcomm's Code Division Multiple Access (CDMA) technology provides clear voice quality in new generations of communications products and services. The success of this company depends on its ability to continually update the technology and to both develop new products and services and find new customers who want to license the technology for products of their own.

Boston Scientific is a global company that makes medical products around a technology concept of "nonintrusiveness." Building instruments that enable surgeons to be less intrusive during operations has led Boston Scientific to develop core competencies around miniaturizing medical instruments using integrated software. These competencies have led to a unique set of medical products that make Boston Scientific a leader in their industry.

Leaders committed to a technology strategy design a solution that utilizes their technology concept. To grow, they find new customers and new products where their technology can be used. They build core competencies in areas such as

For more ideas about core competencies and strategy, go to: www.rbl.net/whythebottomlineisnt.html.

applications engineering, continuously improving their core technology, and watching customers use their technology as a source of new ideas.

Leadership Implications

For core competence or functional expertise to create intangible value, it must be aligned with strategy. Each business strategy requires its own set of core competencies. When the core competencies match the strategy, leaders can make functional investments to ensure that their organization has the know-how to deliver what is expected. These core competencies can then be tracked and measured as leading indicators of future financial performance. They can also be managed as leaders make choices about how to invest time, money, and resources to ensure a continual stream of functional expertise in their organization. The following questions help you assess the current core competence stance of your organization:

1. What are the major opportunities in your industry and market?
2. What is the unique business strategy that you will select to gain position in this industry?
3. What core competencies are required to deliver your strategy?
4. How will you measure each of those core competencies?
5. What specific investments can you make in terms of time, resources, and attention to maintain and build those core competencies?
6. How can leaders assure that core competencies fit with the entire organization with respect to process, technology, and/or organization?

5

Boot Camp: Building Your Talent Base

So far we have covered the first three levels for building intangible value. We have demonstrated that leaders must keep their promises, articulate a vision for growth, and then build technical competencies that are consistent with this direction. The rest of the book is about the fourth level—how to build organization capabilities.

Organization capabilities are the things a company knows how to do well; the ability of an organization to use resources, get things done, and behave in ways that lead to accomplishment. They form the identity or personality of the firm, govern the way work gets done, and

Figure 5.1 Focus on building the organization's capabilities.

help executives create an organization that succeeds. In the following chapters, we propose seven capabilities that leaders use to build intangible value. We begin with the capability of managing people.

"People are our most important asset." Leaders make this claim all the time, to the point where it is either so empty or so complex as to be almost meaningless. On one hand, it's often a slogan with little substance. Leaders talk about the importance of people while pursuing short-term profit regardless of the human cost. On the other hand, analysts use it as the justification for measuring a firm's intellectual capital in elegant and complex ways, but provide no useful hints about building and conserving the asset represented by the workforce.[1]

Without a doubt, organizations with more intellectual capital are likelier to succeed than those with less. At a broad level, intellectual capital represents the collective knowledge, skills, abilities, and motives of all employees within a firm. As an intangible, this success shows up in market value as well as investor, employee, and customer value. Efforts to track a firm's intellectual capital have evolved over time. Over 30 years ago, James Tobin, a Nobel Prize-winning economist, predicted a firm's future economic value based on the assumption that long-term market value must be equal to asset replacement value. In the past decade, Baruch Lev defined knowledge capital as what is left over in terms of market value—that is, the excess of value over the expected amount based on its assets. Lev has made a breakthrough on finding ways to measure knowledge and intellectual capital. Using a complex methodology, Lev and his colleagues[2] have calculated that the three "smartest" U.S. companies are General Electric, Pfizer, and Microsoft; IBM comes in eighth. They have also calculated a knowledge capital scorecard for *CFO Magazine,* where they report the knowledge capital scores for top performers in 21 industries.[3]

The broad concepts of intellectual capital and knowledge capital have been covered effectively in other publications. In this chapter, we focus on what leaders can do to build talent.[4] In the last chapter, we discussed how the technical core competencies of an organization must be identified and embedded in key functional areas; in this chapter, we focus on competencies of the *individual* using a formula for talent: competence × commitment.[5] *Competence* represents the overall knowledge or skills of employees for the future, not the present; *commitment* represents employee willingness to work hard and deploy those skills in service of the goals of the firm. Firms with competent employees who are not committed have bright people who often don't get the job done; firms with committed employees who are not competent have hard workers who make dumb decisions. Both competence and commitment are critical. Leaders who build talent generate both competence and commitment, thereby giving investors confidence in future earnings.

Competence: Assess Then Invest

Competence matters. Although many efforts to identify and upgrade individual competencies have been made, too many of them stop short of linking the competencies to business results.[6] Without this linkage, descriptions of competencies tend to be generic across companies and industries, and work based on them is full of pitfalls. Five ways that we have found to ensure that competencies are results-driven include:

1. *Focus on the future.* Direction is strongest and most clear within organizations when competencies explain not only what or how to do something, but *why*. Competencies should focus on the future and what needs to be done, not on the past and what has been done.

2. *Define measurable behaviors and results.* When put into behavioral terms with a results focus, competencies can be tracked and measured.[7] When employees understand what they need to do and receive consistent, measurable feedback on their behaviors, they are able to change and align behaviors with the goals of their organization.

3. *Specify behaviors that can be learned.* Leaders who define and then invest in desired behaviors rather than general personality traits increase the probability of successful growth.

4. *Tailor competency models to organization goals.* Competencies should be focused on individual behaviors required to help a specific firm reach its business goals. These behaviors thus differentiate and distinguish organizations.

5. *Integrate competency development as a leadership responsibility for all managers.* For competencies to have impact, the leaders of the firm must emotionally and intellectually own them. If the leadership doesn't care, nobody cares. When competencies are appropriately defined with the active participation of the leadership, it is relatively straightforward to align recruiting, performance management, training and development, and reward practices to build and reinforce key-valued behaviors.

Building Your Competency Model

To produce competency models with impact, we have often engaged leaders in a conversation that runs along these lines:

Q: Do you believe that people are your most important asset?
A: Of course, how can I not?

Q: Compared to other areas you need to develop in your firm (creating innovative products or services, serving customers, reducing costs, defining new distribution channels, or investing in technology), how critical is the development of people?
A: It is the most critical because it underlies all the rest. Without people, none of the strategies or technical competencies associated with them (see Chapter 4) will happen.

Q: Would you be willing to have you and your direct reports devote a block of time (four hours in one sitting and two thereafter) to improving the quality of people within your organization?
A: No, we're very busy fighting fires this quarter. Why don't you get the human resources people to develop the first draft and show us something in a few months?

At this point, we push leaders to either commit to doing something specific right now (that is, spend the four hours of their time) or face the fact that they are not fully committed to people as a critical asset. We encourage leaders to spend time because people are their scarcest resource. We suggest dedicating one staff meeting to competence development. They generally then ask what kind of action we suggest, and we describe a two-part process for creating solution-based competency models; competency assessment and competency investment. It is a relatively simple process; yet, it is one that has been successfully used by many clients.

Part 1: Assess the Competencies Needed

In competency assessment, leaders identify the competencies employees must demonstrate to achieve future goals. We believe that leaders and their direct reports should be the primary owners of the competency models they use. To create high ownership while maintaining high validity of the competencies produced, leaders and their direct reports should go through an exercise we call "four hours plus two":

1. *Identify the present technical skills employees possess in the organization* (about 30 minutes). Have the team brainstorm the core competencies that exist in the organization today. What are the functional areas where we perform well? This list of competencies is likely to be tied to the present strategy and to focus on technical expertise (see Chapter 4 for examples).

2. *Identify the present social competencies resident in the organization* (about 30 minutes). Discuss how work gets done in the organization. How are decisions made? How are people treated? How is information shared? How are conflicts resolved? What are norms, orthodoxies, or accepted ways of doing things in the organization? This list of behaviors represents the social pattern within the organization.

3. *Specify the challenges facing the organization looking forward* (60 minutes). In the future, what are the major challenges the organization is likely to experience and how will the organization respond? These challenges may include a discussion of customer expectations, competitors present and future, technology trends, government policies, workforce demographics, economic

conditions, and the like. The responses may be the strategies for growth and competencies associated with them. The challenges and the organization's response to them becomes a lens through which the future can be seen.

4. *Given the future state, identify required technical competencies* (60 minutes). Given the filter of the future, are there some functional or technical competencies that must be maintained? Are there competencies that must be acquired? The competencies that are missing define the gap the company needs to close to go forward. For example, as Harley Davidson shifted toward a more global market, the firm required more employees who understood global market conditions, exchange rates, specific country-buying patterns, and global distribution channels.

5. *Given the future state, identify required social competencies* (60 minutes). Given the filter of the future, are there some social competencies that must be maintained? These social norms represent the emotional heritage of the organization that no one wants to abandon. But what new social norms are required? The social competencies missing for the future define the gap going forward. Harley Davidson focused not only on global technical skills but on global decision making, information sharing, and management of people to accomplish its global strategy. Sometimes in this step it is useful to give leaders and their teams examples of social competencies other companies have derived or lists of competencies from the popular press.[8]

At the end of Step 5, leaders and their teams have identified a set of competencies they require for their organization to succeed in the future. With facilitation, we have found that a half-day session enables leaders to fold the future strategy into present competencies for both technical and social domains. At this point, the sense of ownership to the competencies is high because leaders have crafted and debated them. We have used this exercise with the top teams of multibillion-dollar enterprises, with team leaders of engineering groups, and with grocery store managers. It offers a simple process for thinking and talking about what competence gaps might exist within a firm. However, to upgrade validity, we add two additional steps.

6. *Discuss the list of competencies over the next three to four weeks* (requirements vary, but never more than a few minutes at a time). At the end of the half-day, invite participants to spend time in the following weeks talking about the competencies they have identified. Ask them to debate, discuss, and work to clarify the list of competencies they have identified. Structuring exchanges around desired competencies with larger groups of employees will increase the validity of the proposed requirements.

7. *Review the conversations with the leadership team and refine the competency list* (generally 2 hours). After three or four weeks, when the leadership team meets, take a few hours to share the insights from the conversations. This might remove, add, or clarify items on the list. At this point, the specified competencies become the behaviors employees need to demonstrate for the organization to accomplish goals.

Figure 5.2 provides a template for the exercise. This assessment identifies the gap between what is available and what is required for the organization to succeed. The lists of required competencies may be used for individual assessment or for organizational investment. If you have an academic or heavy-duty consulting background, you may see this methodology as too simple to produce robust results. The validity of the resulting competency model may indeed suffer when compared to what might be prepared by a more rigorous methodology—but the

Type of Competency	Currently We Have	Changes Facing Our Business	In the Future We Will Need
Technical	Step 1	Step 3	Step 4
Social	Step 2		Step 5

Figure 5.2 Competency assessment exercise.

sense of ownership it generates is much higher. The people closest to the situation generally do a reasonably good job of coming up with what they need to be able to do—and they're much more likely to follow through on their own list of requirements than anyone else's.

Part 2: Invest in Developing Your People

With a competency assessment drafted, leaders can make investments designed to ensure that employees have competencies required for the future. We have clustered competency investment choices into five domains: buy, build, borrow, bounce, and bind. These companies have helped us to identify specific options leaders may choose in each of these domains—the 5 Bs—as summarized in Table 5.1.

Buy

The traditional battlefield in the war for talent has been the external labor market. Leaders these days spend more time and effort trying to hire the right people than ever before. Even in a downturn and with increasing unemployment, there is a war for the *right* talent. Top talent becomes even more valuable in a tough economy, where top talent can create more value than average talent. Thus, the war for the right talent has become even more ferocious. A few rules of thumb help leaders "buy" talent:

- Go outside only if you can create an "ah ha" effect. It's worth bringing someone in from outside the firm only if the outsider is 25 percent to 35 percent better than internal candidates. Otherwise, the candidate won't have enough support to work effectively.
- Go outside for talent when you want to create a dramatic change in the organization.
- Build a visible and positive employee value proposition so your firm becomes an attractive organization for the best talent.
- Rely on referral networks to source new talent.
- Spend personal time sourcing, screening, and securing the best talent.

Table 5.1 Leadership Choices for Competency Investment

Strategy	Definition	Action
Buy	Acquire new talent by recruiting individuals from outside the firm or from other departments or divisions within the firm.	Outside hires: • Create a clear identity as a good place to work. • Engage employment agencies and search firms. • Attend job fairs. • Use university recruiting and internships. • Access talent from downsized firms. Internal hires: • Create a succession planning system and have a slate of candidates for key jobs. • Ask individuals to define their own future aspirations. • Have leaders do systematic talent reviews. • Create career plans for each individual.
Build	Train or develop talent through education, formal job training, job rotation, job assignments, and action learning.	• Invest in skills-based inhouse programs that focus on the skills required at a given level. • Invest in action-learning in-house programs for teams. • Send employees to courses available to the public. • Provide coaching for leaders. • Provide feedback such as 360-degree assessment for leaders with development plans. • Use temporary project assignments and community leadership to build individual skills.
Borrow	Partner with consultants, vendors, customers, or suppliers outside the firm to garner new ideas.	• Use consultants on projects and special assignments, and form long-term relationships where feasible. • Create a process for transferring knowledge from consultants to unit. • Manage the process of outsourcing, including when to do it, who to do it with, and how to track it. • Form joint ventures and partner with outsourcing agencies.

Table 5.1 *Continued*

Strategy	Definition	Action
Bounce	Remove low-performing or under-performing individuals.	If involuntary downsizing: • Use early retirements. • Create severance packages. • Learn with and rely on outplacement firms. • Find new ways to accomplish work, as by subcontracting a work unit. • Be strategic: Focus on some units more than others. If performance based: • Have clear standards and expectations. • Ensure that a fair and even-handed due process applies to all performance-based terminations. • Be bold, but follow local laws.
Bind	Retain the most talented employees.	• Customize work arrangements (where and when work is done). • Customize work impact (provide desired levels of authority and power). • Customize skill opportunity (provide chances to learn new skills). • Customize community (build agreeable work associations). • Customize rewards (both financial and nonfinancial). • Study those who leave and find out why—and follow up to see if valuable individuals will return.

A buy strategy works when outside talent is available and accessible. Despite its advantages, the buy strategy also has great risks. You may not be able to find external talent that is better or more qualified than internal talent. You may alienate qualified employees who are apt to resent management carpetbaggers who come into a firm without having paid their dues in lower level positions. You may find it difficult or impossible to integrate diverse external talent into teams of people who know the intricacies of the business and have the ability to work together smoothly with minimal discussion.

Build

A "build" strategy means developing and unleashing the latent talent of people already in the firm. It assumes that current employees have the base competencies required for the future. Build strategies may focus on training or development. Leaders considering training programs should answer questions such as these to ensure results from their investments:

- Who should attend the program (employees, customers, individuals, teams)?
- Who should present concepts (faculty, line managers, customers)?
- Who should design the program (human resource professionals, consultants, line managers)?
- What content should the program present (skills, action planning)?
- How will it be delivered (on site or off site; through technology, case studies, or action learning)?
- How will we tell whether it's working (measures for outcomes, action learning, follow-up)?

These questions will help you ensure that training investments lead to business results.[9]

The other half of build comes from development. Development means giving employees opportunities to learn from experience—that is, from temporary projects, teams, assignments, or postings. Managed well, these experiences give employees opportunities to learn a global perspective or to learn how to behave in new situations.[10] Managing both training and development experiences ensures that current employees have opportunities to learn and to change.

A build strategy for talent works where leaders make sure that development is more than an academic exercise, where training is tied to business results rather than theory, where action learning occurs, and where systemic learning from job experience occurs. The risk of a build strategy is spending enormous amounts of money and time on training for the sake of training and not for the sake of building intellectual capital that creates business value. You may spend a great deal of money and get very little in return. If the employees you have trained feel their subsequent assignments, recognition, and reward levels don't match their expectations, you may find that your competitors who use the buy strategy are happy to snap them up.

Borrow

"Borrow" talent through consulting or outsourcing. The premise of borrowing is that knowledge is an asset that can be accessed without ownership. Sometimes a company needs specific knowledge that would be expensive to own. Besides their factual knowledge, consultants can often draw on their experience in a variety of firms to provide insights not available to existing employees.

In working with consultants, leaders should be careful to *adapt*, not *adopt*. Consultants often want to sell a preexisting solution because that's much easier than adapting their knowledge and insight to a company's unique needs. In addition, leaders should try to lease-to-own rather than rent consultant knowledge. This means putting employees on the consulting team so that over time the knowledge transfers inside the firm.

Borrowing also includes outsourcing when an outside vendor can do the work more effectively and efficiently. In partnering with outsource vendors, leaders need to form relationships based on long-term performance, with clear expectations and contracted relationships. Borrowing external input as a way to increase talent also has risks. You may wind up spending large amounts of capital and time with little return. You may become dependent on the consultant without a transfer of knowledge into the firm. You may suffer by using answers from another setting without appropriate adaptation. However, appropriately used, borrowing competency is a viable way to secure intellectual capital.

Bounce

"Bounce" means remove poor performers. Inevitably, not all employees perform equally. It doesn't matter whether the poor performance comes from a bad hire or from an employee who did not keep current, leaders must have performance standards and discipline to maintain talent. If poor performers are not removed, high performers will grow discouraged and their performance will start to slip.

One way to increase the average talent level is to systematically deal with or remove the people in the bottom percentiles. This requires management courage. It also requires clear standards so that both those who stay and those who leave know why and what is expected of them. Leaders who remove poor performers do so strategically, picking their targets instead of making across-the-board cuts in an effort to sweep out the people they want to remove without calling attention to the decision. They are also fair to those who leave, offering them outplacement and equitable treatment, and they move quickly and decisively, pay attention to those who stay, and have clear support for their actions in the applicable laws.

Removing low-end talent as a way to increase overall intellectual capital also has risks. *Downsizing is not a panacea.* You may lose the wrong individuals. You may demoralize those who stay. If you make any of the difficult personnel decisions on perception rather than fact, you may lose management credibility as a result. However, it is generally worse to keep a poor performer in a job just to have someone do the work. When poor performers are removed, it gives leaders opportunities to upgrade talent.

Bind

"Bind" employees by finding ways to keep existing talent on board.[11] Retention matters at all levels of a firm. Retaining senior managers who have vision, direction, and competence is critical to a successful firm. Retention of technical, operational, and hourly workers also matters because investments made in individual talent often take years to pay back.

A large bank got frustrated because it kept losing its well-trained loan officers to other banks—after three years of formal classroom training coupled with tailored job assignments. This bank was using a *buy and build* strategy, but it was creating intellectual capital for competitors by not retaining the people whose skills it was building.

Another firm facing high labor costs decided that instead of focusing on the 7 percent to 10 percent who might have to be let go, it would focus on the 20 percent to 25 percent whose departure would do the most harm to operations. The managers in this firm began to identify these critical employees, to interview them to find out what it would take to keep them attached to the firm, and then to shape individual employee contracts with these employees so they would not leave. These arrangements allowed the firm to retain its critical employees and increase its intellectual capital.

It's important that leaders know their top talent and bind them to the firm during good and bad economic cycles. During a recession, it can be very expensive to bind those who are not top performers. Further, the binding process should be ongoing and renewable. It is not a one-shot deal. An employee's motivation can shift over the years, and it is possible that today's top talent is tomorrow's deadwood or that what is appealing to top talent might change over time.

Human resource professionals often take the lead in recommending which of the five techniques to implement in any particular organization. It's useful to list the five strategies and the individual steps (from Table 5.1 or direct observation) that the company is already taking. This list makes it easy to analyze how well the company is currently doing with each of the strategies, compared to its competitors and its own market realities, and indicates avenues for future investment.

Commitment: Increase Discretionary Energy

Most leaders worry about ways to increase employee commitment. Most helpful in the evolution of our thought has been conversations with Anthony Rucci, executive vice president at Cardinal Health. With his input, we have discovered that employee commitment consists of two factors: cognitive identity and discretionary energy.[12] *Cognitive identity* means that employees feel a kinship with and identify with the organization—whether defined as the parent firm, a division, a plant, or a team. The employees share the values and purposes of the organization; they accept its policies and practices, want to stay with it, and are proud to be part of it. *Discretionary energy* implies that employees work hard for the organization, do their best, put in extra time if required, accept their jobs in the organization, and otherwise put its interests high on the list of claims on their attention.

Employee commitment produces intangible value. In some ways, commitment is an end in itself. As social systems, organizations have identities. A firm with higher levels of employee commitment is a better place to work than one with lower levels—employees help each other more; they are happier, more excited to come to work, more collaborative, and friendlier.[13]

Beyond these positive social outcomes, employee commitment is a means to other important ends. It builds customer commitment. As we have discussed earlier (in Chapters 2 and 3), customer commitment represents share of targeted customer and reflects a growth strategy. Employee commitment is a leading indicator of customer commitment. When a committed employee serves a customer, the customer senses it and responds positively, becoming more committed in turn.[14] Employees who identify with their organization transfer that identity to customers they interact with. Employee commitment also builds shareholder value in multiple ways. First, employee commitment reduces costs within a firm. It increases productivity, allowing the same number of employees to produce increasing levels of value and thus leading to consistent and predictable earnings growth. The increased customer commitment and revenue per target customer it inspires boosts overall revenues and thereby enhances investor confidence, and investors are also likely to perceive and value the reputation of the firm as derived from committed employees.[15]

Employee commitment counts. It may be tracked and measured in a number of ways. Productivity indices report output per unit of input. The output often reflects the goals of an organization: overall revenue, units sold, market share, or profits. Input often comes from measures of total employee headcount or total employee expense. From 1988 to 1998, General Electric (GE) experienced a gain in productivity from $150,000/employee to $350,000/employee. Some of this shift may stem from a realignment of GE business to industries with higher productivity ratios, but much of it indicates an increased measure of employee commitment as employees worked harder and smarter to produce results.

Retention is a common way to measure commitment (or turnover, the converse). While this is a good index, it also may be misleading. An increase in overall retention may mask the fact that a firm is losing its best talent while retaining its average (or worse, its inferior) talent. Retention needs to be moderated by the quality of employees who stay and leave. Retention of "A" players becomes a critical indicator that the firm is willing to focus on and retain top talent. The *most* strategic human resource decision a leader could ever make is to place the poorest performers with a competitor, then hope they stay a long time.

Employee attitude surveys are undergoing two changes. First, they are shifting measures from *satisfaction* to *commitment*. Satisfaction questions ask employees the extent to which they "like" their boss, pay, career opportunities, coworkers, and work conditions. Commitment questions measure the extent to which the employees have a cognitive identity with the firm (believe in its values) and exert discretionary energy toward it (do all it takes to help it succeed). Commitment surveys should ask questions about overall commitment and about management practices that engender that commitment.[16]

Second, traditional employee attitude surveys include long lists of questions (80 to 100), with factor-analyzed, reliable, and valid questions and scales. We propose that firms create what we call *pulse checks* where they identify 8 to 12 items that capture the essence of employee commitment, then track these items monthly or quarterly with a sample of employees. This information then helps managers monitor the employee commitment of a plant, store, division, or other work unit. When the index trends down, action may be taken to avert the aftereffects of reduced employee commitment. The questions in Figure 5.3 will provide you with a quick snapshot of current employee commitment levels—rather like taking your organization's pulse to see how it's doing on commitment. You can complete this survey in the book or go online to: www.rbl.net/whythebottomlineisnt.net.

Useful as studies are, they're often unnecessary. You can find out much about commitment by simply observing it. When we teach classes on employee commitment, the participating executives often seek precise, rigorous, and trackable measures that they can use for management action. Then we ask those who visit multiple sites how long it takes them to discern the employee commitment level of a unit they are visiting. Without exception, they reply in terms of hours rather than days

Statement	Response 1 = low, 10 = high
1. I am proud to be identified with this organization.	① ② ③ ④ ⑤ ⑥ ⑦ ⑧ ⑨ ⑩
2. This company's mission and vision provides meaning to me and fills my need for purpose.	① ② ③ ④ ⑤ ⑥ ⑦ ⑧ ⑨ ⑩
3. There is plenty of opportunity for me to learn new skills and grow personally.	① ② ③ ④ ⑤ ⑥ ⑦ ⑧ ⑨ ⑩
4. Compared to other companies, this organization affords the kinds of job opportunities that I want.	① ② ③ ④ ⑤ ⑥ ⑦ ⑧ ⑨ ⑩
5. There is a close relationship between my job performance and rewards.	① ② ③ ④ ⑤ ⑥ ⑦ ⑧ ⑨ ⑩
6. I can see the impact of the work I do—my actions and decisions make a difference.	① ② ③ ④ ⑤ ⑥ ⑦ ⑧ ⑨ ⑩
7. I am encouraged to find new, creative ways to do a better job.	① ② ③ ④ ⑤ ⑥ ⑦ ⑧ ⑨ ⑩
8. I feel that the organization does a good job of communicating what is going on with me.	① ② ③ ④ ⑤ ⑥ ⑦ ⑧ ⑨ ⑩
9. I am proud to be part of my work team and a part of this company.	① ② ③ ④ ⑤ ⑥ ⑦ ⑧ ⑨ ⑩
10. The company respects my individual differences, including flexibility with alternative work arrangements.	① ② ③ ④ ⑤ ⑥ ⑦ ⑧ ⑨ ⑩

Figure 5.3 Employee commitment pulse check.

and they refer to dialogues, not data. One fun and simple exercise is to ask a group to think about the conference center or hotel where we're teaching and rate its overall employee commitment on a scale of 1 to 10, measured in raised fingers. The results are almost always nearly uniform—the same number of fingers raised around the room. Different participants, each interacting with staff members in 60- to 90-second episodes, generally derive a shared view about the general level of employee commitment (sometimes high and sometimes low).

Commitment counts and it can be measured in rigorous ways that resonate with analytical managers. The concept of commitment can also be legitimated through personal experience.

Creating Commitment: A New Employee Deal

If commitment matters—to employees inside a firm (productivity and retention), customers outside a firm (share of target customer), and investors (reputation and intangibles)—then what actions can leaders take to increase employee commitment? It isn't enough to simply analyze where commitment comes from.[17] You need a framework for leadership action that will build employee commitment by redefining the employee deal as a new value proposition.

In the bureaucratic tradition that characterized the enterprises that took shape in the early- to mid-twentieth century, leaders wanted to create employee equality, where employees are treated the same by classification (tenure, seniority, title). In the new employee deal, employees who give more value to the firm should get more value back from the firm—equity should replace equality (see Figure 5.4). The vertical axis demonstrates the value that employees give to

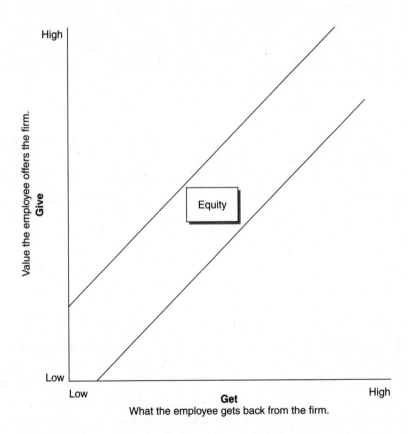

Figure 5.4   The new employee deal: An employee value proposition.

the firm as measured by results such as productivity, customer value, or personal competencies. The horizontal axis represents the value the employees get back from the firm. In this logic, the new employee deal is based on equity, not equality. Employees who give more value to the firm should get more value back from the firm. If there is an imbalance (scores outside the lines in Figure 5.4), then dissatisfaction will inevitably occur. If individual employees give more than they get, they will be likely to either leave the firm or reduce their contributions to remain in an equity position. If they get more than they give, leaders should respond by resolving the imbalance to reduce the unfairness perceived by peers.

Focusing the new employee deal on equity directs attention to both the give and the get dimensions. Leaders must learn to distinguish high- from low-qualified employees through rigorous performance reviews. They must also learn to offer employees value comparable to their contribution. When employees receive value from the firm that has meaning to them, they are more likely to identify with the goals of the firm and offer discretionary energy to accomplishing those goals (thus acting out the definition of commitment).

Taking a condensed view of the academic and popular literature, we see seven key leadership actions that build commitment and offer leaders an integrated view of what they can do to engage employees and deliver on the new employee deal: vision, opportunity, incentives, impact, community, communication, and entrepreneurship.[18] As a mnemonic, think, "leaders build commitment through VOI^2C^2E." Here are the seven practices of VOI^2C^2E that you can use to increase commitment:

1. *Vision*. Many employees want meaning from their work. They want to work in an organization whose purpose they are proud to serve. Employees are more committed when managers give them a purpose for their work. But they're not easy to fool—people soon grow cynical about vision and value statements when they are done as a quick fix, magic pill, or managerial panacea. By contrast, employees who see their organization as having a purpose and leaders as having an agenda devote more time and energy to the unit. Visions are more than slogans; they

allow employees to feel connected to an organization that offers them meaning, thus increasing employee commitment.[19]

2. *Opportunity*. Many employees are more committed when they can develop their skills and abilities. Good employees want to be better. Leaders who invest in training and development experiences that allow employees to develop new skills build commitment. As indicated under the build domain of Table 5.1, leaders may do many activities that enable employees to learn and to grow. As described in the build section of the discussion of competency investments, you have many options for activities that enable employees to learn and to grow. The resulting sense of achievement and accomplishment helps bind employees to the organization.

3. *Incentives*. Regardless of what previous motivation theorists such as Frederick Hertzberg have espoused, many employees are more committed when they share in the gains from the enterprise. Money does affect different people differently, but enough money in the right form is likely to change employee behavior. In boom times, high-tech firms have trouble keeping talented employees because the potential for gain from stock appreciation in start-ups is so great that it draws good employees away from established firms. In economic downturns, employees may return to more traditional companies, again for economic self-interest. Leaders in all firms should be aware of the principles of reward systems that can be used to encourage employees to identify with and work hard for their organization.

4. *Impact*. Many employees are more committed when they work on meaningful projects, participate in decisions that affect them, and experience how their work improves life for others. Shaping governance processes in organizations that engage and empower employees increases commitment.

5. *Community*. Many employees are more committed when they have a positive social setting at work. As social creatures, human beings are more committed when their social structure, or community, offers them positive reinforcements. This means that managers who encourage teamwork, shared experiences, cooperation, and collaboration increase employee commitment.

6. *Communication.* Many employees are more committed when they know what is happening to them and why. When leaders communicate extensively and openly about the business strengths and weaknesses, employees recognize that they are regarded as an essential part of the organization and therefore feel more committed to it.

7. *Entrepreneurship.* Many employees are more committed when they experience a sense of ownership and direction on the job, and when they can influence the way the organization they work in is both changing and adapting to its environment. Generally, this attitude develops when people can define their own working arrangements—hours worked, work-life balance choices, location of work, and the like—and choose their own tasks and priorities within the scope of a goal they accept and support.

We organize these seven factors into our VOI^2C^2E maxim because they are consistent with the commitment research, they each represent leadership actions that will increase employee commitment, and they can all be measured and tracked to create an employee commitment index for a manager or work site.

Each employee may have a unique VOI^2C^2E score. Some employees may favor vision more than opportunity or community more than incentive. But a leader who sees what a talented employee wants to get from the organization (by calculating a VOI^2C^2E score for that employee) can then focus on the items that matter most to that employee. Table 5.2 is a template we have used to assess what a talented employee may want from the firm. Once they determine the employee's orientation, leaders may then provide specific actions that link satisfying the employee's desires to the organization's getting what it requires. When this linkage is firm, the employee stays more committed to the organization.

The VOI^2C^2E model works in public as well as in private sector firms. We applied it in a church setting and found that member commitment strongly derived from vision (sharing the meaning of the theology), impact (doing service work that makes a difference in people's lives), and

To watch a video segment about increasing your talent online or to complete tools and assessments, go to: www.rbl.net/whythebottomlineisnt.html.

Table 5.2   Employee Commitment Worksheet

VOI²C²E		
Leadership Action	Definition	Employee Orientation Score: 1 = Low; 10 = High
Vision	Employees find meaning in their work.	
Opportunity	Employees have a chance to grow, learn new skills with recognition.	
Incentive	Employees receive financial rewards for good performance.	
Impact	Employees engage in work that has an impact.	
Community	Employees are proud to be part of their work team.	
Communication	Employees have knowledge about what is happening and why.	
Entrepreneurship	Employees experience personal ownership in their work because of flexible work policies.	

Source: Tony Rucci and Dave Ulrich, white paper.

community (enjoying being around people of similar values); less relevant was opportunity, incentive, and entrepreneurship. Knowing this profile, leaders in not-for-profit organizations may seek employees who share these orientations. First-line supervisors may also apply the model to their direct reports. It helps tailor specific agreements the leader may forge with employees to ensure higher commitment and productivity.

Leadership Implications

People are an organization's most important asset. Once leaders acknowledge this axiom, they can see how worthwhile it is to develop both competence and commitment. Leaders build competence through assessment and investment. Assessment comes from identifying what competencies are required for the future and determining a competence gap from the present. Investment comes from selecting from an array of activities those actions that will do most to enhance future talent levels. Commitment comes from defining a new employee value proposition where employees who give more value to the firm get more value back from the firm in the form of VOI^2C^2E. VOI^2C^2E depends on the unique orientation and needs of the individual employee.

When leaders manage both competence and commitment, talent becomes an invaluable intangible. With talent, investors have confidence in present and future earnings; they believe that the organization has intellectual capital to deliver growth strategies; they count on the organization to have the ability to turn strategic goals into core competencies.

Here are some steps you can take to ensure that your organization develops and conserves talent and commitment in its workforce:

1. Determine the relative importance of talent for your organization's ability to reach strategic goals.
2. Assess competency gaps with your team (complete the exercise summarized in Figure 5.2).
3. Prioritize competency investments by selecting the highest impact items from Table 5.1—the 5 Bs.
4. Determine the commitment level of employees in your organization by tracking productivity and retention, and by taking a pulse check as outlined in Figure 5.3.
5. Work to improve commitment by offering talented employees VOI^2C^2E—that is, by determining what they desire most among the seven features, and then ensuring that they receive what they value most as long as they produce.

6

Shared Mindset: Creating Unity from the Outside In

A second organization capability in level four sounds familiar—how to build a high-performance culture. Business culture—what it means, what it does for success in operations and in the financial markets—is an important concept these days.[1] With varying definitions, *culture* and *culture change* may refer to:

- Transformation not just turnaround—as when Continental Airline leaders worked to transform their culture and change the way they compete in the airline industry.[2]
- Any firm brand or identity in the mind of target customers— like the one Marriott leaders have created around service, which became their reputation in the lodging industry.[3]
- An articulated set of norms, beliefs, or values—as with Herman Miller or Johnson & Johnson, who are known for value statements that define what they stand for and influence business decisions.[4]

- An organization's *DNA*—for example, Dell proclaims its genetic code is to have low inventories, fast service over the Internet, and demanding profitability goals.[5]
- A firm's personality—as when Southwest Airlines adopted the personality of its founder and decade-long CEO Herb Kelleher.[6]

Each definition implies that culture is more than random or isolated activities. An organization begins to have a culture, a unique identity, when its management approaches outlive any one executive and involve more than any single management practice, fad, or era. We prefer to use the term *shared mindset* for this phenomenon because it represents the essence of what's really happening. First, *shared* implies common, familiar, or memorable. A *mindset* represents a cognition, image, or thought pattern. A shared mindset becomes the identity of the firm in the collective mind of employees, customers, or investors.[7] In this chapter, we share ways that we have found to create a shared mindset that translates into increased intangible value.

Building Culture from the Outside In— A Shift in Perspective

Shared mindset shifts a traditional focus on culture from inside to outside. Instead of just focusing on the patterns inside an organization that affect employee behavior, we focus on how customers and investors perceive and respond to the culture. For example, Dell's commitment to rapid service affects customers as much as employees. Shared mindset also shifts focus to the unity that might exist among employees, customers, and investors and away from value statements about what executives say is important.

A shared mindset exists when customers and investors outside and employees inside have a common view of the organization's identity.[8] Merging internal and external views of identity means that customers perceive the firm in ways that match how employees perceive the firm. At Coopers & Lybrand (C&L), we worked on a program called *Nexus*. This initiative started by identifying target customers, those clients who represented significant current or future business. We helped design a workshop where these clients sat down with the account or engagement teams from C&L who served them. The goal of the workshop was to create a nexus between clients and account teams, as illustrated in Figure 6.1, so the participants of the two groups would gain a shared identity or purpose. The workshop began with each group first identifying its own goals, then working to identify and increase common or shared goals and behaviors. By engaging in the dialogue about what mattered to both sides, employees and clients developed a shared mindset—C&L employees had a stronger understanding of what service meant to clients

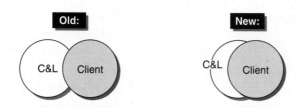

Goals of the Nexus Workshop
- Improved communication and understanding of each other's needs.
- A contract among members of both the engagement team and client team about what is expected from each other.
- Ongoing processes whereby C&L and client teams can have productive conversations to prevent and resolve issues.
- A sense of how to better contribute and commit to each other.
- Behaviors and actions that can be institutionalized to help C&L better serve clients and receive in return more revenue from this service.

Nexus Program Design
1. Introduction: Present the theory of shared mindset and unity.
2. Generate common understanding around values: Identify common and different values of C&L engagement team and client team.
3. Generate common behaviors based on values: Identify common and different behaviors of C&L engagement team and client team.
4. Generate contract for action: Identify actions each team can take to build a shared mindset.
5. Define next steps: Prepare action plans to continue relationship.

Figure 6.1   Nexus at Coopers & Lybrand.

and clients had a better sense of what they could appropriately expect from C&L employees. C&L found that clients who participated in this workshop spent more money with C&L over time, partly as a result of their increased comfort with the relationship that C&L was trying to forge with them and partly because they had a clearer idea of the services available to them.

What's in It for Me—Intangible Value among All Stakeholders

A shared mindset produces intangible value when it creates an identity or reputation in the mind of employees, customers, and investors that is tied not to a person or product but to the firm itself. This mindset becomes a self-fulfilling prophecy when it affects how each stakeholder behaves toward the firm.

Employees self-select into firms where they perceive a fit between their personal hopes and values and the existing mindset at the firm. Employee commitment, productivity, and behavior both shape and are shaped by the identity of the firm. Employees who choose to work for Marriott must realize up front that they will be expected to provide exceptional customer service. Once hired, they find management practices that reinforce the customer service mantra. Employees who don't fit with the service agenda are likely to leave. A shared mindset changes and reinforces employee thinking and action.

Customers also demonstrate their commitment to a firm's mindset or identity. When a firm develops a reputation for quality, service, or price, customers begin to rely on this identity and do business with the firm based on it. This identity of the firm in the mind of its best customers becomes a firm brand and demonstrates the impact of mindset on customer value. Research shows that firms with strong and visible brands, such as McDonald's, American Express, Harley Davidson, Herman Miller, and so forth, create higher shareholder value (see Chapter 3), and day-to-day life often illustrates the same point. Possessing a firm brand becomes even more important for Web-based sales. Firms on the Internet with a known identity and positive reputation attract customers much more than unknown firms do.

Shared mindset also affects investors in two ways. First, investors have a mindset that defines a company and its overall intangibles. This is the essential point of this whole book—a firm's identity positively or negatively affects investor behavior. Investors may gravitate toward firms with positive identities (as with the run-up on Cisco stock in the dot-com bubble) or rush away from those with negative reputations (as with the explosive run-down on Enron stock). Second, investors may be affected by the extent to which employees have a shared mindset. This concept can be a bit of a stretch, and CEOs often ask us, "What are the indicators that our shared mindset will affect shareholder value?" The simplest indicator is that shareholder value will climb as employee mindset promotes its customer value proposition, such as quality or speed or price to the point where investors and customers seek out the company on that basis, get more of what they want, and return again and again. For those who want more concrete data, we offer the following challenge: Invite the largest shareholders (analysts or investors) of your firm to visit any location in your firm for a day. Encourage them to ask any employee any question. The questions might be about strategy, competitors, profitability, what's important to customers, or any other relevant question. At the end of the day, meet with those investors and debrief what they learned. If the firm or unit has a shared mindset, the investors will have found similar answers to their multiple queries. So far, few senior executives have taken us up on this challenge—the process makes them understandably nervous. But it is a test of shared mindset that may evoke confidence in investors, helping them sense that employees throughout an organization have common knowledge of how their actions affect the firm's results.

Shared mindset may exist for an entire enterprise or for subgroups within the enterprise. Any unit where a group of employees engage in shared behaviors dedicated to meeting customer expectations should have leaders dedicated to a shared mindset. Mayo Clinic has a worldwide reputation for patient care built on education, research, and provider support. Each unit at Mayo (cardiology, oncology, obstetrics, etc.) works to make the Mayo reputation real to physicians, nurses, and administrative staff. Leaders in Rochester, Minnesota; Scottsdale, Arizona; and Jacksonville, Florida, each adapt the core values of Mayo to their work operations.

Creating a Shared Mindset

How do you create a shared mindset? We propose a four-phase process (Figure 6.2) that creates a shared mindset that affects employees, customers, and investors:

1. Create the desired identity
2. Make the identity real to customers
3. Make the identity real to employees
4. Build an action plan for implementation

To illustrate the overall logic, let us share a relatively recent experience with a large firm. The firm had experienced a number of labor challenges, including delayed union contracts and a brief strike. The

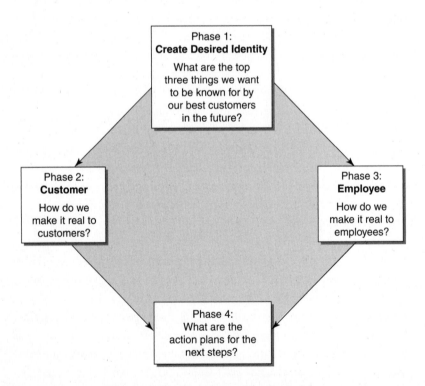

Figure 6.2   Creating a shared mindset.

CEO called Dave Ulrich and a conversation along the following lines occurred:

CEO: Can you help fix our labor problems?

Dave: Not really.

CEO: Why not?

Dave: Typically, a problem like yours is not about your labor policy or contract. Instead, it may be about the underlying culture of your organization.

CEO: Please don't suggest that my team and I go off-site and talk about our innermost values and beliefs, then write a culture or values statement that reads like those from every other firm.

Dave: I'm not suggesting that, though it sounds like you and I define culture differently. To me, a culture is the identity of the firm in the mind of your best customers, your firm brand or reputation.

CEO: What would you suggest then?

Dave: From what you have told me, many of your best customers are disillusioned with you because of the poor service they receive. Poor service typically comes from disgruntled employees who have quit caring about customers. Before you can make changes in labor policies, you may want to deal with the deeper issue of shared mindset.

CEO: Makes sense, but what's in it for the firm to have this shared mindset.

Dave: Firms with a shared mindset, or strong positive identity in the mind of their customers, get more revenue from targeted customers, more committed and dedicated employees, and more investor confidence.

CEO: What is the first step?

Dave: Have your top executives reach a consensus about the question: What are the top three things we want to be known for by our best customers?

CEO: Then . . .

Dave: Then, make this identity real to target customers who come in contact with your firm and to employees who work for the firm. Generate specific and concrete actions that employees and customers experience that reflect this identity.

This conversation captures the essential elements of a shared mindset: It matters, it can be intentionally crafted, and customers and employees can experience it. Let's look at the four phases of creating this shared mindset.

Phase 1: Create the Desired Identity

We have worked with over a hundred executive teams to create a desired identity or shared mindset. Some were at the top of an organization and creating a desired identity that relates to the entire organization; others represented a division, a plant, or a function. Regardless of scope, the process for crafting a shared mindset is similar.

First, ask each individual to write a response to the question: What are the top three things we want to be known for by our best customers in the future? This question turns attention outside rather than inside by seeing the organization through the eyes of the customers. It highlights the best customers, not the average ones. It concentrates the focus by asking for three answers, not an unlimited number. It emphasizes identity by asking what the unit is known for. Finally, it points toward the future, not the past or present.

Second, collect the responses and categorize them. For example, a team of 10 people will give you 30 total items. Sort the 30 into common answers. This might mean that of the 30, you have seven that add up to "service," six "value," and five "reliability," and the other 12 are not in these three categories. It is important to sort rigorously. For example, some people will write things like "service, reliability, or ease of doing business" and imply that they all mean the same thing. Not so. At this point in the exercise, the goal is to see the extent to which a shared mindset exists among the top team, which includes rigor of language and ideas.

Third, add the total number of responses in the top three categories (18 in this example) and divide by total responses (30) for a rough measure of shared mindset (67 percent in this case). Our rule of thumb is that a desired level is 80 percent—which is extremely rare on the first round. Generally, even when firms have strong cultures, executives use differing language and even differ in the aspects of the company they regard as crucial to its success.

Fourth, talk about themes in the results. Cluster and define themes that emerge from the responses and redo the exercise to see if an 80 percent consensus can be reached. Reaching 80 percent consensus generally takes a couple of hours. After debate and dialogue, the executives can usually agree on what they want to be known for by their best customers.

Fifth, put the themes into words that resonate with customers. For example, at Domino's Pizza in the early 1990s, we did this exercise with the top 14 executives. When asked the top three things they wanted to be known for, responses included service, reliability, good product, good value, talented employees, easy access, and many more. The unity score was about 40 percent to 45 percent after Step 2. On discussion, they came up with themes around quality, service, and talent. Then they put these themes into customer language with the following desired mindset: hot, fresh, tasty pizza delivered on time by friendly people who drive safe.

Sixth, check out the articulated mindset with customers to make sure it is right. This final step in building a shared mindset—making sure it resonates with target customers—is probably the most important. If the desired mindset will not cause customers to pick your firm over competitors, it is the wrong one. This means having executives and employees make their mindset real in all customer touch points. Every customer contact should be characterized by the desired mindset.

We have done this process many times. The discussion it evokes generally moves beyond generic values to customer buying criteria and serious debate about the firm brand and identity in the mind of the best customers. In one case, a group of executives and a group of their customers came up with widely different answers for the question of what they wanted the firm to be known for.[9] In this case, the exercise forced executives to face the reality that they were out of touch with customers. That led them to take the powerful step of starting their culture change with customers, not with themselves.

In other cases, creating the desired identity evoked discussions of what should be a shared firm brand across multiple divisions and in multiple countries versus subunit brands and country-specific brands. In these cases, we generally conclude that a firm brand of a large complex organization focuses on processes of how work is done rather than the content of the work, that a firm brand is simple rather than complex, and that a firm brand highlights principles rather than practices. Subunit brands (by product, division, or geography) then focus more on the content of the product, the specific customer requirements for that market niche, and the practices to deliver this brand.

In other cases, the discussion helps executives create a story line about how their business has evolved and how it needs to change for the future. In one company, the exercise helped executives see that they had focused for years on operational excellence with a series of cost-oriented initiatives. But the industry had caught up with them and developed price parity, so they had to shift to another theme—service. With service as a mindset, they were able to craft a story for investors, customers, and employees about how they would differentiate themselves in the future.

In almost all cases, the exercise imposes a clarity and consistency about the desired identity or mindset. Such consensus enables the executive team to combine unity of thought with variety of action.

Phase 2: Make the Identity Real to Customers

Given that the desired identity should have meaning and impact for targeted customers, leaders should find ways to make the stated identity real to those customers. This comes from specifying points of contact—*touch points*—between the firm and the target customer, then finding ways to make the desired identity real in each one.[10]

For example, at Domino's Pizza, executives picked four touch points between the firm and the pizza-buying customer: the call, the delivery, the pizza, and the box. To communicate service during the call, they worked to answer the call by no more than the fourth ring, have a friendly greeting, use caller ID to verify name and address of customer, and make sure they thanked customers for their patronage. The delivery was on time because the drivers had maps and drove in areas they knew, and it was accomplished by friendly people who dressed in clean uniforms, had correct change, and used a positive script in communicating with the customer. The pizza was hot, fresh, and tasty because it was made of good quality ingredients, packed in heat bags to maintain warmth, and delivered quickly after cooking. But as executives thought more about the customer contact, they realized that the call lasted about 30 seconds, the delivery exchange about a minute, and the meal about 10 minutes, but the box often sat around customer kitchens for hours. So they chose to use the box for advertising their firm brand and identity. Rather than merely have the box give their name and say "our drivers carry less than $20 in change"—which might communicate an attitude of suspicion toward customers—they placed coupons, slogans, and commitments about the pizza on the box itself.

Other firms have focused on touch points. For example, Merrill Lynch makes contact with customers by offering consulting services to targeted accounts where the account manager visits with clients annually, doing an account review and offering specific advice for potential investments. The Harley Davidson owners' group (HOG) has a special club sponsored by Harley where owners share information and experiences. All these efforts are designed to make a desired mindset real to targeted customers.

We have run workshops where we ask leaders to think about the firm from the customer point of view: Imagine you are one of your own customers. What are the touch points you have with the firm, from the beginning of the process to the end? We often have leaders go a step further and really be customers so as to experience their firm through the eyes of a customer—to call in for service using normal channels, to shop in a store or dealership without identifying themselves, to stay in a hotel room or eat in a restaurant, to send back a product, or to use competing products. As leaders adopt the eyes of the customer, they begin to make lists of how each touch point might be managed to make sure that customers always experience the desired culture.

We also encourage leaders who work to make the mindset real to targeted customers to also include these customers in management actions. Frequently interview and survey these customers as sources of feedback and include their input for performance appraisal of employees. Invite clients to attend and present at training programs. Share their ideas through employee videos and newsletters. Include their case studies in leadership talks and speeches. Ensure that they participate in compensation decisions and on task forces. Include clients to help redesign products or services. In short, develop touch points for clients in many ways. The more that targeted customers engage in or touch the firm, the more the desired culture is real to them.

Phase 3: Make the Identity Real to Employees

Ultimately, employee daily actions should reflect the shared mindset. We have found three critical factors for leaders who want to make the mindset real to every employee:[11]

1. Articulate an intellectual agenda.
2. Establish a behavioral agenda.
3. Institutionalize an organizational agenda.[12]

Articulate an Intellectual Agenda

An intellectual agenda changes how employees perceive and think about the firm. It affects their top-of-mind relationship with the firm. A good intellectual agenda is woven into a communication plan through four steps: (1) create the message, (2) choose the audience, (3) select a time frame, and (4) identify alternate channels for the message.

Step 1: Create a Simple Message.   People remember simple messages. Complex messages get lost. In politics, candidates strive for simple messages that convey their values and beliefs and why they are running for office. George Pataki (running for governor of New York against incumbent Mario Cuomo) used the slogan "too liberal too long" to contrast Cuomo's approach with his own. Leaders don't run organizations by slogan, but their messages need to be simple to penetrate the boundaries of the organization. In building a communication plan, we often recommend that leaders have three to five messages they hope to communicate as part of their intellectual agenda: What it is, why they have it, and how it affects employees.

At Continental Airlines, Gordon Bethune and his team crafted a plan they called "Go Forward," which highlighted and integrated their approach for the future.[13] This plan had four elements:

1. *Fly to win: The market plan.* They focused on profitable flight routes and abandoned others; they removed capacity or flights so that remaining flights flew full; they reengaged travel agents.
2. *Fund the future: The financial plan.* In overcoming bankruptcy, they invested in cash and forecasting systems to give them accurate information. They also renegotiated leases and payments and focused on making a profit within their first year on the job.
3. *Make reliability a reality: The product plan.* They knew that customers who traveled the most cared about being on time predictably. They installed measures of on-time arrival that were shared with all employees—then they offered employees a $65 bonus each month that the airline was among the top three of on-time arrivals in the industry. They also worked to redesign aircraft interiors to make them more comfortable for passengers.
4. *Working together: The people plan.* They treated their people as important elements of the business equation. They worked to build teamwork, cooperation, and trust.

The overall Go Forward plan and the four subplans became a simple message that employees could understand both conceptually and behaviorally. It became the lighthouse and north star for the Continental transformation.

Step 2: Define Targets of the Message.   The intellectual agenda needs to permeate all levels of an organization. It needs to be heard, understood, and acted on everywhere in the organization. Targets of the message might be the top management, senior management, middle management, first-line supervisors, and ultimately all employees. In addition, the mindset might need to be shared by customers, suppliers, and investors outside the organization.

Step 3: Create Time Frame for Sharing Message.   The time frame for communicating an intellectual agenda is based on understanding that the message will not be understood at any one point in time, but over time. Sometimes, the time frame has a clear ending, as when an upcoming public or union election imposes a deadline when the vote takes place. At other times, the time frame is arbitrary and may be measured in months or quarters.

Step 4: Propose Alternative Ways to Share the Message.   Messages about an intellectual agenda may be shared in many ways. Some of these messages are more impersonal (video, newsletter, chat room); others are more personal (town hall meetings, one-on-one interviews, coaching, team off-sites, and the like).[14] Impersonal messages suffice for information sharing, but attempts to change behavior need as much personal contact as you can give them.

With these four steps in mind, leaders may turn an intellectual agenda into a communication plan (see Figure 6.3). Such a plan enables executives to craft, communicate, and publicize the shared mindset. It must be publicly shared and owned by line managers, not delegated to staff or outside groups. It must be rigorously redundant to ensure that target groups for the communication receive the same message repeatedly. Our rule of thumb is 10:1. Each message (WHAT in Figure 6.3) needs to be shared approximately 10 times before it has impact. This means filling in the cells of Figure 6.3 so that each message (A, B, C, D) is shared in multiple ways for each target group.

Establish a Behavioral Agenda

A new, shared mindset becomes real if, and only if, it changes the way employees behave. Words, phrases, concepts that resonate but don't change behavior, create cynicism. Generally, employees who experience day-to-day business problems know what to do to turn a shared mindset into action. Developing mechanisms to engage employees and to enable them to figure out what behaviors to change creates enduring culture. For example, engage them through listening, town hall meetings, or brainstorming sessions, enabling them to recommend specific changes that will make their work better.

It is our experience that local line managers are the ones who build long-term relationships and embody the values of the corporate leaders. When local leaders change their behavior, employees gain confidence and believe in the new mindset. Local ownership comes when local

Who: Target						
Top management						
Front line managers						
All employees						
Customers						
Suppliers						
Investors						
Other?						
	1	2	3	4	5	6
	When: Timing of information sharing					

What: The messages to communicate
A: Why we do it?   C: Why we do it?
B: What we are doing?   D: What it means to me?

How: How can we share information?

1. Video
2. All hands meeting
3. Newspaper article
4. Q&A article
5. Letter to all employees
6. Documentation manuals
7. Brochure
8. Broadcast
9. Poster
10. Message on paycheck
11. Newsletter
12. Article in local paper
13. Training program
14. Voicemail
15. Q&A town hall meeting
16. One on one meetings
17. Counseling sessions
18. Performance reviews
19. Wandering around (MBWA)
20. E-mail
21. Web site
22. Chat room
23. Off-site workshop
24. Lunchroom chats
25. Mentor relationships
26. Telephone contacts
27. Others

Source: Adapted from Ronald Ashkenas, Dave Ulrich, Todd Jick, and Steve Kerr, *The Boundaryless Organization: Breaking the Chains of Organization Structure* (San Francisco: Jossey-Bass, 1995), pp. 78–79.

Figure 6.3   From an intellectual agenda to a communication plan.

managers are invited to publicly present and engage in the new mindset. At Marriott, each hotel manager engages local employees in what can be changed, kept the same, or removed to improve performance. It's worth repeating: *The employees closest to the work know how to enhance service.* When local managers solicit input, employees develop more commitment to the service mindset. When asked questions, we encourage managers to ask "What do you think?" as a way to engage employees in the solution of problems.

To make change real to employees, tie simple changes to the larger mindset change you intend. Rather than have multiple themes and messages, it is important to cluster behaviors under a common theme. Leaders building mindset have used many themes to unify employee behaviors:

- General Electric: Work-Out
- Sears: Transformation and town hall meetings
- IBM: Accelerating Change Together (ACT)
- General Motors: GoFast
- Unilever: Cleanout
- Phillips: Centurion program
- Aetna: Out of the box
- Armstrong: Trailblazing
- Rolls Royce: One small step
- Continental: Go Forward plan

Regardless of the title or theme, these efforts encouraged and integrated employee behaviors consistent with the desired mindset. Different employee actions could then be bundled under these umbrella themes, allowing employees to see how their behavior aligned with the overall mindset.

Institutionalize an Organizational Agenda

A shared mindset occurs when the principles of the new mindset become embedded in the organization's systems and processes. These processes endure beyond any one leader or event the leader may plan. Processes that institutionalize the new mindset include:

- Talent flow
- Rewards

- Training and development
- Budgeting
- Leadership brand
- Organization processes

Talent Flow.   As we discussed in Chapter 5, the treatment of talent sends messages to employees, customers, and investors. Moving talent into, up, through, and out of the organization communicates the mindset. Hiring new people who embody the mindset and promoting employees who live the mindset—and removing those who don't—become critical tools for embedding culture. Those who are not hired, promoted, or removed observe what is happening and adapt their behaviors accordingly. Southwest Airlines rigorously screens flight attendants. It looks for employees who have technical skills, but even more, it seeks those who are predisposed to engage with passengers, doing the required job with humor and enthusiasm. This type of screening becomes the most critical decision of a merger or acquisition—for the survival of the combined company, it's essential to assess talent and ensure that the right talent stays and the wrong talent leaves.[15]

Rewards.   Reward systems both change and reinforce behavior. The goal of a reward system is to turn goals into measures of behavior and outcomes, then allocate rewards based on the extent to which employees behave in the right way and deliver the desired outcomes.

For a quick look at your firm's current mindset, take a look at its performance management system. The appraisal questions show what your firm values as defined by what it rewards; that is, its real mindset—which may be quite different from the one espoused in vision statements and other earnest pronouncements. It's also useful to invite customers to review the performance management process and report the extent to which the behaviors and outcomes on the appraisal document reflect what they as customers want the firm to be known for.

Training and Development.   Designing and delivering training courses sends messages about what matters. At the same time, it offers leaders skills and tools to act on those messages. An audit of the content of training and development experiences should show that these investments focus on the desired mindset, both conceptually and pragmatically.

The suggestions in Chapter 5 on the "build" option of competence investment suggest that innovative ways to develop employees may be used to share a culture. At one firm we worked with, the first development experience after the merger involved employees from both sides of the deal. We asked members of each firm to capture what they were proud of about their firm; its heritage, history, and culture. They shared these views with one another. We then created mixed groups from both partners and asked them to create a new mindset that would serve the new firm. We asked them to identify things that they needed to let go from each of their old cultures and to spend time discussing and ending the old culture to create the new. Finally, we focused on behaviors of the new culture.

Budgeting.   Mindset affects budgeting in two ways. First, resources need to be allocated to issues consistent with the mindset. When Marriott faces cost pressures, service budgets are among the last to be reduced. Dell constantly invests in finding ever more innovative and creative ways to do direct sales and service through marketing groups, customer datasets, and technology investments. Second, the mindset determines how budgets are set and modified. When Herman Miller faced a downturn in the office furniture business, its leaders knew they had to reduce investment and costs. Even with the worst economic downturn in 20 years, they continued to invest in innovative products and services. Then, they shared their budget-cutting process with employees. For example, they felt it necessary to close a California facility. Rather than do this from corporate headquarters in Michigan, the entire executive team went to the facility and held multiple meetings with employees. They shared market, customer, and performance data. They listened to employee concerns and answered numerous questions. They worked to help employees find alternative work by bringing search firms on site with them. They shared their personal concerns with having to close the facility, but shared the logic behind doing so. At the end of their session, the employees gave them a standing ovation. The Herman Miller executives felt that this open-book budgeting process reflected their mindset.

Leadership Brand.   It's common to see leaders with different mindsets, theories, and agendas about what constitutes effective leadership within the same business and even the same function. There are many reasons this happens—these theories may be age-related. Leadership theory may be consistent with whatever was in vogue during a leader's formative years when he or she received supervisory training. It could also be that a particular theory strikes a chord and strongly influences what a leader values and pays attention to. Some leaders advocate a "Great Man" theory of leadership advocating certain character traits. This could range from a specific Meyers-Briggs profile to "does the candidate shake hands with a nonsweaty handshake while looking the recruiter steadily in the eyes" (consumer products company). Others advocate theory X or theory Y, situational leadership, principle-based leadership, and so on. Multiple theories about effective leadership are not conducive to shared mindset that drives a performance culture. These multiple theories have the potential to confuse because each theory advocates different behaviors and values. Our solution is *leadership brand*. It is an integrative approach that is simple, effective, and makes sense to most leaders.

In Chapter 11, we discuss leadership brand in greater detail. Leadership brand exists when leaders at every level take action to deliver the right results in the right way. Leaders are branded because they stand out from leaders in other companies. They stand out because it's clear what results are desired for all leaders and it's also explicit how these results should be obtained (e.g., accomplish our business results with speed, integrity, and with an absence of bureaucracy). Customers, employees, and investors trust that these leaders will do what they promise to do, now and in the future. A shared mindset about leadership brand is a cultural advantage.

Organization Processes.   Organizations may be seen as bundles of processes of how work is done. When these processes are done in line with the desired culture, the culture will be sustained. Marriott has a number of processes and procedures for keeping rooms clean, managing guest registration and checkout, providing room service, communicating with frequent guests, ordering new materials and supplies, and managing the hotel infrastructure (heating, cooling, lights, etc.). Each of these processes communicates to employees the service mindset Marriott seeks to instill. Leaders who want to create sustained culture must embed that culture in organization systems and practices. The organization agenda becomes a way to ensure that culture is maintained over time even without a specific leader championing it.

In summary, when employees understand the intellectual agenda, see how their daily actions reflect the desired mindset, and experience organization processes that reinforce the mindset, they become more aware of and committed to that mindset. Sometimes, we have seen leaders fail because they emphasize one of these three strands for making mindset real to employees and forget the others. Some leaders focus aggressively on building an intellectual agenda, but don't translate it into employee behavior or organization processes. Others work hard to reengineer work processes but don't engage employees at the same time. Or they engage employees through some form of participative management (quality circles, town hall meetings, or the like), but fail to connect these actions to an intellectual agenda or embed them into work processes.

Phase 4: Build Action Plan for Implementation

Shared mindset changes thinking and action of employees, customers, and investors. When your employees behave in ways that customers would like them to behave, employees, customers, and investors are well served. In the fourth phase, the ideas from preceding phases translate to action. To be successful, action plans need to be specific, start small, and have leadership support.

We often ask leaders to look at the ways that they could make the culture real to customers and employees and pick two or three specific areas they could focus on. Prioritizing a few things and getting them done is more useful than talking about many things and accomplishing little or nothing.

Many times, this means implementing a new mindset with *steps of change*. Each step in Figure 6.4 represents a small, specific action that General Electric (GE) took toward the ultimate mindset. Starting with simple actions works because leaders control the action and employees and customers see something real as a first step. Building step on step

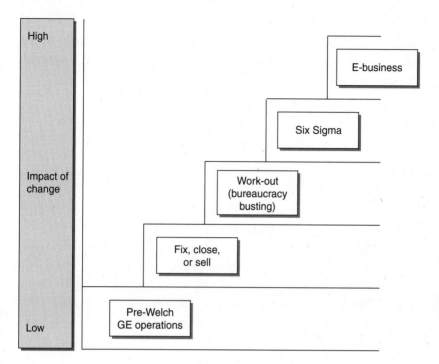

Figure 6.4   Waves of change.

enables leaders to gain momentum for a change and build confidence in the success of the change.

Leadership support requires line managers who sponsor the shared mindset to act accordingly. Their actions need to be public, visible, and consistent. They must take visible ownership of the new mindset and talk about it to employees, customers, and investors. They must make the firm mindset part of their personal leadership style. In their private meetings with their subordinates and peers, they need to express commitment to the mindset they are working to instill. They must find and identify symbolic events to reinforce the mindset, and make sure that organizational changes are consistent with the mindset. They need to stick with

> To watch a video segment or complete online tools related to shared mindset, go to:
> www.rbl.net/whythebottomlineisnt.html.

their espoused mindset over time without wandering from it to new ideas, and to create myths, metaphors, and symbols that reinforce the mindset. They must put a review of the mindset on their management team agenda and hold direct reports accountable for acting on it.

Leadership Implications

Here are some specific steps that will help you build a firm mindset:

1. Invite your top team to do the shared mindset exercise we suggest and create a unity score for your business.
2. Identify target customers and spend time with them to see if your desired mindset will influence their buying patterns.
3. Make the mindset real to customers by specifying customer touch points and finding ways to connect between the firm and customers on each touch point.
4. Make the mindset real to employees by creating an intellectual agenda and building a communication plan to share it throughout the organization.
5. Make the mindset real to employees by encouraging employee behavior through town hall meetings or other forums where employees change behavior.
6. Make the mindset real to employees by changing organization processes to be consistent with the desired mindset.
7. Build an action plan with early successes and first steps.
8. Make sure that you are visible, public, and consistent in your own commitment to the mindset.
9. Ensure that the look and feel of all advertising—and the message it includes—is consistent with the shared mindset.
10. Watch for employees whose behavior is consistent with the mindset, and present both public and private rewards when you catch them in the act.

7

Speed: First Beats Best

An organization's capability for speed of change often determines its overall competitiveness. Just consider the personal computer industry. A business must have a faster internal rate of change than the external rate of change in its industry or else it will quickly be surpassed by competitors. Business leaders often lie awake at night worrying about the volatility and unpredictability of the new economy.[1] Things are changing faster and faster because of accelerating technology, increasing sophistication of customers, competitors, and suppliers, and catch-up efforts on the part of government regulators and financial markets. *Volatility* refers to pace, velocity, and rate of change. *Unpredictability* means the future can no longer be extrapolated from the present. Leaders must respond to unanticipated changes. These changes might come from unexpected events, as when the 9/11 terrorist attacks dramatically changed the world for the airline, financial services, lodging, and tourism industries. Changes come from new technologies, such as the way genetic engineering has changed pharmaceuticals and the Internet has changed publishing and a host of other industries; or from consumer trends, as when demands for comfort and individual expression influence fashion design.

In this chapter, we review ways to best respond to the increase in the speed of change and the concomitant unpredictability of the business road. In particular, we look at a decision-making protocol that our clients have found useful, as well as bureaucracy busting tools created by General Electric and General Motors. We also share with you our own "anticorporate virus" signatures that you might have fun with—and find effective to use.

A Shift in Thinking—Building and Maintaining Speed

Management thinking has shifted from understanding and managing change to building and maintaining speed.[2] Change deals with new ways of doing things; speed focuses on how quickly those new ways are implemented. An organization imbued with speed has intangible value for employees, customers, and investors. Speed excites. Most people like things that move fast—fast cars, fast boats, and fast athletes. When organizations act quickly, employees have a sense of momentum and purpose rather than indolence and lethargy.

Speed enables. Organizations that are first to market gain share and define standards. Speed becomes an adjective applied to the whole range of management strategies: *faster* globalization, *faster* product innovation, *faster* customer service, *faster* operational efficiency, and so on. In one company working to create a strategy for the future, the leadership engaged in a debate between speed versus product innovation—but soon concluded that both were equally critical. Slow product innovation would result in great products that customers would probably ignore because they would already be aligned with competitors. Fast innovation emphasizes that the pace of innovation matters as much as the innovation itself. Customers have more confidence in organizations that consistently move quickly and aggressively into new markets, geographies, and products.

Speed energizes investors. Market leaders who move quickly build investor confidence in strategic, product, and administrative innovations. Firms that quickly deliver consistent and predictable earnings, that quickly define and deliver a growth strategy, that quickly identify and create core competencies linked to strategy, and that quickly build capabilities of talent, shared mindset, learning, accountability, collaboration, and leadership build greater intangible value.

But *unmitigated speed*—speed at the cost of everything else—is not the answer. We see five main issues that leaders need to address in their pursuit of speed:

1. *Emphasize smart speed.* Speed matters, but it must be related to relevant and important issues, not trivial ones. Being faster at a bad idea or incorrect solution only gets wrong things done sooner. Leaders do smart speed when they make speed a way to help accomplish business goals rather than serve as an end in and of itself. Speed varies by business issue; fast in a financial services industry differs from fast in a nuclear services industry.

   It can be useful to ask yourself: How accurate do we need to be on this decision? The answer leads to smart speed. If the decision requires it, take time and be thoughtful and careful. If the decision allows it, be creative and entrepreneurial, learning from successes and failures.

2. *Start small.* For leaders working to increase speed, this means turning large, complex problems into small, daily, and doable actions—and then being consistent and persistent about pursuing those actions until a tipping point is reached and the impact begins to occur quickly.

3. *Recognize capacity.* Capacity deals with how much change an institution or individual can absorb. Leaders need to ensure that change aspirations exceed resources, but not by too much. Managing capacity begins with answering the questions, What do we most want to do? What are we doing that we don't need to do? Separating high- from low-priority issues and being explicit about what will and will not be done frees institutional and individual time and energy. It also helps prioritize the workload so that resources and energy may be directed to the things that matter most.

4. *Identify speed targets.* For institutions, leaders may create a number of key initiatives to accomplish business goals. Speed occurs when these initiatives (e-commerce, quality, customer service, etc.) are done faster with similar or better quality. An indicator of institutional speed would be a 20 percent to 30

percent cycle time reduction for any and all key initiatives such as the time to respond to a new business reality or change to a new business focus.

5. *Recognize that speed also affects individuals.* People spend time. It's often useful to calculate a return on time invested index (ROTI) to track trends in employee productivity, commitment, and engagement in their work. Individuals increase their speed when they are able to focus on work that matters most, when they feel they have control over their work, and when they see how their work aligns with the overall goals of the company. Individual speed would result in employees' taking appropriate risks, feeling more responsibility for action, being able to distort time on important and value-added work, and increasing enthusiasm, commitment, and productivity at work. Speed must be both institutional and individual. If institutional speed occurs, processes may be improved, but if individuals are not feeling engaged in the effort, they may not be committed and productive and over time the speed will slow. If individual behaviors are done with more speed, but the institutional processes remain slow, people will become frustrated and the institutional changes won't be sustained.

Factors That Increase Speed

With these issues in mind, leaders can engage in four practices that increase speed: decision making, bureaucracy busting, speed profiling, and eliminating viruses.

Speed Through Decision Making

Decision making speeds up or slows down work. To encourage speed through decision making, it is useful to ask: What is the decision you want me to make as a result of this conversation or meeting?

This "what decision" question has as a premise that it's the leader's job to make decisions, not create action plans; to cut to the essence of an issue rather than to debate the fringes; and to focus attention, not divert it. We find that most leaders have goals, objectives, or some form of desired outcomes for the next six months to a year, but they're not always as explicit about their role in the process. For example, one executive told us that he wanted his firm to sell more through Internet channels, have more product innovation, and increase customer service. When we asked him to pick the one he worried about the most, he chose product innovation. We then asked our "what decision" question: What are three decisions you will make in the next 30 days that will ensure progress on product innovation? (Three is not a magic number; many situations need only one or two and some need more, but asking for three helps keep the thought process moving.) He immediately began to talk about the action plans that had been developed for innovation. We stopped him and probed again for specific decisions he would make or make happen in the next 30 days to foster innovation. Finally, he admitted that he did not know what decisions he personally would make to advance innovation. We brainstormed the possibilities, and he then committed to make a set of specific decisions that allowed him to cut to the chase in the next month and move things along by making the decisions that only he could make.

The "what decision" query clarifies leadership challenges in many situations. A McDonald's shift supervisor was having trouble managing schedules with employees who had obligations that constrained when they could work. By bringing employees together then framing and asking the question: We have to fill these shifts; what are the options for how to fill these shifts? she was able to reach closure on schedule requirements. An IT supervisor was responsible for selecting and implementing a new computer program. The choice of the program ended up in seemingly endless debates about criteria and vendor options. Finally, the IT supervisor pulled employees together and raised the "what decision" query: What are the criteria for selecting an IT vendor? How do vendors rank against these criteria? By being explicit about the "what decision" that needed to be made (setting criteria and selecting a vendor), he was able to speed decision time.

At times, increasing speed through decision making requires more than the simple "what decision" question; it requires a decision protocol.

For example, when team meetings routinely seem to take more time than they are worth, leaders can promote smooth and efficient operations (and help save everyone's time) if they follow the five-decision protocol guidelines summarized in Figure 7.1.

First, ensure decision clarity: What is the decision we are going to make? One CEO of a large computer company stated that no one could bring him an issue unless it has been boiled down to a "yes or no" response. This means that background information isn't enough on its own; it is imperative to be clear about the decision that the information should help make. By that yardstick, "How do we gain better customer service scores?" isn't a useful question for a meeting with a decision-making authority. Instead, it's best to focus on a few key options and state those options explicitly: "We can improve customer service scores by investing $50,000 in a customer information and response system targeted on the top 10 percent of our customers; therefore, may we have authority to. . . ." This type of specific question then leads to more informed decision making.

Second, specify accountability: Who will make the final decision? Decisions may be delegated to an individual or a team, but it is critical that the individual or team know that they are responsible and that the accountability is public and shared.

The most basic of all accountability tools is "On the count of three, point." A team can learn much about decision clarity by simply calling on all members to point to the person on the team who is accountable for ultimately making a specific decision. Somebody says, "On the count of three, point to the person in the room most accountable and responsible for this decision," and the fingers fly. This exercise may seem simplistic. But we have found that it often makes unspoken misunderstandings public, identifies possible political squabbles before they break out, and allows people to resolve ambiguity with cool heads. Generally, most people point to the same person, who then takes charge. Sometimes, team members delegate up, pointing to the team leader, who in turn is pointing to someone else. The team leader can then make clear who will be accountable. At times, team members split their assignment of accountability and point at different people, which permits a useful discussion about who will ultimately

Keys to Faster Decision Making	
Principles of Higher Quality Decision Making	**Assessment (1 = Low; 10 = High)**
Clarity We are precise about the decisions we are making. We never begin a meeting without being clear about what decisions we will make by the end of the meeting. We don't have reviews without knowing what the decision will be as a result of the review. We can dissect big ideas (such as quality or market share) into specific decisions with clear alternatives. We create decision pyramids of the little decisions that will lead to other decisions.	
Accountability We know who is responsible for a decision and hold that person (or team) accountable if they do or don't make and execute a decision. Consensus does not mean everyone gets equal vote. Somebody (individual or team) must make the decision, but should involve others in it. Ideally, the decision should have the support of those who care about it, and general acceptance on the part of those who don't.	
Timeliness We have deadlines to get decisions made and we stick to those deadlines. (It's often useful to set a limit of 14 days to closure on most decisions.) We are decisive and demanding on getting decisions done and if a team lags, the manager makes it.	
Process We have a method of engaging critical people in key decisions so they share ownership through meetings, technology, or other processes. We take appropriate risk for the decision required. We accept that we may not have total consensus, but move on anyway.	
Return and Report Once we make a decision, we follow up to ensure that it sticks and happens.	

Figure 7.1 Decision-making protocol.

make what decision, and, if the accountability is shared (as in a matrix), how to ensure speedy decision making.

Third, require timeliness: When must the decision be made? Leaders focus on getting decisions made when they're still useful. They set time lines and hold people to them. The best deadlines have a public requirement, for example, a presentation to a senior management group or board of directors. With the commitment to a presentation, decisions are likely to be made to accomplish the decision on time. We saw one effective team leader lay the groundwork for a decision by sending an e-mail message to all his team members on Monday morning, announcing that on Friday at 9 a decision would be finalized for presentation to the executive committee. He laid out the question and parameters and wanted input by Tuesday at 5 P.M. Tuesday evening, he condensed this information and sent out the resulting synthesis Wednesday morning, asking for a second round. This information was collected by Thursday at noon, whereupon he crafted his recommendation for the executives that afternoon and sent a copy to the team. They had a chance that evening to make final comments before he prepared his remarks for the executives.

In this case, the decision and timing was clear and anchored in a real event. With technology, employees have access to information regardless of where they are working that day or week. Employees who did not participate did so at their own risk. The three rounds enabled employees to have a voice in the decision, to have their input shared, and then to recognize the recommendation going forward.

Fourth, pay attention to process: How will we ensure that we make a good decision? The process for decision making may include *who* needs to be involved, *how* much risk the decision can carry, and *what* information is required for a good decision. Using a good process increases both the quality of a decision and the commitment it receives from all concerned.

Fifth, commit to follow-up: How will the decision be returned and reported? Decisions need to stick, to be implemented, and to deliver what is promised. Return and report means that data is collected to track and monitor the decision, that people are publicly accountable for making a decision happen and that follow-up occurs. Decision "stickiness" increases when periodic reviews occur, when measures are tracked, and when incentives align with desired outcomes. At the end of many meetings, we ask the simple question: "What will happen next?"—and then push for clarity about what decisions have been made in the meeting and how they will be implemented.

The simple "what decision" question coupled with the decision protocol offers leaders tools for making fast and effective decisions. The "what decision" question aims to focus attention on the desired set of issues as leaders interact with others. The decision protocol helps a meeting, task force, or project team make sure that decisions are made in a way that encourages speed. These tools are as useful for CEOs as they are for shift supervisors at McDonald's or task for leaders on IT projects.

Speed Through Bureaucracy Busting

Nearly all organizations, whether large or small, have unhealthy levels of low value-added, unproductive, and bureaucratic work. Such work slows down company progress, encourages employees to look inward rather than to focus on customers and competitors, stifles creativity, and rewards those who curry favor through office politics rather than serve customers. Bureaucracy is the antithesis of speed. Bureaucracy is found in many forms, the most visible of which include reports, approvals, meetings, measurements, policies, and practices that add little value but slow things down.[3] Leaders who do not consciously work to reduce bureaucracy inevitably find that employee energies that should be focused on getting important work done quickly are spent fulfilling arbitrary requirements instead.

At General Motors (GM), CEO Rick Wagoner established four major themes: act as one company (leveraging GM's global scale), product and customer focus (innovative products that stimulate customers to buy), stretch targets (meeting aggressive financial and market share goals), and have a sense of urgency. Under the sense of urgency theme, GM initiated a program called GoFast![4] This initiative builds off of work from General Electric's Work-Out program.[5] The goal was to remove bureaucracy by engaging employees in an effort to identify bureaucratic barriers that were slowing down their work. The program encouraged and allowed leaders to take quick and decisive action by making thousands of small changes that would add up to a sense of urgency.

GoFast! was simultaneously a bureaucracy-busting exercise, a culture change initiative, and a workshop where employees could practice problem solving and decision-making skills. A typical GoFast! workshop lasts four to nine hours, divided into five modules as shown in Figure 7.2:

> *Module 1: Call to action.* Leaders introduce the workshop and set expectations, encouraging employees to be open, candid, and willing to identify bureaucratic activities that stifle their creativity. Leaders also encourage employees to focus on issues within their control (asking them to address problems within the scope of the people present rather than to try to solve corporate-wide problems), to offer solutions rather than just complaining, and to be specific rather than generic.

Module	Content
Call to Action (1 hour)	• Set tone and expectations for workshop. • Identify workshop theme. • Talk about speed as enabler of business results.
Gallery of Ideas (2 hours)	• Brainstorm barriers to speed (reports, approvals, meetings, policies, practices). • Prioritize opportunities for impact.
Action Recommendations (3 hours)	• Recommend actions to increase speed by category or topic.
Team on Team (1 hour)	• Synthesize recommendations to be consistent and nonduplicative.
Commitment to Action/ Decision Module (2 hours)	• Present recommendations to leaders who make decisions on the spot. • Prepare champions who will take lead on the effort and action plans to ensure that decisions are carried out.

Figure 7.2   General Motors GoFast! workshop.

Module 2: Gallery of ideas. Participants brainstorm their experiences with bureaucratic work, defined as anything that kept productive work from happening fast. After brainstorming individually, participants prioritize the opportunities for removing bureaucracy that has the biggest impact.

Module 3: Action recommendations. Participants work in teams to prepare action recommendations to remove bureaucracy. The teams discuss past successes and failures in efforts to remove bureaucracy. They then examine root causes for the persistence of some bureaucratic mechanisms, making specific recommendations for each bureaucratic activity: eliminate, partially eliminate, delegate, do less often, do in a less complicated or time-consuming way, do with fewer people involved, do using a more productive technology, and the like.

Module 4: Team review. Teams share their recommendations with one another. In the ensuing discussion, they work to consolidate recommendations so as to address problems in a coherent, high-impact manner and not work at cross-purposes to each other.

Module 5: Commitment to action. Leaders who sponsor the workshop listen to and act on the recommendations. The goal for this decision module is that 60 percent to 70 percent of the recommendations are approved on the spot and implementation plans are derived to assure follow-through.

Under Rick Wagoner's direction, senior GM business leaders have sponsored and championed thousands of GoFast! sessions. Rather than try for one or two major corporate actions to stimulate speed, this process has engaged and enabled employees throughout GM to identify and remove bureaucracy that affects them. Removing bureaucracy in a firm as large and complex as GM takes time, but it also takes *impatience.* The GoFast! effort is pushing responsibility for removing bureaucracy to all leaders and ultimately to all employees.

Employees closest to the work know the bureaucratic barriers to getting work done. When given an opportunity to identify and remove those barriers, employees become excited because they can make a difference and see the results of their work. When leaders publicly and visibly support employee recommendations, both leaders and employees develop a sense of urgency—and speed increases in the organization. The principles behind the GoFast! workshop may be applied by any leader who senses that things are not going as fast as seems necessary. A leader may simply call together employees and open dialogue on what can be done to remove barriers to getting things done quickly, with a commitment to leadership action as the result.

Speed Through Profiling

Speed is sustained when critical business initiatives are managed with a focus on success factors. When leaders of initiatives know what is required to get the job done successfully, they can use that knowledge to move more quickly. Change programs identify what is required to make things happen; a speed success factor approach focuses on how to apply change knowledge to a particular initiative to make it happen faster.

General Electric (GE) has created a success factor process it calls the Change Acceleration Program (CAP) that applies lessons learned about change to any business initiative in an effort to speed things up.[6] Using the metaphor of a pilot's checklist, GE leaders were encouraged to turn what they know about change into what they do to make change happen fast. Through CAP, GE has developed a generation of leaders who make change happen quickly by means of the following tactics:[7]

- Quickly mobilizing key leaders whose tacit and active support for the change is required. (Leading Change, as specified in Figure 7.3.)
- Defining clear business rationale for investing in particular initiatives. (Creating a Shared Need)
- Building both aspirational and behavior-based statements of the desired outcomes of an initiative. (Defining What To Do)
- Effectively involving the key implementers so that their commitment to the change is optimal. (Mobilizing Stakeholders)

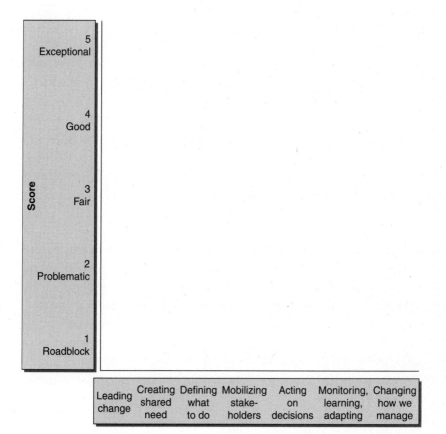

Figure 7.3   General Motors *ChangeFast!* profile.

- Ensuring that resources are allocated to deliver an initiative including people (skills, communication, accountability), finances (money needed to move ahead), and technology (information processing systems). (Acting on Decisions)
- Establishing key benchmark measures that ensure the timely completion of change initiatives. (Monitoring, Learning, Adapting)
- Setting up short cycle time feedback loops that promote learning from both successes and failure. (Changing How We Manage)

The CAP process ensures that knowledge is transferred to action and that leaders help make initiatives happen fast.

At General Motors, the CAP process was adapted to become a speed success factor profiling process.[8] Leaders know more than they think they do about making change happen fast and thus more than they attempt to use in practice. When they are taught to rigorously apply what they know to what they do, they can get things done more quickly.[9] Building on the GE work, GM derived seven critical success factors (shown in Figure 7.3) that encompass an initiative they call ChangeFast! Leaders of any initiative at GM were then encouraged to use the seven critical success factors to ensure that work happens faster by going through the following steps:

Step 1: Profile Critical Success Factors

Any initiative can be ranked on each of the seven critical success factors in Figure 7.3, with scores ranging from 1 (a problem that could derail us) to 10 (we have this completely taken care of). This profile offers a sense of how likely and how quickly the initiative might be implemented. Sometimes, having different stakeholders do the profile also reveals information about probable challenges in moving forward. For example, leaders who sponsor initiatives may score the Leading Change critical success factors high while employees who might be affected by the initiative score it low because they do not see or sense the leadership commitment.

Step 2: Interpret the Change Fast!

The profile captures a great deal of information about the probability of fast change. If all seven critical success factors score low, the initiative will be unlikely to happen quickly and may require more work than it is worth to make it happen at all. If all seven critical success factors are high, the initiative should move forward on time and within budget. We've found that the first three critical success factors focus on initiating change and the last three on sustaining it. To succeed, generally two of the first three scores need to be high and so do two of the last three scores. We have also found that the middle success factor—mobilizing stakeholders—is the make-or-break success factor. If employees who are impacted by the change do not feel committed to it, the change will go forward slowly, if at all.

For example, our friend Buzz Nielson—police chief of the West Valley Police Department (WVPD) just outside of Salt Lake City, Utah—

recently ran into just this problem. Buzz is a very effective leader, personable and driven to succeed. However, he just found out the hard way what happens when the staff doesn't support changes that their management tries to implement.

Last year, WVPD unsuccessfully experimented with Village Policing that is popular in New York City, Los Angeles, and other metropolitan areas. In Village Policing, the city is divided into six, geographical basic car areas. This was a big change for the staff who had been using a specialist system for the past 20 years. That is, the first response was by means of officers who patrolled an assigned area by car, responded to any calls that came in, and prepared an initial report on the incident. This report would go to a central records system, and then—after about three days—to a detective specializing in the specific type of crime (such as burglary), who would begin working on the solution. These specialists continually built expertise by concentrating on the same sort of crime and by networking with their counterparts in other departments.

With Village Policing, the city is divided into areas in which an officer is responsible for all problems in that area. The detectives become generalists rather than specialists. So a burglary report would wind up with one of the detectives assigned to the part of town where the burglary occurs rather than with a burglary specialist. Instead of the report going to central processing and then to a specialist, it goes to a weekly meeting in which all of the officers assigned to the area sit down and look at the problems and identify how they will work together to solve the problems.

After a year of trying to implement this new system, the detectives finally rejected it. They argued:

- We need specialists, not generalists, as technology improves and becomes more sophisticated.
- Quality of work on investigations has worsened.
- Other agencies in this area do it the traditional way and so our specialists are losing out by not staying technically up-to-date. No one gets a chance to attend the countywide specialty meetings.

Buzz and his former boss, Chief Alan Kerstein, agreed to let the detectives return to their old approach. The department is now trying to figure out how to integrate some elements of Village Policing into its operations. No matter how well Village Policing works in other areas, it can't be implemented at West Valley until the detectives and officers there support it.

Step 3: Decide Where to Focus Attention

The ChangeFast! profile makes it clear which critical success factors require more attention. Leadership time, energy, and resources are best used when they flow to those areas where scores are lowest. Leaders frustrated by a slow pace of change often leap to the conclusion that they need to share more information about why to do the change. By contrast, diagnosis and profiling often reveals that the sense of shared need is already high, but people don't know what to do about it. So more videos, newsletters, or town hall meetings about why to change will have far less impact than meetings and surveys that address defining the needed action.

Step 4: Invest in Actions to Master Each Critical Success Factor

Each of the seven success factors may be mastered by applying a set of tools or leadership actions. GM created a toolkit for the seven critical success factors and leaders as well as project teams acted on those that require attention.[10] Here are some of the leadership actions for each success factor:

- *Leading change:* Leaders need to manage their personal attention (time, energy, passion, focus), to develop personal competencies related to effective change implementation, and to understand and adopt roles required for speed (champion, sponsor).
- *Creating a shared need:* Leaders and project teams need to build a case for change based on both opportunity and need, to understand sources of resistance to change and have plans for making the demand for change greater than resistance to change, to help employees see the rationale for change based on data, expectations, or examples (pilot projects, early wins).
- *Defining what to do:* Leaders need to articulate the outcomes of change in specific, concrete ways and to specify actions that move the organization to achieve the future desired state. A key

tool requires leaders and project teams to develop a pithy elevator speech—an explanation so clear and concise that a guest can grasp the plan on the ride between the lobby and the executive suite.

- *Mobilizing stakeholders:* Leaders and project teams need to identify target individuals or groups who are critical for the change to happen, to define influence patterns for them, and to create commitment strategies that will bring them on board.
- *Acting on decisions:* Leaders and project teams need to turn the vision into specific behaviors, to implement the "what decision" query, to use the decision protocol, and to make sure that action plans are in place to implement plans.
- *Monitoring, learning, adapting:* Leaders and project teams need to create indicators to track progress on each change initiative, to hold people accountable for results, to learn from successes and failures, and to tweak and adapt a change effort based on early successes or failures.
- *Changing how we manage:* Leaders need to weave the change into management practices such as measures, rewards, communication, structure, technology, and resource allocation.

When leaders act to fill the gap in the success factor most requiring work, they ensure that all the key factors for successful change are managed and that the change occurs quickly.

The purpose of the diagnostic and profiling exercise is to help leaders turn what they know into what they do in a disciplined way so that fast and effective change occurs, not just change. When leaders apply what they know, they focus attention, act faster, and learn rapidly. ChangeFast! profiles can be crafted for any set of initiatives as a way to turn what is known about change into what needs to happen to make change happen faster and more effectively.

Speed Through Eliminating Viruses

All firms have orthodoxies, sacred cows, norms, and patterns of thinking and behaving that impair their financial health. One way to think about these beliefs and practices is as viruses. If you think of them as natural parts of the firm, it's easy to shrug and accept them as facts of life. But if you recognize the way they can paralyze your operations and block the use of your collective knowledge base, it becomes clear that they're as dangerous to your corporate culture as computer viruses are to your corporate IT systems. They share another feature of computer viruses: they're at their most deadly when they're not recognized. Once you find an antivirus program able to diagnose and detect a computer virus, you can isolate the virus, prevent it from spreading, and repair and restore your files. Likewise, once an organization spots a cultural virus that is keeping things from happening as fast as they should, it can take steps to eliminate the blockage.

For example, in one firm, managers routinely held premeetings before meetings. The original idea had been to speed things up by coming to a decision in a small group and then selling it, but it turned out that the preliminary sessions just hardened differences among the managers. Not only did they not decide anything in advance, they had nothing to sell in the larger meeting and generally wound up postponing matters to yet another meeting. Decisions were so slow that the competition surged ahead easily, and employees who valued getting things done left to work for the faster competitors. By identifying this practice as a virus, leaders of this company were able to articulate the problem and then take explicit action to eradicate it, making the company more success focused, efficient, and agile.

Antivirus programs rely on *signature files*—lists of known viruses and their symptoms, which they use to scan computer systems for traces of the listed viruses in action. You can do the same thing on the job, once you know what to look for. We have fun with these viruses in leadership workshops. We ask leaders to break into groups and identify the two or three most salient viruses in their organization. This is easy to do. Then we ask them to draw a picture that represents how the virus actually works in their organization. Finally, each group shows their picture to the larger group and explains their choice of virus in less than one minute. In one case, we placed all of the flipchart papers with the virus drawings in a large trash container and lit fire to it. In another company, all of the drawings were signed by each group of leaders and then framed and displayed in the hallways of corporate headquarters as a way to communicate to all employees what they were dedicated to eliminating. Here is a basic set of management virus signatures (your organization will have viruses we have not yet named):

1. *Overinform:* We tell everybody and then have a meeting. We make sure everyone has been touched before we meet, which reduces our ability to be decisive.

2. *Have it my way:* We know we don't have much to learn from other units; our ways are always the best. (Also known as NIH—the Not-Invented-Here syndrome.)

3. *Saturday morning quarterback:* We enjoy criticizing everything, even before it happens.

4. *False positive:* We like nice-speak—everyone tries to be subtle, be nice, be kind, even if they disagree. This leads to passive resistance.

5. *False consensus:* We like the feeling of consensus so we ask everyone before we act—but we just go through the motions before we do what we please.

6. *Caste:* We like to label people by grade and then evaluate their contribution by their grade level instead of their competence to address a particular question.

7. *Forward into our past:* We spend a lot of time looking for the future in the rear view mirror. We are so afraid of losing our heritage that we won't change our culture.

8. *Turf wars:* We let units defend their turf even to the detriment of the firm's overall interests. Groups fall into a "my business" stance, ignoring "our business" and defending their ideas and programs as though they were sports teams defending a goal line.

9. *Command and control:* We like senior management to tell us how to run the company so we don't need to feel a personal obligation when things go wrong. This leads to management by memo instead of personal interaction, and exacerbates the effects of the Saturday morning quarterback virus.

10. *Activity mania:* We like to be busy. Our badge of honor is being so busy that we don't have time to think (or in some cases, to get results).

11. *Hero worship:* We like heroes. We like to label projects, initiatives, branches with the individual, not the collective—leaving the labeled individual hero out on a limb and the collective happily off the hook when problems arise.

12. *Results rule:* We like results any way, anytime, anyhow . . . process is nice if we have time, but who has time? (This is the flip side of item 22, Process mania.)

13. *Narcissistic competitiveness:* We're so fond of winning as individuals that we sabotage anyone who seems likely to get ahead, no matter how much good the competitor might have done the company.

14. *Adrenaline addiction:* When in a crisis, we act quickly and decisively, and then we wait for the next crisis to hit. Between crises we kick back and don't worry about the next one—and if things stay calm for too long, we stir them up.

15. *Customer antipathy:* We know more than they do, so they should turn to us; we are invested in our success, not our customers'. (This would be a great place to work if it wasn't for the customers.)

16. *Authority ambiguity:* In our complex matrix structure, we are not sure who has ultimate accountability and authority, so no one really does.

17. *All things to all people:* We never met a good idea we didn't like. Instead of clearly focusing on a few critical priorities, we spend attention and energy on everything that comes up, whether or not it's part of our strategy.

18. *Flavor of the month:* We jump from program to program as separate, not integrated initiatives. Meanwhile, cynicism about new programs mounts.

19. *Dripping with change:* We have a capacity problem—so many changes are going on at once that it is difficult to keep up. People are stressed out, but we never stop to wring out the sponge and make room for new activities and approaches.

20. *Disjointed action:* We don't see the big picture and how our unit's work fits in with an overall strategy or purpose.

21. *Obedience:* When told to do something, we do it, even (or maybe especially) when we know it's going to cause trouble down the line.

22. *Process mania:* We're so consumed by process that not much actually gets decided. (This is the other end of the scale from item 12, Results rule.)

23. *What more than why:* We like to think about what needs to happen, but we don't look at why it should happen or who should do it.

24. *Kill the messenger:* We tend to fire or sideline any employee so incautious as to point out bad news.

25. *Glacial response:* We just can't seem to get decisions made quickly, so we might as well go on as before.

26. *Engineering oriented to a fault:* We're sure that any problem has an ideal technical solution, and no stopgap or administrative action is worthwhile.

27. *What have you done for me lately?* We make sure that no good deed goes unpunished, and respond to all successful efforts with requests for more.

Figure 7.4 is a worksheet for our antivirus program. Use it to prepare a virus scan and plan for your organization. Sit down with your team and hand out a list of viruses, including the ones we note here and any others that occur to you. It helps to discuss the virus concept with others, especially with new employees, who bring fresh eyes and are likely to spot dysfunctional practices that old-timers simply don't notice. Ask each team member to identify five to seven of the most common or pressing viruses in the organization.

After each team member picks a set of viruses, tally the choices in the Frequency column of Figure 7.4. With some discussion, the group should be able to reach a consensus about which viruses are most prevalent and damaging to the organization. At that point, turn the discussion to probable causes: Why do we do things this way? When was the first time anyone can remember us doing this? Who wants to keep it this way? What purpose is this virus serving?

Virus	Frequency	Cause	How to Eliminate
1. Overinform			
2. Have it my way			
3. Saturday morning quarterback			
4. False positive			
5. False consensus			
6. Caste			
7. Forward into our past			
8. Turf wars			
9. Command and control			
10. Activity mania			
11. Hero worship			
12. Results rule			
13. Narcissistic competitiveness			
14. Adrenaline addiction			
15. Customer antipathy			
16. Authority ambiguity			
17. All things to all people			
18. Flavor of the month			
19. Dripping with change			
20. Disjointed action			
21. Obedience			
22. Process mania			
23. What more than why			
24. Kill the messenger			
25. Glacial response			
26. Engineering oriented to a fault			
27. What have you done for me lately?			

Figure 7.4   Virus detector worksheet.

The cause may suggest the cure. In many cases, eliminating virus practices is a simple matter of labeling them and agreeing to stop doing them. Sometimes they require more attention, in which case it can be useful to assign someone to monitor the dysfunctional behavior. Process mapping—gathering participants to trace the process that includes the virus from beginning to end—may be required to sort out the cause and the remedy. You may also find it necessary to provide incentives for avoiding or consequences for engaging in a virus practice, and to draft communication plans to eradicate the virus.

> To see a video segment on speed or to complete tools or assessments online, go to: www.rbl.net/whythebottomlineisnt.html.

Whatever you do to identify, understand, and remove viruses, bear in mind that they have a tendency to recur. It's essential to be persistent and consistent in avoiding dysfunctional behaviors to keep the level low enough for organizational health.

Leadership Implications

Speed of change is more important than change itself. Being fast or first becomes an intangible value inside the firm to employees (who grow more engaged and excited) and outside the firm to customers (who get products or services quickly when they want them) and to investors (who develop confidence in fast-moving firms). Speed must be smart, start small, recognize capacity, and be targeted to both institutions and individuals. Leaders may apply decision-making, bureaucracy-busting, speed-profiling, and virus-destroying tools to make speed happen.

Here are some questions that are useful to ask as you address the question of speed and how to get it:

1. What is my organization's predisposition to speed? Are we generally behind, equal to, or ahead of competitors in going to market with new products or services, doing administrative innovations, and forming strategy?

2. What is my organization's reputation for speed among customers and investors? Are we seen as leader or laggard in our industry?

3. What decisions should be decided slowly, with high quality and low risk, and what decisions should be decided faster than we now do them?

4. How can I apply the "what decision" question to people I meet with, to teams I lead, and to units I direct?

5. How well does my team apply the decision protocol in gaining closure? Where are we strong? Where are we weak?

6. What elements of bureaucracy persist in my organization? How can I engage employees across the company in identifying and removing bureaucracy?

7. What are the top two to four initiatives we are working on in my organization this year? Can we apply the speed success factor profile to these initiatives to see how fast we are likely to do them? Do we have the success factor to turn what we know about change into ways to deliver speed of change?

8. What are the recurring viruses that attack my organization's effectiveness? How can we identify and eliminate them for good?

8 | Learning: Changing the Game

Everyone has firsthand experience with learning—in school, at home, and at work. In organizations, learning also occurs. Learning differs from change and speed of change that we discussed in the previous chapter. Where change deals with doing something new and speed focuses on the pace of doing new things, learning implies transferring knowledge from any single change experience to another. Some organizations seem to have the ability to learn better than others, creating intangible value in the process. These organizations are not only able to change but to learn from each change experience so that cumulative progress occurs.

Investors recognize intangible value in organizations with a learning reputation because these organizations not only create new ideas, they share those ideas throughout the enterprise, building knowledge networks where technology and communities of practice transfer experience from one setting to another. These organizations operate on the leading edge of the half-life of knowledge within their industry. They keep updating what they know and abandoning what becomes obsolete, so that the time interval from any given date to the point where half of that date's knowledge has been replaced grows shorter and shorter. The impact is that their lead over their competitors grows longer as their intangible value increases. In this chapter, we explore how you create learning environments as intangible value in your firm. We look at some companies that have nurtured learning, as well as invite you to assess how well your organization fosters individual, team, and organizational learning.

A Learning Equation—Three Building Blocks of a Learning Organization

Much has been written about organizational learning, beginning with Chris Argyris and Donald Schon in the 1970s and more recently by Peter Senge and his groundbreaking book, *Fifth Discipline*. Many others have defined the concepts and constructs of learning organizations and infused our thinking. The following simple equation can represent the extent to which an organization has developed its learning capability and can help leaders assess their firm's overall ability to learn:

Learning capability = Generate × Generalize ideas with impact[1]

Examine each element of the equation. *Generate* deals with creation of new knowledge through discovery, invention, experimentation, or innovation. *Generalize* deals with movement of ideas across boundaries. Some companies may seem more adept at doing new things before others, yet merely having an idea (generate) is not sufficient for learning. Learning requires that the idea transfer across a boundary, such as time, geography, or business units. *Impact* means that something substantial has changed, and change implies that learning has happened. For real-world business purposes, we define impact as adding value to the firm's stakeholders (investors, customers, and employees) over a long period of time.

Learning as an intangible requires all three building blocks. True learning organizations both generate and generalize ideas and ensure that the ideas will have impact. Matsushita is a good example of how this process works. Its Cooking Appliance Division generated new concepts in designing a product (the Home Bakery). The company then generalized the concepts and methods to other divisions and finally to the whole corporation.[2] The successful development of Home Bakery— the first fully automatic bread-making machine to allow users to make quality breads comparable with those of a professional baker—provided an exciting learning experience for Matsushita, a company known up to that point as a price-based competitor for relatively standard products in mature markets.

To begin with, the development process for Home Bakery represented a sharp break with the conservative and status quo–oriented culture at Matsushita. It dissolved the usual boundaries within the organization through formation of interdepartmental project teams. Engineers also reduced the amount of time they spent competing with each other to conjure new fancy products and concentrated their efforts on creating products with genuine quality that met real customer needs. The development of Home Bakery inspired Akio Tanii, CEO at the time, to adopt the Human Electronics program, focusing Matsushita's strategic and product-design energy on developing more human products that incorporated high technology. The fully automatic coffee maker with an integrated mill and the new generation of rice cookers (such as the Induction Heating Rice Cooker, which cooks rice in a manner similar to the traditional Japanese steam oven) are other examples that have entered the marketplace. Based on our definition, Matsushita has high organizational learning capability.

Leaders who want to build learning into their organization strive to generate and generalize ideas with impact. Such learning occurs at three levels: individual, team, and organization (Table 8.1). When each of these three learning targets employs the building blocks effectively, an organization creates intangible value.

Foster Individual Learning—The First Target Group

As managers, you have probably noticed that some individuals are predisposed to learn. By nature they are inquisitive and curious; they're always experimenting, trying new things, and seeking ways to improve. These individuals have a constant stream of fresh insights and ideas. They see

Table 8.1   Overall Model for Learning Capability

Targets of Learning	Dimensions of Learning	
	Generate New Ideas	Generalize across Boundaries
Individual	1. Ensure that people are creative and innovative.	2. Ensure that people see patterns in behavior, then do things in new ways.
Team	3. Ensure that teams encourage creativity and approach problems in new ways.	4. Ensure that teams learn lessons from successes and failures.
Organization	5. Ensure that organizations find ways to bring new ideas into the organization.	6. Ensure that the organization has the ability to share ideas across units.

alternatives others don't see and connections not readily apparent to others. These natural learners are valuable employees because they generate new ideas and offer alternatives for the future not grounded in the past.

Leaders should identify these individuals both as they come into and as they move through the organization. Natural learners offer novel responses to preliminary screening questions. A number of companies (Microsoft comes to mind) have thought-provoking interview questions to tease out an individual's predisposition to learning, for example:

- How much water flows through the mouth of the Mississippi River in a day?
- Why are manhole covers round?
- Who in history would you like to visit with for an hour? Why? What would you ask?
- What is the future of our industry? What are the threats? Challenges? Opportunities?

The goal in each case is to see how a prospective employee responds to these questions. The correct and factual response, where there is one, matters relatively little. The intent is to identify how the candidate thinks about finding an answer to the problem. Natural learners see alternatives that others don't see.

Other questions explore the applicant's past, since personal history is often the best predictor of present state, and natural learners have also probably engaged in creative activities, taken risks, and had unique experiences. In screening for natural learners, leaders may also explore issues such as these:

- How did you approach selecting your college major?
- What was unique or unusual about your college studies?
- What array of jobs or experiences have you had?
- What are some of the riskiest tasks you've taken on? What did you do when you failed?

Screening the applicant pool and securing natural learners may sound enticing, but bear in mind that what makes these individuals creative on one hand may make them difficult to manage on the other. Creative people need space to experiment and try new ideas.

Train Everyone to Be a Learner and to Generate Ideas

Natural learners are a real resource for companies that know how to handle them, but they're not absolutely essential for the development of a learning organization. Even people who aren't natural learners can master the tools of learning, and any organization is well advised to help them do so because there are never enough natural learners to fill all the available jobs.

Most individuals go through a learning cycle that has three steps: choice, consequence, and correction (Figure 8.1). Natural learners go through this learning cycle by instinct, but nonlearners can also master it and make it run more smoothly for them.

Step One: Choice

Learners seek alternatives. They see what might be, not what has been or has to be. They are able to quickly brainstorm multiple ways of approaching and defining problems rather than relying on old methods of solving them. Here are some tools to help individuals increase their ability to make choices:

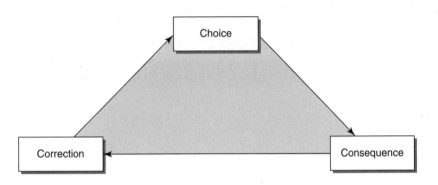

Figure 8.1   Individual learning cycle.

- *Comparing:* Learners look around and see what others do. They encourage their own creativity when they identify alternatives by examining how other people have approached similar problems; benchmark both successful and unsuccessful people and draw conclusions about the two groups. Leaders increase learning when they develop mentors who offer formal and informal counsel about their experiences; and encourage staff to ask for advice from those who have relevant experience.
- *Experimenting:* Learners are willing to try new things and take risks. They create alternatives by testing new ways to do things even if the old ones are still working; by setting up mini-experiments where they do something one way and see the impact, then try another. Leaders can assign staff to projects that are not within their comfort zone.
- *Being willing to look stupid:* Learners accept that they probably won't get it right the first time. They see alternatives, are willing to make mistakes, and don't become captive to the mistakes. When learners make a mistake, they take it in stride, figure out why it happened, adapt, and try to not make the same mistake twice. They don't blame, they reflect. By contrast, perfectionists have to have things right the first time and often don't create as many alternatives as those who try something even if it is not completely finished. Leaders encourage learning when they model

successive experimentation by admitting their own mistakes and
sharing their lessons learned.

- *Volunteering for tough assignments and projects:* Learners increase choices by taking on assignments that stretch their thinking and approaches. One leader encourages learning by having
  manufacturing employees spend time (a day every quarter) in
  sales to get a better look at the customer point of view. Another
  leader puts new employees onto tough projects and asks them to
  share their ideas before the seasoned employees speak up; this
  both gets the benefit of an outside eye and helps the new employee learn by surfacing misunderstandings.
- *Asking what if?* Learners moderate fear of failure and facilitate
  generation of new ideas by thinking through "what if" questions:
  —What if I don't succeed? What is the worst possible thing that
  can happen? Am I okay with that?
  —What if I don't try something new? How will I feel about my-
  self in the future?
  —What if I try to do this project another way? How would
  someone else approach this project? What insights can I gather
  from seeing this project through someone else's eyes?

Individual learners create choices and seek alternatives. They act on
their own behalf—and recognize that choices always exist. They seek
novel and unusual ways to solve problems. They see existing challenges
through others' eyes. They have new ways of doing things.

Step Two: Consequence

Every choice has a consequence, some good, some not. Natural learners instinctively connect choice and consequence. They see the impact
of their choices, both positive and negative. They constantly play the
"if, then" game: if I make this decision, then such and such is likely to
happen. In the "if, then" game, they can see future consequences of present decisions. They envision a future and fold it into the present.

Often employees fail to learn when they cannot connect choices to
consequences. Employees who won't work on tough projects, who
won't take difficult assignments, who don't work well on teams, or

who do the minimum to get by are surprised when they don't have opportunities for promotion or long-term success. These employees have
not connected choice and consequence; they are not able to envision a
future and fold it into the present.

The choice-consequence connection implies understanding risk.
Risk focuses on the probability that an action will lead to a reaction. Managing risk comes from having a clear path between choice
and consequence. Effective learners assess probabilities and take informed risks.

Step Three: Correction

Learners adjust and adapt to the choices and consequences they experience. They constantly need to take corrective action to inform the next
cycle of choices. Effective learners are feedback junkies—they always
want to know how their work is seen by and affects others. They ask
what worked and what did not so they can adapt and improve their
work. Sometimes they seek formal feedback on their general behavior
(as with a 360-degree survey). At other times, they seek informal feedback by watching how others react to their work. They do not make
the same mistake over and over. Rather than being satisfied with the
status quo, they always want to improve and make things better.

Leaders can find natural learners through the rigorous talent selections that we laid out in Chapter 5 and by using effective interview
techniques, or they can develop individual learners by helping employees
master the choice-consequence-correction cycle we have described. In
either case, leaders want individuals in their units who seek new ideas
and are able to experiment and try new things.

Create Opportunities Where Individuals Can Generalize Ideas with Impact

Sometimes the most creative people don't have the impact that they
should or would like to have. Some creative people who generate new
ideas fail to generalize the ideas they create. Their personal creativity does not lead to sustained innovation. They do not see patterns,

connections, or integrated solutions. They are not able to generalize their knowledge beyond isolated actions or applications.

Effective learners build on the past. They also see patterns in activities and work to build in positive directions. Whereas isolated failures tend to disrupt or discourage nonlearners, learners see the pattern and do not let isolated events get them down. When effective learners see relationships between activities, they transfer knowledge from one setting to another. This kind of transfer is best if knowledge is adapted, not adopted; if ideas from one setting are rearranged to suit another and not simply imposed on it. Learning to see connections of ideas from one area to another enables leaders to accumulate knowledge and experience.

By integrating solutions, learners can avoid fixing one part of a problem only to find that other problems arise all over again. Sometimes, nonlearners fix the symptoms, not the underlying problems. In basketball or soccer, coaches who want to build teamwork may emphasize that players pass before they go for a basket or a goal. However, coaches who really build teamwork help players learn that teamwork is more than passing, it is a way to think about the game. When this learning finally takes hold, players begin to work as an integrated unit rather than as individuals and the team's success tends to soar.

Leaders want to harness individual creativity by ensuring that the most creative people deliver on their ideas. When those who generate also generalize their ideas, they turn energy, action, and creativity into sustained innovation and results.

Create Team Learning Opportunities—
The Second Target Group

Increasingly, companies perform work through task forces, projects, groups, account teams, and the like. Teams as collectives of individuals may be scored on their ability to generate and generalize ideas with impact. High-performing teams begin their learning journey by generating new ideas, which come both from the composition of the team and from the way the team operates.

Build Teams That Generate Ideas with Impact

Teams striving for new ideas select diverse members. When team members each bring a unique point of view, the entire team benefits—and so does the organization it serves. When the members are all looking at problems from the same perspective, by contrast, they're likely to fall into groupthink and miss many useful possibilities. That makes it important to orient new members to encourage debate and dialogue. One of the most effective team leaders we know uses this briefing for new team members: "You are on this team because you are different from me. If you and I think alike all the time, one of us is not necessary. And it won't be me."

Teams may operate to encourage generation of ideas. Successful teams brainstorm alternatives before reaching a conclusion, set stretch goals that demand new ways of doing work, do risk assessment to examine probabilities between actions and outcomes, orient new members rigorously to norms and listen to new members for new ideas, use time well to ensure that progress is made, allocate rewards based on team performance, and manage their group process to promote smooth teamwork.

When leaders use teams well, they are sources of new ideas and new ways of thinking. Teams have the ability to generate more alternatives than any one individual can perceive.

**Create Opportunities Where Teams Can Generalize
Ideas with Impact**

High-performing teams not only generate new ideas, they generalize those ideas by rigorously improving their team process. Team process checks enable teams to audit and improve how well they are working. By so doing, they learn about their own processes and improve on them, thus enhancing the team's ability to generalize from previous experiences in future idea generation activities. Four processes are critical for team effectiveness: defining purpose, making decisions, managing relationships, and learning. Table 8.2 summarizes the key questions for reviewing team processes.

Table 8.2   Team Audit

Purpose:
- Are our goals clear?
- Is our identity clear?
- Do we know what we need to accomplish?

Decision making:
- How timely are our decisions?
- How well do we involve everyone?
- How effectively do we implement our decisions?
- How good is our decision process?
- How well do we follow up on decisions?

Relationships:
- How well do we get along?
- How well do we show that we care for each other?
- How well do we manage conflict?
- How well do we encourage diversity?
- How well do we ensure unity?

Learning:
- What has worked or not worked well in last time period and why?

Purpose

A team needs a purpose, a vision, mission, strategies, goals, agenda, intent, aspiration, or raison d'être. Although team purposes evolve with changing business conditions, they also remain consistent over time.

We have seen different ways to craft a purpose statement. You can simply pick a purpose and stick with it for a long time, until it is accomplished, or you can pick one and allow it to evolve, as conditions require. In today's high-participation work groups, however, it's often most effective to lay out an array of goals and ask members to pick the ones that work best for them. Examples of purpose statements are: "Our team's purpose is to test new software products and identify any defects before they are introduced to our customers"; or "Our team's purpose is to design and develop action-oriented leadership experiences that allow participants to experience new and desired behaviors in positive ways."

Decision Making

A team functions through the decisions it makes. Good teams spend time sharing information, discussing issues, and building relationships, but teams make decisions. As we discussed in Chapter 7, good decisions have clarity, accountability, timeliness, processes, and follow-up (see Figure 7.1).

Team leaders facilitate decision making by focusing attention on the decisions that need to be made in any one time period, and by keeping priorities straight and not getting bogged down in issues beyond the scope of the team's charter. Team leaders also decide who decides on decisions. They must make some decisions, then assign and delegate others to those primarily responsible for those areas. They do decision process checks frequently to assure that time in meetings is well spent.

Relationships

Effective teams foster relationships that nurture trust, tackle issues, and validate differences. Building relationships means caring, expressing thanks, and managing conflict and differences. Teams work well when members acknowledge and care for each other. In team meetings, time can and should be spent finding out how members are doing personally and being sensitive to events outside work. Teams also need to be forums for gratitude. When people see their work appreciated, they work more willingly and effectively. Effective team leaders do set standards and demand performance—but they acknowledge success whenever they find it rather than simply pointing out weaknesses. Effective team leaders also encourage differences and manage conflict. Some teams ask "what if?" to see how others might respond to an issue. But ultimately, teams must deal with tough issues and deliver results. This comes from honest and direct feedback and talking about differences and sharing performance standards.

Learning

Teams always do some things that work and some things that do not work as well. The choice-consequence-correction cycle also applies to teams. Teams need time to reflect and assess: What did we do since last meeting? How did it work? What was successful? Why? What was less than successful? Why? What can we learn that we can apply to the next project or assignment? Teams, like individuals, also identify patterns of common errors and work to resolve those errors. When mistakes are made, it is important to acknowledge them quickly and directly, and then move on.

Team leaders must be role models of learning by being inquisitive, asking questions, seeking new solutions, looking for alternatives, encouraging creativity, and having fun with new ideas. Team leaders learn from failure and allow others to do likewise they are willing to say, "I goofed on this" and apologize. Team leaders do formal learning audits with their teams to periodically check on how they are performing. These might be 15 minutes once a quarter to review purpose, decision making, relationship building, and learning.

We have had the opportunity to take a number of teams—from the top team in a company to project teams to account management teams to shift teams—through the type of team audit outlined earlier, in Table 8.2. This is a valuable process, as it enables the team to generalize from previous experiences to enhance its chances of success in future experiences.

Develop the Capacity for Organization Learning— The Third Target Group

Organizations as entities also have the capacity to learn. By so doing routines or patterns become adopted and shared throughout an organization.

Build Organizations That Generate Ideas with Impact

Our research on learning organization identified four learning styles that represent ways in which organizations generate ideas with impact: experimentation, competency acquisition, benchmarking, and continuous improvement.[3]

Learning Style 1: Experimentation

Some organizations learn by trying many new ideas and being receptive to experimentation with new products and processes. The primary sources of learning are direct experiences from customers and employees. They aim to achieve organizational learning through controlled experimentation, from both inside and outside, rather than through exploiting the experience of others. 3M, Sony, Hewlett-Packard, and Unilever are companies known for their experimentation strategies. They follow guiding principles like these:

- We constantly seek new ideas, even before old ones are fully implemented.
- We constantly seek new ways to do work.
- We try a lot of new ideas; we want to be known as experimenters within our industry.
- We want to be the first in the market with a new idea or concept.

Learning Style 2: Competency Acquisition

Some organizations learn by encouraging individuals and teams to acquire new competencies. Learning is a critical aspect of business strategy, and focuses on both the experience of others and an exploration of new possibilities. By investing resources in training and development, these organizations provide cutting-edge materials and concepts to their members through consultants, line managers, and faculty. The intention is to help organization members acquire relevant knowledge that may accelerate their subsequent assimilation of new knowledge and stimulate them to develop innovative products and processes. Motorola and GE are well known for their competency acquisition strategies. Guiding principles:

- We encourage individuals to acquire new competencies.
- We encourage teams to acquire new competencies.
- We learn by hiring people from other companies who have skills we need.
- Learning is a critical part of our business strategy.

Learning Style 3: Benchmarking

Other organizations learn by scanning how others operate and then trying to adopt and adapt this knowledge into their own organizations. Learning comes from organizations that have demonstrated excellent performance or developed the best practices in specific processes. Benchmarking companies primarily learn from the experience of others and exploit successful technologies and practices that already exist. Samsung Electronics, Xerox, and Milliken all emphasize benchmarking. Guiding principles:

- We learn from others, entering a product market or applying a process only after it has been fully tested.
- We learn by broadly scanning what other companies do.
- We learn by focusing our scanning on specific activities done by other companies.
- We primarily benchmark the competition, measuring our progress against competitors' performance.

Learning Style 4: Continuous Improvement

Other organizations learn by constantly improving on what has been done before and mastering each step before moving on to new steps through a disciplined process like Six Sigma. They often emphasize employee involvement groups (i.e., quality control circles or problem-solving groups) organized to resolve issues identified by internal and external customers. These are organizations that both rely on learning through direct experience and the exploitation of existing practices. Toyota, Honeywell, and Honda are continuous improvement companies:

- We master new ideas before moving on to the next round.
- We upgrade the way we do existing work until we have it right.
- We want to be known as the best technical experts in our industry.
- We primarily benchmark ourselves, measuring progress against our previous performance.
- We use Six Sigma and other quality tools to continually improve how we do our work.

Implications of Learning Styles

These four styles are the ones we've seen in action. They're not abstracts that we've invented either as strawmen or as recommended goals. Real as they are, however, the descriptions represent ideal types only. Just as individuals never conform to one personality type, companies—especially large corporations with diverse businesses like GE and Motorola—seldom engage exclusively in just one learning style. Typically, organizations mix all four (as individuals do on the Myers-Briggs), but in different combinations and to varying degrees. In addition, learning capability profiles can change over time within organizations, depending on particular situations.

In general, our research indicates that competency acquisition and continuous improvement are the most popular learning styles, followed by experimentation and benchmarking.

Leaders who want to generate new ideas would be well advised to use multiple learning styles. Leaders might ask which of the four styles are most prevalent in their unit, and to look for ways to build up experimentation and competency acquisition if they're currently underemphasized in relation to continuous improvement or benchmarking. Likewise, if the more cautious approaches are largely ignored, it's apt to be useful to make sure they get a measure of attention, or the organization may miss out on some good ideas.

Create Opportunities Where Organizations Can Generalize Ideas with Impact

Many more organizations generate ideas than generalize them, and yet from the learning capability perspective, it's not enough to be awash in new ideas. For example, all too many companies have succeeded in creating pockets of excellence, then failed to transfer the achievement across boundaries to the rest of the firm. They never established best-practice forums to codify and disseminate lessons from one site to another. For generalization of ideas, *implementation* of what has been learned is essential.

Leaders build learning capability, therefore, not only by generating ideas but by sharing them within—and even beyond—the organization.

This has direct impact on the intangible value of the firm. It's a focused set of leadership actions and accountabilities, and not just an academic exercise and experience. The primary leadership task in generalizing ideas is to create an infrastructure that moves ideas across boundaries. When at General Electric, Steve Kerr,[4] chief learning officer and vice president of management development, created a *learning matrix* (Figure 8.2) that identified the source of good ideas for sharing across geographic, functional, or business boundaries and proposed a disciplined process for moving ideas across units.

		Step 2: Critical Success Factors for X				
Proposition Step 1: To be world class at X, we must . . . (identify critical initiatives).						
		a	b	c	d	e
Step 3: Location: Where work is done.	1					
	2					
	3					
	4					
	5					
	6					
	7					
	8					
	. . .					

Step 4: In each cell, score 0 (not applicable) to 1 (low) to 5 (high).
Step 5: Repeat for each part of the business.
Step 6: Build a plan for how to move best practices across the businesses.
Step 7: Generalize the learning capability across the organization.

Source: Adapted from General Electric.

Figure 8.2   Learning matrix form. Adapted from General Electric

Completing the learning matrix involves five steps:

1. Identify an important initiative that is in the process of being "rolled out" in the company and that the company is committed to doing well such as service, quality (Six Sigma), customer focus, cycle time, training, and so on. Let's call this initiative X. Complete the sentence in the matrix (Figure 8.2), "To be world class at X _____ . Fill in the X.

2. Identify critical success factors for X. Complete the statement, "To be world class at X, we must _____ ." The outcome of this step should be the identification of eight to ten critical factors for this corporate initiative to succeed. Arriving at this outcome might involve a small research team, task force, or other group to define these critical success factors. Put these critical success factors in columns labeled a, b, c, d, e, . . .

3. Answer the question, "What are the locations where these critical success factors are demonstrated?" The units generally are discrete work settings (plants, divisions, business units, or regions) where work is performed. Put these locations in the rows labeled 1, 2, 3, 4, 5, 6, . . .

4. On a scale of 0 to 5, score each cell of the matrix: 0 = not applicable; 1 = no skills at all; 2 = some skills; 3 = average; 4 = we think we are good; 5 = others think we are good, that is, world class. Either an organizational unit leader or a rating team external to the organization should do this assessment of the unit (such as a corporate group who inspects the unit or an outside rating agency). Members of the unit can provide scores of 0 to 4, but a score of 5 must come from someone outside the unit. (*Note:* Scoring in this step will help a leader diagnose the extent to which the unit exhibits the specific actions required by the overarching initiative.)

Scoring: The unit leader should complete the scoring of the matrix. This completed companywide matrix can help pinpoint pockets of excellence (scores of 5 in a cell) and provides an overall corporate score on any initiative. The overall score may provide feedback for a corporate person assigned to pursue initiative X. The matrix itself indicates the baseline for how ideas are generalized across these different units.

The leader then can then proceed to Steps 5, 6, and 7. These steps are: to repeat the scoring for each part of the business (Step 5), to build a plan on how to move best practices across the businesses (Step 6), and to generalize the learning capabilities throughout the organization (Step 7), respectively.

One beauty of Kerr's learning matrix is that it simply and elegantly shows where pockets of excellence exist, and suggests how to move ideas from one unit in the firm to other units. There are many ways to share ideas and knowledge based on the high-score cells in each column and apply them to the lower-score cells in that column. In other words, generalize, or transfer, knowledge and best practices from one unit to another. You can use any of these mechanisms for generalizing knowledge and experience from one cell to the entire column.

- Make the high-score cells best practice sites where others can learn. The best practice site opens its doors to the rest of the company and invites others to visit, observe, and take ideas that might be moved to another unit.
- Create case studies from the higher score cells for others to draw on. The best practice site might be written up for a company newsletter, or used as a case study in a development class. Participants from other units can be encouraged to question leaders from the best practice site to draw out knowledge that might be transferred.
- Move talent from higher to lower score cells. In one company that used this matrix, the corporate executive would ask the business leader to identity six individuals who were instrumental in making the unit a best practice site. Once these individuals were named, the corporate executive would then ask, "Which three do you want to keep?" The expectation was that the other three could be moved to other units to share their experiences. When visiting the other units with lower scores, the corporate executive could refer to this pool of available talent as a way to improve performance.

- Create an incentive system to encourage those in high-score cells to share knowledge. People do what they are rewarded for. In one company, each year leaders of units were offered bonuses by the number of 5 scores in a column. These financial bonuses provided an incentive, but it turned out that the nonfinancial rewards counted even more as the leaders of best practice sites gained visibility and credibility for their successes.
- Assign someone from corporate headquarters to oversee the entire matrix process, ensuring that a larger percentage of cells achieve scores of 5 each successive year.

This learning matrix offers a simple methodology for generating and generalizing ideas with impact within an organization. Leaders who use methods like this ensure that good ideas are not hidden within a unit but quickly and rapidly disseminated across units.

Another popular tool for generalizing ideas across units relies on technology. Through technology individuals in different parts of an organization may be connected to form a community of practice. Most companies have a lackluster history of deploying learning technology only to be disappointed by its failure to live up to expectations of increased productivity and effectiveness. How do you avoid the potential traps of technology and appropriately apply technology for maximum learning impact?

The following sections list traps to avoid and effective steps to take.

Avoid	Do
Convert content to the Web or CD-ROMs and tell employees that it is available for their use (often referred to as "pushing" it at them). This approach depends on employees' taking time away from their daily work to go through the learning exercise—and staying engaged throughout the exercise. Most of the time CD-ROMs sit on the shelf and stand-alone. Web-based courses remain unused—especially the ones aimed at training executives and senior managers, who always have more urgent demands on their working time.	Design learning technology with these barriers in mind and try to create a lure or pull for users. Technology with the best pull is integrated into daily work and organizational processes; it is not a separate activity that users must remember to use.

Avoid	Do
Eye-candy—sexy technology that incorporates video, animation, and sound for the sake of an impressive production. These solutions tend to be quite expensive to build or customize and not relevant to a user's work. Most of these solutions share a fatal fault: They ignore adult learning theory and are not designed to create specific business results. Another danger is that these exercises are usually one-on-one with the computer; the computer becomes the expert and whatever the computer says is perceived to be right, so valuable dialogue and sharing of experiences can be lost.	Remember that technology cannot totally replace face-to-face classroom time. Most learning experts are touting a term called blended learning—a combination of classroom discussion and Web-based tools. At the very least, opportunities for networking, the reflection part of action reflection, dialogue, and Q&A need to be fully integrated into any learning solution.
Spending too much on the initial creation of a knowledge base. Most knowledge bases work only if leaders are interested enough to stop their daily work and access the information. Leaders must then search through it and with any luck, find data or case studies that illustrate learning that they can apply directly to current work. Unfortunately, many knowledge bases are not used or maintained on an ongoing basis because they are static, one-way communication vehicles and lack the pertinent information to be useful on the job.	Try using a moderated knowledge base. Internal or external consultants interview the senior executives and write the cases for the moderated knowledge base, rather than relying on the senior executives to make time to write up their own cases. This ensures that the cases are timely, complete, and objective (recounting both successes and failures) so that everyone in the organization can learn from the action-learning project. Any executive reading a case in the moderated knowledge base can post a question for the action-learning team or consultant about the project. The reader can also view all past questions and answers for each case study.

In brief, by adopting the to-do items in the preceding sections, you can use technology to help move knowledge from one setting to another. In fact, technology has many benefits to sharing ideas. Technology enables people in geographically dispersed units to connect and share; it costs less than face-to-face meetings or training; it focuses attention on key concepts and applications; it allows for preliminary work and follow-up to surround traditional training activities; and it develops as it is used, becoming a way to continually share ideas over time.

In one company, we used technology to leverage the five-day leadership-training program we offered. Each of the five days of the program focused on how leaders could and should deliver a specific result (employee, customer, investor, organization). Faculty (both internal line managers and external customers and professors) presented materials at two levels. First, they offered a brief synopsis of the theory, or content, of their topic. Faculty who worked on employee results developed a perspective on how to build employee commitment through providing employees clear and accountable standards, communication of ideas, flexible work practices, and team-based organizations. The theory for each of these modules was taught in the course, and then synthesized into a one-page summary.

Second, for each module, faculty provided a tool or worksheet on how to apply the theory. For example, the concept of employee accountability was tied to a performance improvement tool that had been used by others and could be used by participants to increase employee accountability. The concept of effective teams translated into a team effectiveness instrument that could be used to assess and improve team functioning.

These concepts and tools became part of a leadership knowledge base that participants could access after the course. On the last day of the course, participants were introduced to this knowledge base and taught how to access it from their desks. Using problems they were likely to face in their next year as leaders (e.g., how to build employee, customer, investor, and organization results), they were shown how to find the concepts and tools used for resolving the challenge.

Since each module taught in the course had a concept and tool, anyone who accessed the module and used the tool could add that experience into the knowledge base. For example, the module on holding employees accountable had been taught for the last three classes. Five participants in those courses had used the concepts and tools to build performance improvement plans for their employees. Their experiences were also in the leadership knowledge base, which generalized this knowledge to those more recently in the course. Any participant could access the knowledge base twice free of charge and find out how others had used the concepts taught. However, to have access after these two freebies, participants had to put their personal experience with the concept and tool into the knowledge base. In this way, the knowledge base grew over time.

A key to the knowledge base's effectiveness was that course participants were not expected to remember everything it included, they merely had to recall that they had learned some ideas and tools. In the ensuing months, participants could recall that the event gave them ideas on employee, customer, investor, and organization results. They could then access the knowledge base to recover the concept taught (the one-page summary) and find applications of those tools written up by other participants based on first-hand experience. With this focus, the event-facilitated generalization of ideas over time. The leaders learned by doing as they used information when they needed it. They had access to others who had used similar ideas within the firm so they could test their ideas. They shared their learnings and the learnings of others so that the received feedback on their effort. The knowledge base was integrated into daily work activities because it was organized around business issues and challenges the leaders would be facing, offering them real-time, live examples of how to respond to those problems.

Whether through a learning matrix or technology, leaders who generalize ideas gain a broad commitment to organization learning.

> To watch a video segment on learning or complete any tools online, go to:
> www.rbl.net/whythebottomlineisnt.html.

Leadership Implications

Leaders build learning into their organizations by generating and generalizing ideas with impact for individuals, teams, and organizations. Here are some specific leadership actions that you can take to build learning into your organization:

1. Bring natural learners into the organization and encourage all employees to learn through the choice-consequence-correction cycle.

2. Encourage employees to look for patterns and to transfer knowledge from one setting to another.

3. Provide forums (meetings, training, and the like) where people have permission and the opportunity to reflect on better ways to do their jobs.

4. Help teams become more creative and insightful by bringing new people onto teams and by operating teams in a way to encourage debate and dialogue.

5. Allow teams to generalize learning through team audits on purpose, decision making, relationships, and learning.

6. Encourage units to create new ways of doing work through experimentation, competence acquisition, continuous learning, and benchmarking—making sure that all receive at least some attention, and that experimentation and competence acquisition aren't overshadowed by the more cautious approaches.

7. Share knowledge and ideas across organization boundaries through building the right culture and a disciplined learning process.

8. Frequently audit for internal best practices in relevant areas and find ways to export these best practices to other parts of the firm.

9. Use your intranet to create chat rooms and e-mail lists focusing on important issues, making it easy to discuss important ideas across geographic boundaries.

9 | Accountability: Making Teamwork Work

Some managers are gifted at making excuses. When missing financial, customer, or employee results, these managers make creative explanations ranging from competitor responses to bad customers to government regulations to bad weather. What we generally find is that once an organization begins to tolerate excuses, they mount month after month and quarter after quarter. They almost take on a life of their own and it becomes the norm to miss numbers, rant and rave with great justification, then move on.

These organizations lack accountability.

Accountability exists when leaders and employees deliver what they promise, on time every time. Accountability means that goals are accomplished and plans executed. It means that when failure occurs, excuses are replaced with acknowledgment of mistakes followed by lessons learned for the future. Accountability comes from discipline and rigor. It is more than assigning someone to a task; it is ensuring that they do the task. Accountability, as we define it in this chapter, is a culture or way of work that shapes how employees behave. It sets a standard about what must be done that compels employees to do it. When accountability exists, high performance matters.

University faculties impress newcomers to their ranks with a simple mantra: Never miss class. They tell stories of professors making special efforts to teach, including working while sick, walking through ice and snow when the roads were blocked, and turning down important consulting engagements. All these stories reinforce the ethos of teaching and communicate a clear accountability. A similar ethos applies in the airline industry, where pilots likewise tell stories that reinforce the need to make every flight. At the Ritz Carlton, the commitment to service led to accountability as individual employees worked to meet targeted customer requirements. For example, when a guest asks any employee "Where is the pool?" the employee takes personal responsibility to escort the guest to the pool, not to point and direct. These simple stories capture the essence of accountability. When people know what is expected and do it, they are accountable.

Accountability can be a source of intangible value for any organization. Some organizations develop cultures around delivery and execution. It is simply not tolerated to miss numbers, offer excuses, or fail to deliver as expected. Stories of exceptional customer service abound in firms where this accountability mindset resides. A friend once drove two cartons (eight cans) of tomato sauce four hundred miles to a Domino's restaurant that ran out of the chain's prescribed high-quality sauce one Saturday. Domino's leaders felt accountable to their customers to have pizzas ready for the Saturday evening rush that met the chain's standard in every respect, and that meant that the local supermarket or convenience store tomato sauce just wouldn't do. Federal Express delivers on time with guarantees tied to service, a commitment so strong it made up one of the story lines of the movie *Castaway*. Caterpillar will ship a part anywhere in the world within 24 hours to keep its equipment working. Southern Company, one of the largest electric utility firms in the world, prides itself on being accountable for having power working after a storm faster than any of its competitors.

When investors sense a firm's commitment to delivering on promises, they have confidence in consistent and predictable earnings (Chapter 2). Investors also believe in firms with a culture or mindset focused on execution, delivery, achievement, and performance. Customers value accountable firms because the products or services are reliable and available on time. Firms with accountable reputations both attract employees who deliver results and find it easier to remove employees who do not. Leaders who ensure accountability build trust among employees because these leaders are predictable, consistent, and responsible.

Accountability is both a culture or mindset and a set of management practices that create and sustain that culture. Leaders worry about accountability for both individuals and organizations. At the individual level, accountability deals with finding and applying ways to motivate and engage employees. It focuses on what leaders can do to assure that individuals remain committed to the firm and allocates their attention and energy to the firm. (See Chapter 5 on talent, where we talk about building individual commitment.) At the organization level, accountability assures that the systems and practices of the organization focus, drive, and reinforce employee behaviors and organization actions.

Steve Kerr, the Chief Learning Officer at Goldman Sachs, brilliantly captured the accountability issue as "hoping for A while rewarding B."[1] Often a leader hopes that employees will do tasks A, B, and C, then builds reward systems for D, E, and F. Leaders hope that employees will focus on quality, but reward on-time delivery. Leaders hope that employees will learn new skills, but reward them only for deploying old skills. University deans hope faculty will teach well, but reward them for publishing. Inevitably, employees do what they are rewarded for more than what leaders hope for. Accountability exists when the things leaders hope for are done (because they are the right things to do based on strategy or business goals) and are built into the reward system.

The model for accountability falls into four phases: strategy, measures, consequences, and feedback (see Table 9.1).[2] Leaders who use these four phases sequentially ensure accountability. Sometimes, leaders make mistakes by skipping one of the phases. For example, some leaders try to build creative incentives (in the consequences phase) without having clear measures. If it is unclear what is expected, it is difficult to enforce consequences. Likewise, it is difficult to have measures without strategy.

The logic in Table 9.1 applies to both individuals and organizations. At an individual level, my child and I have a strategy. Strategy deals with allocating scarce resources, in this case, her time. Of all the

Table 9.1   Phases of Accountability

Phase	Question	Individual Application	Organization Application
1. Strategy	What are we trying to accomplish?	Where should an individual focus attention and energy?	What are the goals or priorities of an organization unit?
2. Measures	How will we recognize success? What are our standards?	What indicators will tell us how we're really doing?	What are measures that can be used to track performance? How can they be woven into performance appraisal process?
3. Consequences	What are positive or negative consequences of meeting or missing measures?	What happens if the individual does not meet goals?	What are the reward systems that deliver value?
4. Feedback	How do we know how we are doing?	How can we provide individuals feedback on their performance?	How can we build organization feedback mechanisms to track results?

things she could do, I would like her to clean her room. Part of my strategic challenge is getting her to agree that this is a good strategy for her. To help her agree (or acquiesce) to this room-cleaning strategy, I know I cannot ask for too many things or she will just resist completely; nor can I ask for too few, or she might not learn the responsibility I feel obligated to teach her. Now, we have to set agreed upon measures. My measure or indicator of a clean room may vary dramatically from her measure of clean. She defines "clean" as out of sight, out of mind, even if that includes under the bed, in the closet, or otherwise hidden from obvious sight. My definition differs. We finally agree on measures. Then, we have consequences. Consequences deal with "Why should I care?" The consequence has to mean something to her. In fact once she said to me, "Why should I clean it, you are gone for two weeks and no one will notice?" The consequence needs to be related to the effort. Ideally, the clean room is an end in and of itself, but more realistically, if I tie negative or positive consequences to her clean room, it is more likely to be clean. Cleaning does not seem to be an innate ability. Finally, we agree on feedback and follow-up on how she has done. This includes positive feedback for a clean room and learning feedback when improvement is needed.[3]

These same four phases apply to leaders wanting to build accountability into their organization.

Phase 1: Strategy/Goal—What Are We Trying to Accomplish?

Opportunity should exceed capacity. Neither individuals nor organizations can do all they would like to do. Leaders make choices to allocate resources to areas where impact is greatest. Strategy is the process of making choices about devoting resources to issues that matter most. Strategy focuses on setting a future direction that implies resource allocation in the present. As Yogi Berra said, "You've got to be very careful if you don't know where you're going, because you might not get there. If you don't know where you are going, you will wind up somewhere else."

Many concepts or phrases have been used to dissect strategy. Leaders frame visions and picture what the organization ultimately chooses to achieve. Leaders have missions that tell employees what business they are in. Leaders pursue goals that define what outcomes to work on. Leaders accomplish objectives that define how to get where they are headed. Creating strategic clarity requires the leaders to define a future state in ways that engage current behaviors. At Microsoft, after Bill Gates describes his epiphany about the Web, there was a strategic emphasis shift beyond desktop applications to more Web-based applications. Behaviorally, this meant increased entrepreneurial emphasis in the new areas. Without such clarity, accountability wanes.[4] We have identified six keys for testing a clear strategy or objective (see Table 9.2).

Aspiration

Clear strategies envision a future state that defines what can be, not just an extension of what has been. A leader establishes an aspirational strategy by creating a mental image of what might be. Regardless of whether it's called a vision, dream, goal, or mission statement, a strategy offers a point of view about how the organization will be positioned in the future. The aspiration should exceed resources, but not so far as to create cynicism.[5] We were once in a firm where leaders stated a bold aspiration "to be worth $20 billion in five years." Unfortunately, the path from the present $10 billion to the aspirational $20 billion level was unclear.

Table 9.2   Criteria for Strategic/Goal Clarity

Dimension	Definition	Rating 0–10
Aspirational	Defines a desired future state that is a stretch where aspiration exceeds resources but is still within possibility.	
Behavioral	Turns the ideas of the strategy into day-to-day behaviors that employees can do.	
Customer focused	Emphasizes value added to external stakeholders, particularly customers of the organization; focuses the strategy from the outside in.	
Disciplined	Woven into the fabric of the firm, including hiring, training, resource allocation, compensation, decision making, and technology.	
Energizing	Inspires and excites, creating emotional energy and passion for the goals.	
Focused	Focuses a few critical priorities rather than an unlimited number.	

Employees did not think they could accomplish it, so they shrugged cynically and went on with business as usual. At the other end of the scale, leaders who define a future state as an extension of the present lack a unique point of view about the future. Employees grow apathetic about the future of the business, figuring that good enough is good enough, and there's no need for extra work or thought. Aspirations need to be distinctive, showing how the organization is uniquely positioned to define a future state.

Behavior

Aspiration statements need to be translated into employee behaviors. Behaviors show up in how employees spend time: what they do, whom they meet with, where they work, and how they get work done. Absent a focus on behavior, aspirations inspire but don't endure.

In our work with Sears, we helped leaders define their aspiration as establishing a positive selling environment through becoming a compelling place to shop, work, and invest. This aspiration focused on a passion for customers, a commitment that people add value, and performance leadership. Sears had many other corporate initiatives, but launched a series of town hall meetings designed to make this aspiration real to all employees. Local leaders facilitated these meetings to ensure commitment and kept the group focused on specific issues within the employee unit without complaining about corporate policies and conditions outside the unit's control. They made it clear that they understood that employees closest to the work knew what to do to make the aspiration real and encouraged each group of employees to identify activities that should be stopped, started, or simplified. They also made it clear that small changes that could be implemented were more important than large changes that required enormous resources, and they assigned champions to follow up on approved recommendations and make sure they were implemented.

With these steps, leaders at Sears were able to create strategic clarity and distributed ownership of it. Once employees were engaged in an effort to define how they could behave to make the aspiration happen, they felt ownership of it and accountability to it.[6]

Leaders shape aspirations, but employees specify behaviors. The best way to build a shared aspiration is to present the initial ideas interactively, allowing employees to respond to them and define what specific things they could do more or less of in the next month to implement the vision. This invariably gets better results than a one-way forum where the leader speaks and the employees take notes. It's also effective to ask employees attending the session to send personal messages to the leader outlining what they plan to do to implement the vision, to have meetings with their own employees to discuss the vision and how to implement it, and to talk about the vision with everyone they meet to gain commitment to it.

Customer Focus

One easy test for an aspiration is to ask: "How would our target customers or consumers respond to it?" This question helps you reframe traditional internally-focused business shorthand (service, quality, low cost) in terms of goals that matter to external customers. Service might mean answering phones in four rings or less, resolving customer problems within 24 hours, or having a personal contact with target customers each quarter. One firm we worked with adjusted its definition of on-time delivery in customer terms. The old measure of delivery was the shipping date—when the product left the building—and employees were meeting this target a satisfactory 95 percent of the time. But what customers cared about was the date they could use the goods in question, and the company was on time by that measure on only about 70 percent of orders. Between transit delays, repairs required before installation, and other factors, about a quarter of the orders were in trouble when the old measure reported they were fine.

Gaining a customer focus to ensure strategic clarity means taking the aspiration to target customers and asking them a series of questions:

- What does this aspiration mean to you?
- How will it change your behavior toward the organization?
- How does it compare to what competitors promise you?

- If you could change it, what would you say or do?
- What do you need to see us do before you will believe in what the words say?

Another way to make an aspiration customer focused is to create images or stories about how customers should respond to the vision. When you give aspirational talks, it's useful to focus on a single customer as a case study. Describe the way that customer currently experiences your firm and how you envision the customer experiencing the firm in the future. Personalizing an anticipated customer experience helps focus the aspiration on customers.

For example, Jeff Smulyan, founder and CEO of Emmis Communications, has built an aspirational vision to "Emmisize Global Media." The company (based in Indianapolis, Indiana) owns a variety of television and radio stations, as well as a number of regional magazines—*LA Magazine, Texas Monthly,* and so on. Part of Emmisizing is to remain in all three media (television, radio, and publishing) when conventional wisdom is to specialize. Most of Emmis' competitors are much larger and still consolidating. Jeff does a great job of capitalizing on these differences in size and direction when he speaks with employees, customers, and investors. Jeff is a very effective communicator. When he wants people to understand what he means by his vision for Emmis, he invokes Emmis history to describe what he means by his vision:

> Emmis has always been the trendsetter in radio. Years ago, everybody in radio had a list of 3,000 songs that they would faithfully play through every week. The problem with that model is that audiences love only a few hundred songs out of that much larger list. In addition, most listeners don't listen to the radio all day. They listen in 20-minute chunks of time. We understand our listeners better than the others, so we can buy a station that is not successful and turn it around quickly by playing their favorites over and over. This same model works globally.

Based on that insight, Jeff builds audiences that build sales. His knowledge of what people want translates smoothly into sales for advertisers—and to sales of advertising in his media.

Discipline

Aspirations require organization processes that align with the aspiration. Programs like Six Sigma, reengineering, and manufacturing excellence offer disciplines to make an aspiration real. Leaders who draft aspirations should follow up quickly with initiatives that validate the aspiration. These disciplines consume resources, but they also communicate commitment in a way that makes them well worthwhile.

At Sears, as the vision was laid out, the senior leaders demonstrated corporate commitment through specific initiatives tied to their aspirations:

Compelling Place to Shop

- Consistent in-stock performance
- Implement market focus
- Customer service training
- Improved merchandising
- Competitive pricing strategies
- Product service strategies
- Customer information systems
- Total store marketing

Compelling Place to Work

- Associate communication
- Gain-sharing compensation
- Employee idea system
- Team-based management
- 360-degree feedback
- Economic business literacy
- Learning maps

Compelling Place to Invest

- SG&A cost reduction
- Strategic sourcing

- New business development initiatives
- Logistics cycle changed
- Inventory management updated
- Maintain/launch credit strategies
- Cash flow management strategies
- Improved cost accounting

These initiatives become the means of accomplishing and measuring the aspiration. The resulting measures created a discipline for the aspiration. Employees knew the leaders were serious because of the resources they allocated to tasks associated with attaining the vision.

Energy

Strategies and aspirational goals inspire. They create emotional response. They induce passion, energy, and enthusiasm. They excite. Energizing aspiration statements give employees a sense of opportunity, duty, and honor. They help employees feel part of a larger purpose that has meaning for them and others.

Building an energizing statement depends a great deal on the leader. Some leaders are gifted with language and can use words and images to motivate employees. Others use personal stories to show how the aspiration will affect them and by extension their employees. Others tell stories about employees who have implemented the aspiration the leaders intend. These stories become examples others can relate to. Others are personally active, visiting employees and connecting personally with them. Others rely on values and issues of personal meaning showing that the aspiration is a reflection of their personal identity and value statement. Charisma can take many forms, but leaders have an obligation to create energy and enthusiasm in those they lead. At a minimum, this means expressing pride in employees and the work they are doing.

The test of an energizing aspiration statement is the enduring commitment it induces:

- Do employees who will enact the strategy feel a personal passion for it?

- Do they feel it is part of their identity?
- Do they share it proudly with their associates inside and outside the firm?
- Do they put their discretionary energy to accomplishing the vision?

Focus

In Chapter 3, we talked about the importance of focus for a growth vision. Focus applies to *any* aspiration. When we talk to executives, we ask, "What is the message you want employees to know about your strategy?" When the answer is a crisp: "We are trying to turn business A around through cutting supplier and product costs and grow business B through product innovation," we have confidence in these strategies. When we hear a litany of good ideas, we worry about focus. Simplicity, redundancy, and consistency increase focus. Simple messages fit into memorable symbols or icons. Redundant messages repeated consistently assure focus.

At Sears, the theme was the 3 Cs (Compelling place to work, shop, and invest). This focus was an easy mantra that employees could understand and relate to. It helped Sears' executives integrate and bundle initiatives and focus attention. At Emmis Communications, the "Emmisize Global Media" slogan serves the same purposes—it's an unforgettable phrase that keeps everyone's eye on the company's goals.

Phase 2: Measures—How Will We Recognize Success?

Too often, managers measure what is easy, not what is right. Right measures align with strategy and turn strategy into concrete, specific indicators that can be tracked. Incorrect measures can hurt the business by misdirecting employee attention to focus on the wrong things because they are measured. Or they can cry wolf so often they mask real problems when they occur. Leaders have the obligation to create effective measures that focus both individual and organizational attention. An old axiom suggests that management gets *what it inspects, not what it expects.* The concept of inspection suggests measures that can be tracked and monitored.[7]

Steve Kerr has proposed criteria for effective measures that provide a useful test to see whether measures lead to accountability (Table 9.3). *Important* measures pick up information that tracks with strategy rather than what is simply easy to measure. It's always tempting to measure what is easy, even when it's not necessarily what is right. One firm we worked with tracked the percentage of managers who received 40 hours of training per year. This provided a simple, easily interpreted number that masked the reality, which was that many people were opting for irrelevant programs in pleasant locations, perhaps improving their outlook by extending vacation time, but having very little impact on the quality of their work.

Table 9.3   Criteria for Effective Measures (Steve Kerr)

Criterion: Effective measures are . . .	Definition: The extent to which a measure . . .
Important	Connects to strategically relevant business objectives rather than to what is easy to measure.
Complete	Adequately tracks the entire phenomenon rather than only some aspect of the phenomenon.
Timely	Tracks at the right time rather than being held to an arbitrary date.
Visible	Is visible, public, openly known, and tracked by those affected by it rather than collected privately for management's eyes only.
Controllable	Tracks output created by those affected by it, who have a clear line of sight from the measure to the results.
Cost-effective	Is efficient to track by using existing data or data easy to monitor rather than requiring a new layer of procedures.
Interpretable	Creates data that is easy to understand, make sense of, and translate to employee actions.

Complete measures track all aspects of a strategy, not just one piece. For example, in one consumer goods company, employees were measured on revenue, so they increased revenue, only to find that profits fell. Leaders need to recognize all the elements of the strategy and create measures that capture such complexity.

Timely measures are taken when the information can still make a difference. Often companies do excellent autopsies—that is, they use measures that report results after the fact. Better measures are leading indicators that predict and anticipate future outcomes. The Sears data showed that employee results preceded customer results and customer results preceded financial results. Leaders who know the leading indicators intervene on those issues that matter most.

Visible measures are tracked and observed by those whose work they are intended to influence. If no one sees the measure, it has little impact. Publicly posted measures garner attention and shape behavior.

Controllable measures provide a clear line of sight from strategy to behavior. Measures need to center on issues that people can affect, rather than things so high-level and abstract (such as earnings per share of a large company) that employees far inside the company cannot see how their work drives the measure.

Cost-effective measures gather data efficiently. Sometimes the process of collecting data is so burdensome that it is not worth the investment to collect the data. Ideally, data collected for other purposes in a setting can be used to track results there.

Interpretable measures are generally easy to understand. As we suggested in Chapter 2, earnings as a measure is often misunderstood because it is not clear what causes the earnings outcome. Retention is often an easy indicator of employee commitment, but may be hard to understand: which employees are retained? High or lower performers? Overall retention rates may not report real employee commitment. If you and your team build measures that meet these criteria, the measures will operationalize your strategy.

It's useful to think of measures in terms of two dimensions—target and indicator—as outlined in Figure 9.1. The target is the unit whose work is being measured, shown here as the individual or collective, and the indicators are what is being measured, which may be behavior (actions) or outcomes (results). This leads to four types of measures that an organization can track:

1. *Individual behavior measures* (Cell 1) focus on how people behave in a company. Leaders might track how employees demonstrate competencies (e.g., with 360-degree feedback results), how people spend time (e.g., time logs), or where people spend time (e.g., with time sheets that track clients served in a consulting firm). Measures in this cell often apply when outcomes are difficult to define (such as in R&D operations).
2. *Individual outcomes measures* (Cell 2) focus on the results employees deliver. Leaders might create a management-by-objectives measurement system where the specific outcomes for each employee are specified. These types of measures work best where individuals produce results independently (as in sales).
3. *Collective behavior measures* (Cell 3) focus on how teams or organization units work together (e.g., with quarterly team reviews). Leaders may create measures of team effectiveness (see Chapter 8 for an example of team effectiveness index). These types of measures are important where teamwork is critical to success.
4. *Collective outcomes measures* (Cell 4) focus on the results of the organization unit. Leaders may define outcomes of a unit in terms of volume, margin, quality, or service. These types of measures emphasize the outcome of the entire unit. Cell 4 is the domain of the Balanced Scorecard.

	Behavior Focus	**Outcome Focus**
Individual	1	2
Collective	3	4

Figure 9.1   Choices in a measurement system.

A major challenge is to make the explicit linkage from cell 4 back to cells 1, 2, and 3. For a quick assessment of your organization's current measurement practices, divide 100 points across these four measures. Allocate the points based on the measurement efforts used now. If the majority of your points fall under the outcome focus, then flags should be raised whether you have behaviors in place to make the outcomes repeatable. If the majority of your points fall under the behavior focus, then flags should be raised about whether the behaviors are connected to a clear outcome. Is the resulting distribution supportive of facilitating behavior that drives outcomes that deliver your strategy?

The process of setting measures also defines the impact of the measures. When employees who are accountable for the measures help define them, they are more committed to accomplishing them. Allowing employees to set and monitor performance may take more time than imposing standards on them, but the result is that employees accept ownership of the measures and care about them.

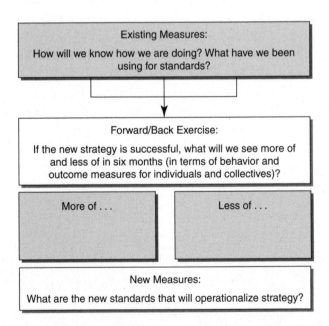

Figure 9.2   Building a measurement system (adapted from Steve Kerr).

With the measurement criteria and these types of measures, the logic sketched in Figure 9.2 helps leaders define their strategy and review the existing measures. Then they can identify what measures could be defined to better align with strategy.

Two questions often help move the discussion along:

1. If we execute the strategy successfully, what will we see more of (in terms of behaviors and outcomes for individuals and organizations)?
2. If we execute the strategy successfully, what will we see less of (in terms of behaviors and outcomes for individuals and organizations)?

The brainstorming session that results from these queries gives a large list of potential measures, out of which it is possible to define a simple, robust set of measures that best meet the criteria in Table 9.3. The steps in Figure 9.2 offer a process for creating measures that typify strategy. With these measures, accountability is more likely.

Phase 3: Consequences—What Happens if We Meet or Miss Measures?

Often leaders like to tinker with rewards while ignoring measures. In reality, if you don't have effective measures, you can't effectively design rewards. If you have good measures, good rewards generally follow. Rewards without measures only randomly drive accountability. When strategy translates into measures that then drive rewards, accountability follows.

Consequences may be broadly defined as negative or positive. Negative consequences imply that missing a standard leads to some form of punishment. Negative consequences generally have a short-term impact, driving behavior because of fear of punishment. When those pressures are removed, the behaviors often come back because every unwilling act of obedience was accompanied by thoughts of what would be done if punishment wasn't imminent. Positive consequences tend to have a longer term effect on behavior, as it's likelier that behavior repeatedly reinforced by desirable results will become a habit.

In teaching, for example, a professor can impose negative consequences by docking points from students who are tardy to class. Students are motivated to get to class on time to avoid losing points. Alternatively, the professor can reinforce arriving at class on time by occasionally opening the session by giving out a few questions that will be on the final. Students are motivated to get to class on time in the hope of picking up something that will directly benefit their final grade. They don't just show up on time, they show up without resentment, prepared to listen to the professor.

At work, negative consequences include taking something away (salary cuts, dismissal) or removing opportunities (loss of a promotion or job opportunity). Positive consequences vary by individual, providing more of whatever the individual employee wants from the working environment. Individuals may have different needs that make some rewards more valuable than others. Some individuals may be more driven by financial rewards and others by opportunities for impact. These individual drives may evolve over a career cycle or as a result of other personal factors. Overall, they have a more lasting impact on accountability than negative consequences do because they focus on the future and what can be, and they encourage learning. Leaders are more likely to drive accountability through positive consequences than negative ones.

Positive consequences may be divided into financial or nonfinancial. Financial incentives may be further divided into cash or benefits, short or long term, base or at-risk pay, and individual or team based.[8] Nonfinancial rewards generally deal with the work itself or how the work is organized and performed. Financial rewards may build accountability, but if the organization does not have the resources to cover them easily, it is useless to keep them as the centerpiece of a reward program. For example, if a down business year undercuts an organization's profits, the organization can't (or at least shouldn't) give employees money that does not exist. Promising money when it is not available creates dissonance and discouragement. Rather than focus on nonexistent financials, leaders can productively switch the emphasis to nonfinancial rewards.

Deciding whether to use negative or positive consequences and whether to use financial or nonfinancial rewards depends on the criteria for the rewards. Steve Kerr has suggested six criteria for effective rewards (see Table 9.4).

1. *Availability* implies that the reward supply is large enough to have an impact. When companies have a bonus pool averaging 4 percent of salary, with a range of 2 percent to 6 percent, it is unlikely that the total available cash will have significant impact on employee behavior. Nonfinancial rewards are more readily available in most cases than financial rewards, which may be constrained by economic conditions.

2. *Eligibility* refers to the extent to which groups of employees are included in a reward opportunity. For example, sometimes executives have unique retirement plans not accessed by most employees, who rely on 401(k) or other retirement plans. Nonfinancial eligibility might mean things like attendance at senior leadership meetings. Generally, these meetings are held for the top 1 percent of employees determined by hierarchy. In one firm, we recommended that 15 percent to 20 percent of the slots for this senior

Table 9.4   Criteria for Effective Rewards (Steve Kerr)

Criterion: **Effective rewards have . . .**	**Definition: Rewards are effective if they . . .**
Availability	Are available throughout the firm.
Eligibility	Are awarded based on clear criteria at each level (hourly, union, executive).
Visibility	Are made known to the recipient and the rest of the organization.
Performance contingency	Vary depending on the performance of the individual or the organization results.
Timeliness	Are allocated close to the time that measurements are made.
Durability	Have sustained impact over time.

management meeting be allocated to employees not in the top 1 percent based on their performance the preceding year.

3. *Visibility* implies that the rewards need to be known to both the recipient and the rest of the organization. When rewards are shared only with the recipient, it is only the recipient who changes behavior, not others. Public disclosure of salary results creates equity challenges for leaders because those who did not receive the salary increase may feel mistreated, but it also motivates people not receiving rewards to learn what matters most. Again, nonfinancial consequences are often more visible, such as an employee attending a conference, getting a promotion, or being assigned more interesting work.

4. *Performance contingency* implies that the reward is connected to meeting standards set in the measurement phase of accountability. No one doubts that financial rewards should be tied to performance, but sometimes financial rewards have such a narrow range (as when the company has a salary increase of 3 percent to 5 percent across the board with a 4 percent average) that they do not reflect the variance in performance. High-performing employees often deliver two to three times the value of low-performance employees.[9]

5. *Timeliness* requires that rewards be distributed close to the time that the performance driving the reward occurs. Annual bonuses require individuals to trust leaders to remember their good performance for the first 10 or 11 months of the year.

6. *Durability* refers to the extent to which the reward has impact over time. At times, annual salary increases are seen as an entitlement and woven into the household budget even before they arrive. Financial rewards cannot be taken back. Nonfinancial rewards, on the other hand, endure as employees have opportunities to change how work is done.

As discussed, these criteria apply to both financial and nonfinancial rewards. In many cases, the tendency to think of rewards primarily in financial terms (some form of money) limits the array of reward options. Yet, if financial rewards meet the criteria, they drive accountability. A number of innovations in financial rewards have been adopted that help leaders meet the recommended criteria, including:

- *Spot awards:* Leaders in some firms offer on-the-spot bonuses (either cash or stock options or grants) to employees or teams who perform well. These are one-time windfalls for excellent performance.

- *Skill-based pay:* Compensation systems may be based on the extent to which employees learn and master competencies or skills required for their job. These skill-based pay systems are contingent not only on outcomes but on behaviors.

- *Long-term incentives:* Leaders are finding ways to connect short-term employee behavior to long-term firm interest through stock grants or options or bonuses tied to the preceding two or three years' performance.

- *Pay at risk:* Increasingly, a higher percent of overall compensation comes from pay at risk instead of base pay. This practice enables leaders to hold constant or offer incremental increases in base pay (which limits the long-term liability of the firm) and offer bonuses, incentives, or other cash gains based on performance.

- *Team rewards:* When the work requires teamwork, measures of teamwork can be crafted (Cell 2 of Figure 9.1). Financial rewards may be allocated to the team and not just the individual. Team-based compensation encourages teamwork and collaboration.

- *Customized deals:* Moving away from traditional Hay points where employees receive pay based on know-how, problem solving, and accountability scores built into their job descriptions, leaders are shifting to customized employee deals tied to competence and performance. The focus is more on equity (pay for performance) than equality (everyone with a given job description gets paid the same).

- *Benefits:* Employee benefits have financial implications. Leaders are finding new sources of benefits (see Figure 9.3), and they are linking the receipt of these benefits to meeting standards— not just giving them to all employees who meet the eligibility criteria.

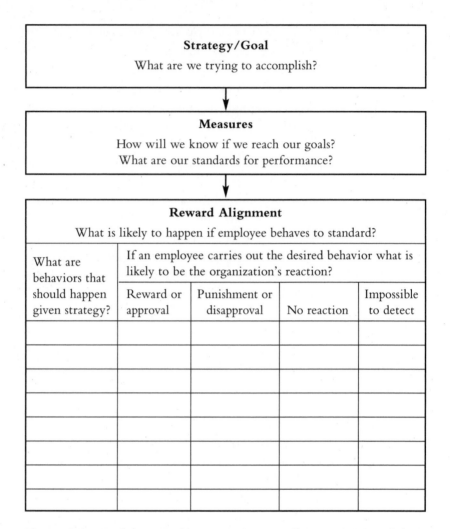

Figure 9.3 Worksheet: Building rewards to match strategy (adapted from Steve Kerr).

As these and other innovations occur, leaders can use financial rewards to ensure accountability.

Nonfinancial rewards also affect performance. Many of the nonfinancial rewards show up in the way work is organized. After decades of research, leaders have learned that empowered work has the following features:[10]

- *Autonomy:* Many employees value the right to make their own decisions, have control over their work environment, and have license to act. Autonomy comes from sharing decision making, authority, and responsibility. It may fall to individuals or teams.
- *Feedback:* Many employees like to know how they are doing on the job.
- *Task identity:* Many employees have pride in the work that they perform by identifying with the goals and values of the firm. When employees have the opportunity to complete an entire task (end-to-end process), they receive value.
- *Task significance:* Many employees want to be involved in work that has an impact on the lives of others.
- *Skill variety:* Many employees want to work on jobs that offer opportunities to learn and deploy new skills and talents. The chance to learn and grow motivates employees.

Leaders can use an array of nonfinancial rewards as positive and negative consequences for employees' meeting or missing standards. Alfie Kohn, who claims that financial rewards don't work, encourages leaders to use choice (give employees choices about what they do and how to do it), collaboration (create teams to have a positive social setting), and content (the five dimensions just listed).[11] Bob Nelson has captured numerous ways to reward employees outside traditional financial incentives in his *1001 Ways* books.[12]

To align rewards to measures and strategy, we suggest completing the worksheet in Figure 9.3. This *Reward Diagnostic* discerns the extent to which the behaviors implied by measures relate to positive employee outcomes.[13] Once the strategy and measures have been determined, the leader and team can then identify the behaviors required to deliver strategy and accomplish standards. Individuals or a team then answer with one of four outcomes that might follow the behavior: (1) reward or approval (a good thing happens either financially or nonfinancially), (2) punishment or disapproval, (3) no reaction, or (4) impossible to detect. As employees check one of these four outcomes, they begin to see the extent to which consequences align with behaviors. We have used this exercise with a number of clients. In one case, after we identified the desired behaviors, we found that most of the checks occurred in the "no reaction" or "impossible to detect" columns. In these cases, employees felt that even if they behaved in ways congruent with the strategy, the probability of their receiving any reward was low. The reward system failed to sustain accountability.

Consequences work. People generally do not act randomly; they act because a positive consequence reinforced the behavior or a negative consequence deterred the behavior. As leaders become clear about strategy and measures, they can creatively craft financial and nonfinancial rewards that change and sustain behavior and ensure accountability.

Phase 4: Feedback—How Do We Know How We're Doing?

Without feedback, employees don't have the capacity to reflect, change, and learn. Accountability requires that employees know how they are doing, in clear and unambiguous terms, so that they can modify what they do in the future. Perhaps the greatest flaw in feedback is not giving or soliciting any at all. Leaders may hesitate to share negative news for fear of offending or for lack of courage. Employees may not want to solicit feedback for fear of not being able to respond and with the often false hope that unspoken mistakes may not really have mattered in the first place.

Leaders who want accountability need to step up to the feedback challenge and learn to both give and receive feedback.

Like consequences, feedback can and should be both positive and negative. Managers are often pulled toward negative feedback, focusing on employee mistakes and what has gone wrong. Effective leaders balance positive feedback, focusing on what employees do well and how to enhance it, with constructive feedback, talking candidly to employees when they need to improve. One leader set an agenda among his team to "focus on what people do, not what they don't." He coached his leadership team to always find something positive that employees were doing, acknowledge it, encourage it, thank the employee for it, and ask the employee what could be done to maintain performance at that level.[14] Leaders who deliver effective feedback follow the criteria in Table 9.5.

- *Immediate* feedback is easy to understand because it is closely tied to the event deserving feedback. When feedback is delayed, it loses impact. This is one of the reasons that annual performance reviews don't work as a sole surrogate for feedback. Employees need feedback throughout the year, not at a one-time event.
- *Consistent* feedback focuses on patterns and explores why undesirable patterns occurred and what can be done to turn a pattern into an event or eventually avoid the event all together. When a mistake is an isolated, unique, and single experience, leaders need to not overreact. Leaders need to be consistent in their feedback, not shifting from advocating quality to cost to customer share. Consistency comes from strategic clarity and operational measures. Periodically, leaders are well served by asking employees, "What are the messages I am communicating?" and receiving feedback on the consistency of their messages.

Table 9.5   Criteria for Effective Feedback

Criterion: Effective feedback is . . .	Definition: Feedback is more effective when it . . .
Immediate	Is offered as soon as behavior warrants it, not delayed to some future date (such as an end-of-year appraisal).
Consistent	Focuses on patterns of behavior, not any one individual behavior and offers one or two areas for improvement, not a long list.
Self-monitored	Is defined and monitored directly by the recipient, not by someone else.
Honest	Is blunt, candid, and straight, and includes specific examples.
Behavioral	Focuses on future behaviors, not the person.
Followed-up	Encourages follow-up to ensure that changes occur.

- *Self-monitored* feedback enables employees to track their own performance, which helps them monitor how they are doing and make improvements. This logic applies to almost any personal change (lose weight, stop smoking, wear seat belts). When individuals track what they do, they become more aware of the changes required and more willing to internalize the processes for change.[15]
- *Honest* feedback is direct and candid. Peter Drucker is credited with the definition of intellectual integrity that captures a Taoist perspective: "See the world as it is, not as you would want it to be."[16] Leaders who offer employees candid, honest, direct, and at times blunt feedback provide a mirror that helps the employee learn and change.
- *Behavioral* feedback offers specific suggestions for the future, not obsessing about what has been done but constructively addressing what should be done.[17] Often feedback fails when it focuses on the person or on generalities. In an interview about how to coach leaders through feedback, renowned executive coach Marshall Goldsmith said, "When I do coaching, I give the person suggestions. I focus my suggestions on the future, not the past. People tend to get upset and defensive and go into denial when you talk about their previous behavior. If you focus on the future, they are much more likely to accept what you say."[18]
- Seldom do single events create sustained change. Epiphanies may excite the soul, but they don't create long-term behavior change. Sustained change comes from feedback that is *followed up*. The follow-up may be as simple as a phone call or e-mail connection to recall and review a change agenda or as elegant as a management by objectives performance management process. Regardless of the intensity, accountability flourishes with follow-up and wanes without it. These criteria for effective feedback may be applied in both formal and informal settings.

When receiving feedback, leaders begin by creating a personal willingness to listen and to change. It is not helpful to receive feedback without being willing to sincerely listen and respond. The value of feedback is enormous. Most people see the world through their own eyes and are not able to perceive how their actions may affect others. Marshall Goldsmith has observed that successful people often overrate themselves because they do not have a regular forum for candid feedback.[19] *We consider feedback a gift that can be opened on demand to enhance personal performance.*

Effective leaders seek informal feedback from multiple sources. They observe how their ideas affect others; they find valued employees who are willing to offer them candid observations; they look for patterns of where things worked and where they did not; they do team audits to check up on how their teams work; and most common of all, they ask for it. In asking for feedback, leaders need to make it clear they're willing to receive answers nondefensively (framing questions in terms such as "I know there are areas I need to improve, can you help me?"), to ask specific questions (i.e., "How can I improve in getting decisions made in the meeting?"), to listen carefully to the answer and seek clarity when required (saying things like, "What is it that shows I come to the meeting with my mind already made up? Can you give me an example? What specifically do I do to communicate this?"), and to thank those who offer the feedback.

In formal settings, leaders also have access to feedback through processes such as the 360-degree assessment.[20] When receiving a 360-degree feedback report, the best approach is to acknowledge the feedback, thank those who provided it, focus on one or two specific behavioral changes that will be based on the data, then build in a follow-up method to monitor progress on the behavioral changes. For example, one of our clients found from the 360-degree report that his employees were frustrated when he answered the phone while they were meeting with him. They found this degrading. He was not aware of the behavior, or the impact it was having on his employees. After the report and resulting dialogue, he worked to change the annoying behavior.

Leaders who effectively receive informal and formal feedback will put themselves in a position to give persuasive feedback to others. They model what they preach and demonstrate what they advocate. When leaders

To watch a video segment about accountability or to complete tools or assessments online, go to:
www.rbl.net/whythebottomlineisnt.html.

give feedback using the criteria in Table 9.5, they improve accountability. Employees know where they stand, how their work is meeting or missing expectations, what they need to do to improve, and what the consequences (positive and negative) will be if they do or do not improve.

Leadership Implications

Accountability matters for individuals. When people at work, at home, or in another setting have strategic clarity, operational measures, relevant consequences, and feedback, they deliver what they promise. These simple principles help parents hold children accountable for household chores or teachers hold students accountable for learning.

Accountability also matters for organizations of all types. There is an accountability movement in education, where districts, schools, and faculty work to deliver better-educated students. This accountability comes through the same four phases: strategic clarity where goals and outcomes are clearly defined; operational measures where everyone knows the standards expected of them; relevant consequences for meeting or missing standards; and feedback to follow up and improve on performance. Accountability in the U.S. government has been mandated (Government Performance and Results Act) because public agencies feel increased obligation to deliver on their promises. In industry, accountability is an intangible because it instills a mindset of commitment. Leaders at all levels need to create accountability through the processes we propose. When investors discern accountability in an organization, they have more confidence in its prospects for long-term success.

Leaders who deliver accountability do so by engaging in the following activities:

1. Understand the overall accountability within your organization by tracking the extent to which goals set are met.
2. Include time on your agenda to publicly acknowledge goals that are accomplished and key people who made success happen.

3. Assess strategic clarity by asking stakeholders (customers, investors, employees) to articulate your strategy and its implications for them.

4. Establish strategic clarity by creating words, phrases, symbols, or icons that capture how you will position your organization in the future.

5. Assess the extent to which measures align with strategy by looking at your performance measurement system and determining if you can discern your strategy from it.

6. Identify outcome and behavioral measures for employees that tie to your strategy.

7. Ensure that you offer positive and negative consequences that align to your measures. Determine what happens to employees who meet standards and what happens to employees who do not.

8. Ensure that these consequences are both financial and nonfinancial (time off, praise, etc.).

9. Offer ongoing feedback to individuals so that they can learn and improve.

10. Employ multiple methods for giving and receiving feedback—such as 360-degree evaluations, performance reviews, and after-action reviews.

10 | Collaboration: It Takes More Than Two to Intangible

As organizations grow, leaders inevitably face the challenge of making the whole more than the sum of the parts. Small companies have clear and simple lines of authority, goals are easily shared, and employees generally feel personal accountability and connection. We have used the metaphor of bumper cars to describe how things frequently get done in small firms. In a normal bumper car experience, most of the bumper cars both randomly and naturally bounce off each other. Likewise, in small firms, in a daily, weekly, or monthly time frame, most employees will interact with each other without formal structures requiring them to do so. Ideas are shared, visions communicated, and unity exists among employees. As an organization grows through multiple divisions, acquisitions, or globalization, the employees no longer naturally touch. Larger, complex organizations require formal mechanisms to share information and create unity across the organization.

Collaboration refers to different parties working together toward a common purpose. In an organization, these different parties may be individuals, teams, plants, divisions, businesses, or geographies. Each part is a part; collaboration makes the whole more valuable than the sum of the independent parts. As organizations grow, they develop more parts. While each part must stand alone and produce independent results, the whole should be more valuable than merely the sum of the independent parts.

In organizations, making the whole more than the sum of the parts has been a leadership challenge for decades. Figure 10.1 lays out the basic dimensions of the collaboration leadership challenge. On the one hand (vertical axis), leaders want consistency that leads to efficiency; on the other hand (horizontal axis), leaders want to manage differences that lead to effectiveness. Many concepts have been used to describe these two extreme alternatives to organizing (see Figure 10.1). Paul Lawrence and Jay Lorsch, two prominent Harvard Business School professors, laid

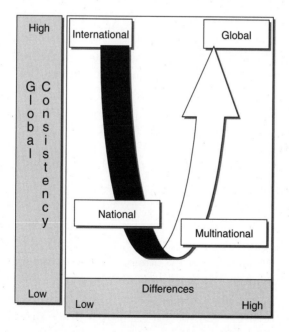

Figure 10.1   Collaboration basic framework: Making the whole more than the parts.

out the dilemma as differentiation/integration many years ago.[1] Firms have to integrate and be focused to have a common agenda that elicits unity, but they also must differentiate into alternative markets to achieve a balanced portfolio.

Firms that are only integrated and focused may be unified but risk their product, geography, or service facing a business downturn exposing them to economic liabilities. These firms may be efficient through costs, but ineffective with tailored solutions to customers. On the other hand, firms that are too diversified become holding companies. Most of the pure holding companies have a break-up value greater than the sum of the parts. This means that if the different businesses comprising the holding company were sold to those interested in this business, the sum of those divestitures would be worth more than the current market value of the firm. We have seen a rule of thumb that when the sum of the parts is greater than the whole by 25 percent to 30 percent, the firm is a likely takeover target because the new owner could then sell off pieces and gain more value for the shareholders.

Collaboration exists when leaders have the ability to make the whole more than the sum of the parts, to make larger and more complex organizations more competitive by making them smaller while retaining the advantage of scale, and to ensure that parties work together on common goals while maintaining their independence. Some thoughtful leaders have said that they want the leverage of scale and the speed of being small. At General Motors, CEO Rick Wagoner talks about being one company—big *and* fast. In both cases, they are working to ensure collaboration, or the capacity to manage efficiency (and all its requirements for standardization, control, and consistency) simultaneously with effectiveness and its focus on flexibility, customization, and responsiveness. As we have said, collaboration is not new, as leaders have worked on issues of governance as long as large firms have existed.[2]

Many have talked about a continuum between high integration and high differentiation. The words for this continuum have become ways to describe how leaders manage between efficiency and effectiveness (see Table 10.1). Generally, what happens is that a firm swings from one extreme of this continuum to the other. Centralized firms—where decisions are made at the corporate level, where the headquarters sets

Table 10.1 Concepts of Parts and Whole

Integration (Focus on the Whole)	Differentiation (Focus on the Parts)	Type of Organization
Efficiency	Effectiveness	Matrix
Centralized	Decentralized	Federated system
Corporate	Business unit	Loosely coupled
International	Multinational	Global
Standardized	Customized	Shared services
Uniform	Flexible	Network
Single product	Holding company	

standards that are then implemented throughout the firm, and where assets are allocated through a corporate process—end up being unresponsive to local conditions, slow to react, and not able to adapt. Managers then shift, often dramatically, to the other extreme and the decentralized organization follows. Decisions are made at the local unit, authority rests with the general manager, and firms are encouraged to adapt and respond to location conditions. Over time, these firms end up with duplication and redundancy that increase costs without learning, so the cycle begins all over again. The vicious cycle between centralized and decentralized organizations only adds value to consultants who offer the counsel and those who create ever-changing organization charts.

In this chapter, we review general principles and processes of collaboration that can be used at different levels of the organization, as well as for the entire company. We look at three common applications of collaboration: mergers and acquisitions, globalization, and shared services. We have worked with companies to help them maximize the benefits of these applications and share with you what we have found to be keys to success.

Before we explore the applications, let's take a quick look at some of the ways that organizations typically collaborate within themselves and with external stakeholders—customers and investors—to gain both efficiencies and increased effectiveness. Some of these processes, discussed in the shared services section on page 221, are important to discuss within this context of collaborative processes.

General Principles and Processes of Collaboration

Here is a sequence of processes that an organization can choose to share across boundaries, arranged from the simplest to implement to the most complex:[3]

- *Standards:* Leaders share a set of expectations and measures across boundaries about what is expected. These expectations might include output measures (e.g., financial returns) or input measures (customer loyalty, employee satisfaction, or organization capabilities). Wal-Mart shares standards for many of its processes, and McDonald's does likewise. Customers going to either establishment expect to have the same shopping experience wherever they are. Standards may come in the form of requirements that businesses follow or in templates that everyone uses in processing information.

- *Information:* Leaders share information through knowledge (IT) databases, through case studies, or through site visits to collaborate. The McKinsey Consulting firm has created a knowledge base to share experiences across client engagements. Partners can access the knowledge base to find out if other McKinsey partners have had similar client queries, to learn how others responded to similar challenges, and to share tools for consulting excellence.

- *Expertise:* Leaders share expertise and competence in the form of moving people from one unit to another, either on full time or temporary assignment. General Electric is renowned for its ability to move talent across organization units. Through systematic reviews, individuals who both need and can deliver skills are transferred to make the best use of available talent. Leaders may identify best practices and those experiences with others.

- *Authority:* Leaders collaborate by sharing authority to solve problems with cross-functional teams or problem-solving teams or boards. Zurich Financial has created global practice boards for customer segments (small client, consumer, wholesale) and for functions (human resources, communications, information technology). These practice boards share experiences, leverage knowledge, and help solve problems with cross-functional expertise.

- *Business processes:* Leaders collaborate on business processes to reduce costs and share knowledge about accomplishing work. Business process reengineering has been critical to Boeing as the company moves from one aircraft to the next. Lessons learned from one experience move to another with each succeeding generation of aircraft done better, faster, and cheaper. Leaders also collaborate on behalf of their customers to make it easy to do business with their company (e.g., to provide a seamless interface and common identity). To accomplish this, leaders at multiple sites might have to collaborate to provide one solution and one invoice for a customer.
- *Innovation and design:* Leaders build collaborative ventures to innovate and create new products or services. 3M people collaborate to maintain their design and innovation heritage. Collaboration is both inside as scientists are encouraged to "steal" resources for innovative projects and outside as customer focus groups help define and refine possible innovations.

Collaboration occurs within an organization when different units share some of these items. Zurich Financial's U.K. subsidiary, Eagle Star, created some innovative distribution channels for personal lines of insurance. Through Zurich's practice boards, these ideas were communicated and shared with operations in over 50 countries. This collaboration increased both efficiency (no need to reinvent the product ideas in each country) and effectiveness (the idea was adapted, not adopted in each country). The "whole" in this case is the firm and the connections between the parts (businesses, divisions, geographies) make the whole more than the sum of the parts.

Collaboration also occurs between a firm and external stakeholders. Firms and suppliers can collaborate to reduce purchasing costs and design products more easily adopted by the firm. Firms and customers can collaborate to share knowledge, expectations, and standards so that firms can develop new products that customers' value and need. Firms and competitors can even collaborate to set industry standards that build performance for the entire industry. By collaborating with external stakeholders, the firm redefines its boundaries and builds a value network of alliances and partnerships. Grocery stores have collaborated to create a universal code for scanning at checkout counters. Automotive companies, with government support and oversight, have collaborated for similar environmental standards. Universities have collaborated to form an accreditation body that ensures that each university meets professional standards.

Collaboration appeals to investors as an intangible, because they want to know that leaders can work together and make the whole more than the sum of the parts. They want to see that when a firm grows through mergers, joint ventures, alliances, or product innovation, the growth always makes the entire enterprise more successful, not just some individual part. They want to know that bigger and more complex organizations are gaining more than size and scale; they are offering clear opportunities for innovation, design, and leverage.

Customers value collaborative firms because they get both personalized service from the part of the firm they work with and institutional support from the larger parent firm, which inspires confidence. Employees get value from firms that collaborate because they have opportunities to learn and grow in different subsidiaries of the overall firm while gaining the credibility and respect of the parent firm.

The principles and processes of collaboration apply at all levels, from the two-person team to the largest multinational. *Information Week* published a list of innovators in collaboration—companies that practiced the principles of collaboration effectively as they set standards, shared information, transferred talent, assigned authority, designed business processes, and encouraged innovation through collaboration.[4] Three common applications provide the most mileage for leaders seeking intangible value through collaboration: merger or acquisition, globalization, and shared services.

Collaboration Application 1:
Mergers or Acquisitions

Mergers or acquisitions look like a simple and straightforward way to reduce costs and grow the business.[5] Almost every industry has consolidated in the last decade. Often these consolidations occur within a single geography (say, the United States), and then become global. The automotive industry moved to three major U.S. players, then each of these players formed global alliances as industry consolidation continued (Ford with Mazda, Volvo, and Jaguar; General Motors with Saab, Daewoo, Isuzu, and Fiat; Chrysler with Daimler-Benz). Airlines, pharmaceuticals, lodgings, oil, and financial services have each followed the same track by consolidating through mergers within a single geography, then moving to global alliances.

Despite their prevalence, mergers often fail to meet their sponsors' financial expectations. Mark Sirower, a professor at New York University, found that about 65 percent of the 168 deals between 1979 and 1990 destroyed value for shareholders. The acquirer's stock trailed the S&P by about 9 percent one year after the deal was announced.[6] Mercer Management Consulting examined 270 mergers and acquisitions over a 10-year period and found that most did not deliver industry average shareholder value.[7] More recently, and in contrast to the previous studies, the Conference Board interviewed top human resource managers from 134 companies that had a merger or acquisition experience since 1990. They found that about 65 percent reported a "very successful" or "successful" outcome.[8] The debate about the viability of mergers has shifted as leaders of alliances have become more cognizant and capable of making the whole more than the sum of the parts.

In a merger, making the whole more than the sum of the parts means finding ways to integrate the merged firms. This is difficult for employees because they typically remember the entrepreneurial zeal of the "good old days" in their previous firm and have not yet experienced the potential value of being part of a larger entity and brand. Their typical response is to resist attempts by the new entity to integrate, and to spend unproductive time reminiscing about the past. It is critical to get past this resistance and find new ways to create customer value or the merger, acquisition, or roll-up is doomed.

In our work on mergers, we have found two major paths to merger collaboration. It's helpful to think of them as two different kinds of arithmetic—neither the sort your grade school teacher would have approved:

1. *Efficiency (1 + 1 = 1):* The merger synergies make the whole more than the parts by increasing efficiencies and reducing costs.

2. *Leverage (1 + 1 = 3):* The merger synergies come through finding ways to grow the two companies beyond what they were as independent entities.

These two approaches occur sequentially, with the efficiencies coming before leverage (see Table 10.2).

Creating Efficiencies in a Merger or Acquisition

The efficiencies gained from mergers often attract leadership attention particularly during an economic downturn, when it seems necessary to take costs out of an entire industry. Here are the most common approaches for efficiency:

- *Headcount:* Reducing headcount becomes the most obvious and telling efficiency gain of merger integration. Duplication of roles exists for senior line manager jobs and for many staff jobs. Most mergers promise a headcount reduction where duplication of jobs will be removed. In making headcount reductions, however, it is important to move quickly or the benefits may be lost. One firm announced in February that 7 percent of its workforce would have to leave in July. Probably 60 percent thought they were in the 7 percent, creating five months of disruptions—with most of the real downsizing targets hanging on for dear life, and many of the people the merged company needed to keep heading off to more stable pastures. Within legal constraints, a faster resolution

Table 10.2   Merger Collaboration
Integrating Mechanisms

Efficiency: 1 + 1 = 1	Leverage: 1 + 1 = 3
Headcount	Customer
Facilities	Product
Technology	Strategy
Supplier relations	Ideas and knowledge
Distribution channels	Talent
	Reputation

would have been both more ethical to those leaving and more reasonable for the competitiveness of the firm. When downsizing, it is important to be strategic, not generic. Generic across-the-board reductions of some set percentage fail to focus on functions or groups where either more or fewer resources would be required. Even with the most demanding and severe head-count reductions, some departments probably should grow.

The process for reducing headcount becomes almost as important as the size of the reduction. Fairness in headcount reduction means involving people, setting clear standards, and giving people from both firms the opportunity to bid for key jobs. Often mergers or acquisitions derive significant productivity gains through reduced headcount—but it doesn't happen by accident, or by the simple logic of the combination.

- *Facilities:* Mergers or alliances generally allow facility consolidation. Physical space is generally correlated with headcount. As eliminating duplicate jobs leads to fewer people, physical facilities may be merged to reduce costs. But physical facilities often influence the quality of work life for employees, so leaders need to take care in shaping physical space that not only reduces costs but also increases morale and productivity. It is tempting to postpone redesigning the remaining office space to reduce costs, but this step should be considered very carefully for its possible negative effects on the surviving workforce.

- *Technology:* As computer investments grew, some firms used the survival-of-the-fittest approach. Each unit could buy its own technology, both hardware and software. Over time, those systems that worked best were able to garner attention and resources; they grew, while those that did not work well faltered and failed. To gain strategic efficiencies, leaders can initiate technology integration. Integrated technology usually means finding a dominant hardware and software provider who can be used throughout a merged enterprise to support the desired capabilities in the company. This results in cost savings through both scale of purchasing and reduced redundancy in support for the technology. Consolidation in the banking industry is a good example of how integrated technology can reduce cost and provide greater overall capability.

- *Supplier relations:* Purchasing often becomes a major source of cost savings in mergers. Volume purchases usually have lower per unit prices. Improved relationships with large suppliers can also yield cost savings through sharing resources, reducing inventories, and streamlining processes. Also, managing the purchasing process often reduces costs when firms and suppliers are connected through technology. Wal-Mart reduces inventory by having suppliers connected to its databases. When customers buy products, the rate of purchase and stores where the products are purchased are reported to both Wal-Mart and its vendors simultaneously. This ensures fewer inventories in process and more cost savings.

- *Distribution:* A merged organization can focus its attention on how to go to market. Sometimes this means consolidating alternative channels (Web-based sales, account teams, middlemen, and the like). When firms merge, they may be able to put similar channels under one leadership team who save duplication of effort. In addition, distribution may help focus on targeted customers to reduce the cost of serving a larger audience of customers.

- *Keys to efficiency:* In any efficiency strategy, the goal is to reduce costs through people, process, and project investments (see Chapter 2). In mergers, most of the early collaboration focuses on identifying such efficiencies. When leaders want to build efficiency, they need to act boldly and aggressively, make tough calls with a fair process, and ensure that actions are consistent with values.

One myth is that people will voluntarily cut costs. This is generally not true. Even when employees know costs are too high, they are unlikely to recommend actions that impair their personal status or career (altruism exists more in books than reality). Therefore, leaders who want to ensure collaboration through merger or acquisition should make vigorous decisions that drive efficiency. Waiting to reduce costs only delays the inevitable. In a competitive economy, organizations with lower cost structures are more flexible, making it more probable they will survive downturns and have the resources to grow in more prosperous times. Leaders in these organizations must be bold and focused to accomplish efficiency goals.

Ways to Leverage Results

In the leverage phase, the power of combined resources shows up in a number of areas. This is where collaboration really makes the whole more than the sum of the parts through sharing ideas or insights that increase revenue. Others have noted the importance of growth in mergers and acquisitions.[9] Cost savings, though important, will not fully justify the collaboration that should emerge from mergers. Growth is what gives mergers the opportunity to create long-term value. Here are the common approaches for merger leverage:

- *Customer/product matrix:* Mergers or alliances should allow growth in either customers or products or both. Figure 10.2 illustrates a tool that helps leaders of a merged firm put things together. The two firms may have been selling different products to different customers. As the leaders look at the present state,

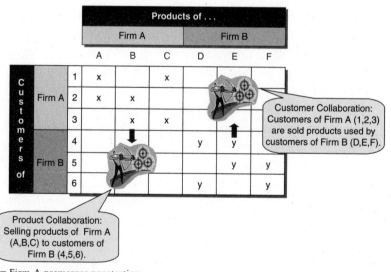

x = Firm A premerger penetration
y = Firm B premerger penetration

Figure 10.2   Product/customer merger strategy chart.

they identify ways in which products from Firm A (A, B, C) can be sold to customers of Firm B (4, 5, 6) and ways in which customers of Firm A can be sold products used by customers of Firm B. The grid highlights empty cells (post-merger) that can then become a basis for future strategic investments in getting more revenue from target customers and more product sales to new customers. This simple analysis leads to profound growth opportunities. For example, Citibank and Travelers executives created a full-service financial provider when products from Citibank were sold to Travelers' customers and when share of targeted customers for overall financial services went up because of products from both Citibank and Travelers.

- *Strategy:* Strategy often deals with allocating resources to win. In a merger or alliance, leaders need to define what businesses they are in and not in. Tools for managing the portfolio of businesses have been created. Businesses may be *divested* to gain cash for growth businesses, *invested in* to assure growth, or *milked* to draw off resources for other businesses. In any merger, portfolio decisions need to be made to enable targeted businesses to grow by drawing on resources from other businesses. Pruning a tree or shrub generally enables it to grow more quickly and in a desired direction. Pruning a company enables a focus on targeted businesses and helps it grow in a desired direction.

- *Talent and people flow:* People make decisions, organizations do not. Growing a business means getting the right talent in the right job. Sometimes mergers are made to ensure that the talent exists to nurture and grow a business. Much of Cisco's growth was through mergers and many of those mergers were made to attract talent that would lead Cisco into new revenue-producing markets. In merging for talent, leaders need to make sure that the merger deal includes retention and production bonuses that keep the desired people on board—there's nothing so disappointing to investors as an expensive acquisition whose most desirable assets have left to join new employers.

- *Ideas:* Ideas for innovation come into companies through mergers by enabling employees from each company to share new processes, products, or services that might grow revenues. Leveraging ideas often comes from moving people, but it can also come from forums and structured knowledge management systems where ideas are generated and generalized (see Chapter 8 on learning). When Boeing acquired McDonnell Douglas, its managers relied heavily on the latter's training center in St. Louis as a forum for ideas. They brought together leaders at all levels from both firms into training programs to manage the transition. These mixed groups shared ideas and practices in an attempt to create a stronger Boeing out of the merged companies.

- *Reputation:* A firm's reputation, or brand, becomes a mindset to targeted customers. Customers with a positive firm mindset may pay more for the product. For example, when Marriott acquired Residence Inn as a long-stay alternative, it used its name (Residence Inn by Marriott) to add value to the Residence Inn brand and charge a premium for the newly branded product. Marriott also brought a series of services and disciplines to the new firm to justify the new firm brand. However, when Marriott bought Ritz Carlton, the brand was not "Ritz Carlton by Marriott" because the Ritz Carlton brand had premium value without the Marriott addition. Should the firm brand be added to a merged product? We believe there is a relatively simple answer to this question when thinking about leverage: If adding the brand creates enough additional value to customers, they will be willing to pay a premium for the product or service.

- *Keys to leverage:* Successful mergers and acquisitions come as leaders find leverage that allows the new firm to expand, not just cost collaboration that provides savings unavailable to the original companies. Leverage means picking one or two ways in which the whole will be more than the sum of the parts and investing heavily to ensure that leverage works. For example, leverage might mean starting with one customer and showing how customer share increases with products from the merged firm. It might mean sharing talent across the boundaries of the newly merged firms to help increase revenue. It might mean discovering one idea with high impact that can be used from one firm to another. Starting small ensures quick, visible wins that build confidence. Although efficiency may require more directive leadership, leverage requires leaders who engage and nurture their employees. Leverage can seldom be imposed by edict—it must be fostered in an environment of openness and sharing. Because efficiency and leverage require different leadership styles, making mergers work has become very challenging.

As leaders collaborate in mergers and joint ventures, we often ask for a road map to show where the collaboration will occur. Leaders often want to skip efficiency and move directly to leverage. That approach is intellectually and emotionally more exciting, but it tends to miss some fundamentals that are critical to sustained collaboration. On the other hand, reducing costs without having a blueprint for growth may save money, but it is unlikely to fulfill the collaboration promise.

Collaboration Application 2: Globalization

As firms become global, making the whole more than the sum of the parts requires leaders who can balance the efficiency opportunities of global scale with the effectiveness demands of location adaptation (Figure 10.3). Globalization has been discussed by many authors.[10] Global collaboration means figuring out a number of capabilities to simultaneously gain global efficiencies and local leverage.[11] Let's take a look at several of these key capabilities.

Identifying Core and Noncore Issues

In a successful global company, some things are globally integrated while others are locally adapted. Consequently, the first critical capability is being able to determine what is core to the organization and what should be integrated and standardized throughout its worldwide operations and what can be locally adapted.

Core issues generally relate to principles that give the firm a global identity. For example, Disney has identified a set of principles for its theme parks. When Walt Disney created the first theme park in Anaheim, he did so focusing on the values of providing a clean, safe, and fun

Global Integration	High	Worldwide business Highly integrated (R&D, finance, product development, procurement) (International)	Transnational, partnered, distributed (marketing) (Global organization)
	Low	Single country/ licenses (National)	Strong country/geography manager (sales, advertising, Human Resources) (Multinational or multilocal)
		Low	High
		Localization Local Responsiveness	

Figure 10.3 Framework for evolution of global organization.

experience for families. This experience was in stark contrast to the seedy carnivals of the time. This core focus is the same throughout every Disney theme park from the oldest one in Anaheim to the one on the drawing boards for Hong Kong.

Just as leaders determine what is core and therefore common across the firm's worldwide operations, they must also define what is noncore and therefore open to local adaptation. The world is too big and too diverse to even entertain the notion that every policy or practice, let alone product or process, could be the same everywhere. Disney demonstrates this principle. Based on the belief that alcohol and a safe, fun experience for the family did not mix, Disney banned alcohol from the parks. However, guests at Disney's park in Paris complained about the rule. The leadership team in Paris had to decide if the assumption that the consumption of alcohol would get in the way of a clean, safe, fun family experience applied in Europe.

Identifying policies, practices, and so on that are clearly noncore can eliminate the time and energy that otherwise would go into debating, politicking, and arguing over the issues. Some issues will be gray or decided only on a case-by-case basis. To some extent, we might think about this general capability as being able to distinguish means from ends. For Disney, the end was a clean, safe, fun experience for the family. Not serving alcohol was a means to this end. However, it had been a means for so long that in the minds of many leaders it had been transformed into an end in itself. Success on this particular issue for Disneyland Paris came only when leaders recognized that regional and country differences required adaptation to reach the desired global ends. Consequently, while alcohol is still not served in the majority of Disney theme parks (including the park in Tokyo), beer and wine are now served in Paris.

Demonstrating Consistency and Flexibility

A second global capability is that of achieving consistency while also allowing flexibility. In achieving consistency, the first required step is determining what is core to the organization. Still, it makes little difference if Disney determines that clean, safe, family fun is a part of its core values if it cannot apply that core consistently across its worldwide operations. This capability centers on understanding what guides people's behavior when no one is looking. In achieving consistency, several specifics are required. First, executives need to be able to help employees understand the core. People cannot consistently honor what they don't understand. This understanding is typically achieved only when there is an explanation of both *what* the core is and *why* it is that way. In addition to understanding, executives need to be able to engender a high level of commitment to the core. In other words, both the head (understanding) and heart (commitment) must be engaged. With understanding and commitment, employees are well on their way to consistent behavior concerning the core.

Disney achieves this consistency through two principal human resource activities. First, it selects individuals to work in all its parks around the world who already believe in the core values of clean, safe family fun. Disney carefully screens candidates to determine if they have dispositions toward providing guests with friendly service and believe in the importance of cleanliness. In fact, Stephen Burke, who was sent to help fix the problems at the troubled European park, determined that one of the problems was that park employees (*cast members*) had not been selected strictly enough for dispositions consistent with Disney's core values. One of the first things he changed was to increase the care with which cast members were selected. In addition, Burke increased the intensity of the detailed orientation Disney provided for all new cast members. These orientation sessions were the first critical opportunity for the company to explain the core values. In combination, the selection and training efforts were effective in creating the requisite understanding and commitment to achieve the desired consistency.

For those issues identified as noncore, flexibility and adaptation must be allowed. In particular, this requires tolerance and even encouragement of differences. One of the greatest obstacles to effectiveness for leaders working outside their native country and culture is a lack of tolerance of the inevitable differences they encounter.[12] However, simple tolerance of differences is only the beginning. True flexibility for the organization requires managers to be able to generate variety in response to local conditions.

Building Global Brands While Recognizing Local Customs

A third collaboration capability focuses on managing the tensions between building global brand equity and honoring local customs. If a company is going to be globally collaborative with a common core that is consistent throughout its worldwide operations, it needs the ability to build global brand equity. For example, Richard Branson is dedicated to building a firm equity in the Virgin brand. He believes that Virgin must have an identity, or stand for something, in customers' minds. The Virgin brand has four key dimensions: a positive buying experience, outstanding service, continuous improvement in products or service, and economic value for each transaction. Branson has applied this firm brand to records, airlines, soft drinks, and railroads.[13] This global firm brand is based on the assumption that a customer of Virgin anywhere in the world will have a similar overall experience—and will value this overall experience and all four of its distinct elements.

Despite the need for building global brand equity, differences in local customs will persist. This requires capabilities not only in observing local customs but in understanding their origins and drivers. Unilever began enjoying real success in India with its laundry soaps after it spent time studying the local washing habits. Many people in India still wash their laundry in rivers on rocks or washboards. Unilever's traditional boxed laundry soap just didn't make any sense and wouldn't work in these conditions. Also, few households could afford the large boxes even if the soap would work. Success for Unilever came when executives recognized that for most people in India, laundry habits were not going to change quickly because of both economic conditions and cultural traditions. After recognizing this, they changed the form of the soap from powder to small bricks and then sold them for pennies each. People could hold the small soap bricks in their hands as they scrubbed their laundry on the rocks or washboards. Though they had to purchase these bricks much more often than their counterparts in developed countries would purchase boxed laundry soap, executives came to recognize that their Indian customers did not view this as an important inconvenience.

Creating Opportunities for Shared Learning and New Knowledge

A fourth set of capabilities centers on knowledge. Global success requires both being able to take advantage of learning across a firm's worldwide operations and, at the same time, being able to create new knowledge wherever incubation conditions exist (see Chapter 8 on learning).

Economies of scale that spread existing knowledge about productivity, sales, competitors, suppliers, distribution, systems, and so on gain the revenue-enhancing benefits of the knowledge across the firm's worldwide operations. In fact, the larger the organization, the greater the cost and revenue benefit potential from sharing knowledge. Consequently, maintaining a competitive position as the firm globalizes requires developing the ability to share knowledge throughout the firm's far-flung operations.

Many organizations have found that the key to this is overcoming the "not invented here" syndrome. Local supervisors, managers, or executives resist incorporating best practices from outside for fear of an erosion of their power base. To the extent that knowledge, technical answers, or solutions of any type are a source of power, then these sources of power coming in from the outside can be interpreted as threatening.

Successful companies have found that the key to widespread learning is overcoming the "not-invented-here" syndrome and providing a variety of different means by which information and insights are shared across the global organization and celebrating those that effectively incorporate these lessons.

Although sharing learning across a global organization is no small task, for many firms it is easier than creating new knowledge on a worldwide basis. To hold down costs, firms increasingly are concentrating R&D centers in a few targeted locations. This makes great economic sense. However, many organizations experience a natural and negative consequence—undistributed knowledge creation. Often when knowledge creation centers such as R&D labs are strategically located in only one or two places for the entire global organization, people tend to grow a bit lazy and think that those are the only places where great ideas can be generated and that the people working there are those primarily charged with innovation.

The world is just too big and there are too many bright and capable people in it to think that key innovations can happen only in a few places with a few people. Thus, even though organizations need to foster the ability to take in and employ knowledge generated elsewhere and avoid the negative consequences of the not-invented-here syndrome, they also need to foster the ability to generate new ideas everywhere. They need to know how to help employees everywhere develop the motivation to generate new ideas and the willingness and desire to generalize them.

Supporting Both Global Perspectives and Local Accountability

This last capability brings us full circle. Global success requires the capacity to view the organization from both an orbital and ground-level perspective and thus to feel a sense of belonging to the worldwide entity while at the same time feeling a fervent sense of accountability for your own plot of land.

Whatever aspects of the company are going to be integrated must be seen in their global entirety. IBM provides an interesting example. Just before Louis Gerstner took over at IBM, the outgoing CEO, John Ackers, had proposed dividing IBM into 13 operating units (mainframes, storage, PCs, and other product-based divisions) and letting each unit compete much like an independent company. Gerstner set forth a strategy and structure that was the exact opposite. He believed that IBM was stronger as an integrated company. The new strategy focused on integrated solutions for customers, including global solutions for global customers. He created new groups called *industry solution units* designed to be global and integrated in nature and focus their efforts on targeted industry customers. The underlying notion was that although banks might need solutions that differed from the ones used in oil and gas companies, banks in Japan and banks in New York had similar needs. Furthermore, many of the banks in Japan or New York required integrated software and hardware solutions for their worldwide operations. This strategy and the resulting structure required IBM employees to coordinate and work together globally as they never had before. In the past, strategy and structure, and therefore employees' perspectives, were largely country-based.

Helping employees, especially middle managers, stretch their minds beyond the provincial boundaries of a single country to include a global perspective was a major challenge. One of IBM's executive education programs is worth special attention. Of the nearly one thousand participants in the program, IBM made sure that almost half came from outside the United States. In most sessions of 25 to 30 participants, 10 to 15 nationalities were represented. IBM also held some of the sessions outside the United States to help many of the North Americans gain a more international, if not global, perspective. In addition, during the 10-day program, at least three senior executives worked with the groups as instructors. Classroom time was spent on cases and conceptual material that helped participants understand and think about the global environment and IBM's strategy in that context. But traditional classroom time was only a small part of the overall design. Participants were also given projects to work on during the program. By design, these projects required participants to think from a more global perspective. Finally, participants were divided into teams and engaged in an interactive, computer-based global business simulation. Each team made decisions from sourcing raw materials to allocating advertising dollars across multiple products and international markets. With six or seven teams competing in an interactive and intense simulation, participants quickly (and sometimes painfully) learned lessons about exchange rate fluctuations and pricing decisions, local manufacturing and global product mix, worldwide brand image and regional customer preferences, and so on. None of these aspects of the program magically produced global leaders, but they did go a long way toward enhancing a more global perspective on both IBM and its competitive environment.

Global collaboration makes the whole more than the sum of the parts in each country. When leaders can manage the paradoxical challenges inherent in the tensions between global and local conditions, they gain both efficiencies and leverage on a worldwide scale.

Collaboration Application 3: Shared Services

Shared services turns collaboration principles inward, with the goal of figuring out how to collaborate across units of an organization to gain both efficiency and leverage.[14] The process begins with a simple challenge: How to connect sources of knowledge (called centers of expertise) with clients (business unit leaders). Most organizations have pockets of functional competence in finance, technology, law, human resources, marketing, safety, design, marketing, and a host of other fields. These sources of expertise add value to business decisions. Traditionally, functional expertise either resides at the corporate center and is pushed to the rest of the organization (centralized) or it is distributed throughout the organization (decentralized). Shared services changes the discussion from *centralize versus decentralize* to *value added*. In this model, resources may be delivered through standardization (as with technology or call centers), centers of expertise, outsourcing, or integrated solutions (see Figure 10.4).

Shared services organizations are neither centralized nor decentralized. Instead, they're offered as resources, and the business units choose to use them (a pull model instead of the push model of centralization) when their expertise is more cost-effective than competing sources of assistance in solving local business problems.

Shared services isn't a new concept. Professional service firms have organized their operations along these lines for many years. For example, law, accounting, and consulting firms generally assign an account manager to each client. This individual's job is to work with the client to identify what is wanted and provide what is needed. To deliver value to the client, the account manager draws on the service firm's centers of expertise, groups of specialists whose personnel are assigned to account teams as required. For example, an account team within a consulting firm may be led by the account manager, with individuals from

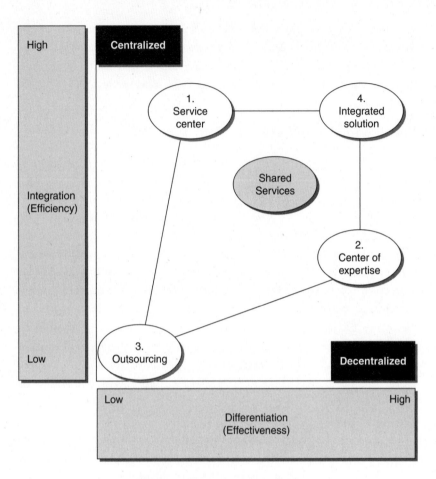

Figure 10.4   Shared services.

specialty areas (information technology, human resources, or whatever) who add value according to the unique needs of the client. At the end of the engagement or the solution of a specific problem, the specialists return to their centers waiting for another assignment.

This logic from professional service firms has moved inside large companies in the form of shared services. Unlike old-line staff groups, which either push knowledge into the businesses or decentralize staff knowledge by placing representatives in the business units, shared services organizations deliver expertise through service centers, centers of expertise, or outsourcing to provide expertise in the form most useful to the business unit.

Strategies for Shared Services

One strategy for shared services involves setting up *service centers* that share transaction staff work. Every staff group delivers transaction work; this is work that is routine, administrative, and standardized. Service centers find ways to deliver staff work better, faster, and cheaper by standardizing the work through common systems, by automating work or by using technology to accomplish work. For example, human resource service centers can streamline benefits processing through common administrative systems by setting up groups of benefits specialists at an 800 telephone number, and by putting benefits administration online and allowing employees to become self-sufficient in that area.

Centers of expertise accomplish work by allowing business unit leaders to draw on their expertise to solve business problems. Those working in centers of expertise become global process leaders, creating and adapting knowledge about financial, human resources, technology, marketing, or other processes to meet business requirements. Principles of collaboration underlie centers of expertise. Experts in the centers seek best practices from both inside and outside their firm to ensure that competencies exist within the firm. They standardize and encourage businesses to follow accepted practices in the quest to share knowledge and ideas. They distribute talent to different units depending on the requirements of those units. They share knowledge and experiences from one unit to another. They create menus of choices about what practices could be done and monitor performance on those practices so that menus are continually updated. They seek innovation by sourcing ideas, incubating them, and then investing in them (see Chapter 3 on innovation). Centers of expertise can work only with exceptional collaboration. Zurich Financial Services, for example, formed centers of expertise called practice boards.

A third strategy for shared services collaboration is *outsourcing*. By outsourcing, leaders can access expertise without ownership. In outsourcing, collaboration shifts the vendor to a partner, generally offering integrated solutions rather than piecemeal outsourcing. As a partner, the outsource supplier forms relationships of trust with the firm and brings external knowledge into the firm. Exult has become the largest supplier of human resource outsourcing, with partnerships with BP, International Paper, Bank America, and Prudential. In the Exult business model, partnerships with clients are based on principles of collaboration. Exult standardizes the processes to ensure consistency, then seeks global best practices for each critical human resources process and weaves that knowledge into the service delivery model. It invests in technology to reduce costs and shares knowledge across clients to seek learning and continuous improvement.

A fourth strategy for shared services is to offer *integrated solutions* by using multiple staff groups to solve a common business problem. A number of firms have created crisis teams that prepare for probable but unpredictable events. The teams include members from a variety of centers of expertise (finance, strategy, safety, marketing, human resources, etc.) who come together to offer integrated solutions to business problems as they arise. For example, oil firms work to avoid major oil spills, but they also recognize that such spills may occur. When one happens it creates a demand for an integrated solution; therefore, the companies maintain shared service organizations that make that solution readily available.

Collaboration principles allow shared services to work. Shared services are neither centralized nor decentralized, but provide a way to govern work that adds value to the corporation by reducing costs and gaining efficiencies and to the individual

> See a video segment on collaboration or complete tools and assessments online at: www.rbl.net/whythebottomlineisnt.html.

businesses by adapting ideas and leveraging ideas and knowledge. The whole organization is once again stronger than the sum of its parts.

Leadership Implications

Collaboration is a valuable intangible. It makes the whole more than the sum of its parts. Any large, complex organization must ensure that the principles of collaboration apply. These principles include the ability to set standards, share information, transfer expertise, allocate authority, improve business processes, and deliver innovation and design. These principles can be applied to consolidate mergers and acquisitions to make $1 + 1 = 1$ by gaining efficiencies, and to leverage them, making $1 + 1 = 3$ to gain effectiveness. These principles can also be applied to global organizations by building capabilities that ensure both global economies of scale and local adaptation. The same principles also apply to shared services in organizations where work can be delivered through service centers, centers of expertise, outsource vendors, or integrated solutions.

When collaboration principles are applied, intangible value is created. The collective enterprise is more valuable than any of the independent parts. Investors in these organizations value the scale and scope of the enterprise as well as its ability to adapt and respond. Customers in collaborative organizations value personal as well as comprehensive service. Employees in collaborative organizations have opportunities to gain diverse experiences through mobility across businesses, divisions, or geographies, and are still encouraged to respond to local requirements.

Leaders who build collaboration do so through the following activities:

1. Defining company practices that are core and should be shared across all units of the company.
2. Creating menus of choices that may be adapted to local conditions, then monitoring how items from the menus are adapted.
3. Setting standards for minimal performance on a business process.
4. Gathering information about best practices from both inside and outside the firm.
5. Creating disciplined processes for moving people from one unit to another where their talents can be used to help the unit succeed.
6. Identifying and reengineering business processes that connect parts of a business.
7. Seeking innovation and new ways to design and deliver work that might fall between businesses.

11 | Leadership Brand: Captains Everywhere

Leadership matters. In sports, which coach do you select? The one with the track record of proven victories in different programs, or the one who's never managed to get anything done? In drama, which director would you invest in? The one who has pulled together an ensemble and has a reputation of success or the one who has not? In politics, comfort level is higher with leaders who have a track record of success either in state or international affairs. In industry, investors have followed General Electric and McKinsey alumni into leadership positions.[1]

Leadership matters in business. As we have seen in this book, the leader makes the commitment and builds the architecture to create increased intangible value. When an organization has favorable leadership intangibles, employees, customers, and investors have confidence, continuity, and commitment. A leadership value proposition exists when leaders add value for each stakeholder.

Consider the value that a leader such as CEO Mike Volkema brings to Herman Miller. He knows many employees by name. He talks to them about their personal concerns. He writes them personal thank you notes. He works hard to serve them. In return, he has a repository of leadership goodwill that he can draw on to ask employees to do hard things.

Customers build commitment to a firm when leaders know and respond to them. Leaders who spend time getting to know key customers learn how to serve them better. As we discussed in Chapter 3, this knowledge can come from personally conducting focus groups, interviews, or surveys with customers. Leaders can also act as customers to experience the firm as the customer does. Customers perceive more valuable intangibles when they experience sensitive and thoughtful leaders who know their needs and are committed to meet them.

Investors also need to know and believe in leaders—simply being very good at the leadership job isn't enough to maximize intangible value. The more that analysts and shareholders know of a genuinely effective leadership team, the more confidence they have in that team. Investors who meet only the CEO or CFO do not appreciate leadership bench strength and depth. Inviting leaders at multiple levels to meet and present to investors increases investor confidence.

In today's turbulent business conditions—where the future is not predictable from the present, where customer loyalty is fleeting, where employees have choice about where they can work, and where investors have impatient capital—leadership matters more than ever. Leaders are the public, visible symbol of the firm or unit they represent.

Two Jobs of Leaders

Leaders have two jobs relative to leadership intangibles: *be* and *build*. First, leaders must be the leaders they expect others to become. Leadership by example is a given, not an option. One of the consequences of leadership is that you are watched and mimicked—whatever you do. Employees take their cues from leaders. The personality of the leader at the top generally becomes embedded throughout the organization. Leaders who work hard generally have employees who work hard. Leaders who seek input generally produce leaders who seek input from their employees. Leaders who commit to personal learning generally instill this belief and behavior in other leaders so that it cascades through the orga-nization. Leaders send cues that others act on.

Second, leaders must build other leaders. The ultimate test of a leader is what happens when that leader departs. Will the next genera-tion be stronger or weaker than the present? We worked once with a leader who always seemed to hire subordinates who were just a little less capable than he was. He could process information a little faster, communicate a little better, and set direction a bit more clearly. Un-knowingly, he'd allowed his insecurities to take him down a dangerous leadership path, one where the next generation was not as good as he was. When he left his leadership role, the organization faltered because the next generation was not prepared. In the short-term, he looked good by comparison. His subordinates did not threaten him; they re-spected and admired him. But in the long term, his legacy was flawed. Building other leaders requires shaping leaders at all levels of the firm.

Table 11.1 is an exercise that demonstrates the role of leadership throughout the organization. Assume your organization has five levels of management—call them A through E to avoid getting tangled in job titles. How much does leadership matter at each level? Take a moment to divide 100 points across the five levels in the exhibit depending on the relative importance of leadership at each one.

When we ask participants in seminars to do this, some put most of the points at the top levels. These individuals assume that leaders at the top of the organization create ideas that others implement. In one firm,

Table 11.1 Leadership
Importance Worksheet

Levels	Points
Top	
A	_____
B	_____
C	_____
D	_____
E	_____
Bottom	
Total:	100

this was characterized as "designed by the geniuses at the top and im-plemented by the idiots at the bottom." Other participants put most of the leadership points at the bottom. These individuals believe that those closest to the day-to-day work have the most impact and that as leaders move up the hierarchy, they become more distant from the real work. These individuals seem to want to keep top managers in workshops, seminars, and other activities that keep them from interfering with the real work. Both these approaches can seem to make sense in practice, but we advocate a third option—we'd put 20 points at each level. Lead-ers should have impact at each level of the organization. Encouraging leaders at all levels ensures accountability by those who do the work and creates a leadership bench for the future.

Building quality of leadership throughout an organization comes from three activities: creating a theory of leadership brand, assessing quality of leadership against the leadership brand, and investing in fu-ture leaders. We examine each activity in this chapter. What you may find particularly valuable are the references to other chapters in the book, as well as our discussion of a new definition of leadership that we introduced in a previous book, *Results-Based Leadership*,[2] written with Jack Zenger.

Creating a Theory of Leadership Brand

Focusing on leadership as a brand creates value for investors, customers, and employees. As discussed in Chapter 6 (Shared Mindset), brand is a powerful concept. The Olympics have become a brand. Firms pay mil-lions of dollars to have their brand associated with the Olympic inter-laced circles and to have their products and services affiliated with the Olympic tradition. When the brand clearly, accurately, and powerfully represents the intellectual capital of the firm, buyers have greater con-fidence in branded products and services. Customers are often willing to pay a premium for the top brands instead of taking a risk with untested or unknown brands. Intel on the Inside, the Windows icon, Mickey Mouse, the Golden Arches, and the Nike Swoosh are examples of brands that have succeeded in embodying the intellectual capital of their owners. Outstanding brands have become increasingly global. The appeal and success of airlines such as Singapore Air, British Airways, Cathay Pacific, and Quantas go beyond their respective local populations; they have become global brands. Travelers from all parts of the world choose them because of their reputation for service, safety, and reliability.

On another level, when the external brand consumers prefer reflects the internal culture experienced by employees, brand becomes a major source of competitive advantage. McDonald's employees who receive good service from the firm (opportunities for training and growth, equitable compensation, and fair treatment) will in turn render good service to customers. Nike's ability to innovate products for customers through employees' commitment to find fast, innovative ways to do their work is now reflected in the brand identity. These firms have learned that you cannot treat employees one way and then expect them to create a different identity with customers.

Thinking about a firm's brand as its culture and set of management practices, however, does not fully explain the power of brand. The brand of a firm should also be embodied in each leader throughout the firm. When leaders embody the firm's brand in their actions and results, they communicate that brand identity to employees—who then convey it to customers. Leadership brand occurs when a sufficiently large number of leaders exhibit distinct leadership practices over time. As a result, the organization creates leaders who are distinct from leaders in other firms.

Leadership brand lies at the heart of a firm's identity. Imagine observing two leaders at any level doing much the same job at competing firms. How long before an investor, customer, or employee could distinguish one firm from another? Branded leadership communicates to all stakeholders both the means (how work is done) and ends (what the goals are) for any firm.

Toward a New Theory of Leadership

Conceptualizing a firm's brand to include the image of branded leadership helps us to extend the current thinking about what makes an effective leader. We often start leadership workshops by asking participants to fill in the open-ended statement, "In the future to be successful at this firm, a leader must. . . ." The responses are consistent with current thinking about how to be better leaders: set a vision, have energy, energize others, mobilize commitment, manage teams, coach, have integrity, think globally, and so on. After we generate this list of *attributes of leadership,* we ask, "Who is surprised by this list?" No one is. The list makes sense and can be turned into behaviors, which can then be assessed through 360-degree feedback and woven into development experiences. But then we ask, "What if we did this exercise in 20 companies?" Or, "Compare your list of attributes with the competency models of other companies. Do they differ?" The answer we inevitably get is, "No, they are much the same."

Many of the current efforts to be or build better leaders have fallen prey to *generic models of leadership.* Even the rigorous competency models based on key informant methodologies with high reliability and validity tend to generate similar lists of behavior-based competencies that might be expected of leaders in any number of firms. These competency models fall short because they are not linked to customers, shareholders, and business results. They are often tied to past behaviors and not to future performance. They focus on what leaders are like rather than on what they accomplish. (See discussion of competency models in Chapter 5.)

For leadership to be a brand, leaders must exhibit more than generic competencies. Generic brands do not receive a premium price; they do not attract customers; they do not commit employees. Likewise, generic leaders who demonstrate universal competence can not deliver the unique results they are expected to deliver. Turning generic into branded leadership is both simple and complex.

At a simple level, branded leadership requires a new definition of leadership that includes *attributes* times *results.*[3] Our redefinition of leadership as the outcome of both attributes and results explains some of the causes of ineffective leadership and the challenges faced by effective leaders. Leaders who either embody attributes or achieve results will not have sustained success.

Leaders who score high on the attribute (or character) side of this equation but low on results do not truly lead. These leaders do good work, relate well to others, and act with honor and integrity. However, even when people exhibit the behaviors most expected from leaders, if they fail to deliver desired results, they will not be seen as effective leaders. They are generic and not branded leaders, having mastered the language of leadership but not the essence. Other leaders who score high on results but low on attributes also face enormous risks. They often take or receive credit for results they did not produce, so they have difficulty replicating or extending those results. They lack the leadership goodwill required to get results in the face of obstacles. They find the going tough when they try to focus attention on new initiatives or strategies. These leaders do not create a long-term legacy because their results cannot be sustained by their behaviors.

Effective leaders need to have both attributes and results. All the integrity, character, and goodwill in the world will not cover a lack of results. But in delivering results, leaders must also do it in the right way. Building character sustains results, particularly when the getting of results is difficult. To leaders who get high scores on employee surveys or 360-degree feedback, we say, be wary. Leadership is more than a popularity contest. Without clear and visible results, leadership can not endure.

Leaders who demonstrate attributes and deliver results become *branded leaders*—they possess appropriate attributes; they have a point of view about the future of their business, build teams, manage change, and have personal integrity. They are also able to turn attributes into specific results required for their business to succeed by answering the "so that" query for each attribute they demonstrate. Focusing on results requires understanding the unique competitive requirements of a firm. Firms win with strategies that differentiate them to customers and the financial markets; results should reflect these differences. For example, leaders at Quantas have a vision *so that* traveler satisfaction will stay high enough to gain a sizable share of frequent travelers' dollars spent. Leaders at the Olympics have a vision *so that* they attract committed employees and volunteers who will manage the large masses of event attendees. Leaders at Disney have a vision *so that* guests will return home from the Disney theme park experience with positive memories and stories for their friends. Each "vision" becomes branded when it is coupled with a "so that" statement that makes it specific to the unique requirements of the business.

At Herman Miller, the leadership brand calls for leaders who act with diligence and integrity so that they can deliver innovative products that create great places to work. Here's how the concept plays out at each level, beginning with CEO Mike Volkema, who models this brand. He allocates time carefully among the various stakeholders he serves, informing the board of directors about future directions, engaging his top team in crafting business strategy, sharing his vision with employees, meeting with dealers, and listening to customers. His example sets the expectations for how leaders should behave and what results they should deliver throughout the company. Plant managers listen to employees frequently, yet remind employees of the obligation they have to investors and customers. First-line supervisors take pride in their work setting. They constantly seek ways to improve the work processes they are responsible for, to care for employees while reminding them of business commitments, and to make Herman Miller a great place to work. Throughout the leadership cadre of Herman Miller, you see common behaviors and commitment to results. This Herman Miller leadership brand builds unity of purpose among employees and confidence in investors who support Herman Miller in up and down markets.

Building a Leadership Brand: Five Steps

Building a leadership brand can be done in five steps. First, you need to be clear about your strategy. As discussed in Chapter 9 (accountability), strategic clarity exists when leaders, employees, and customers have a clear and shared sense of the how the firm allocates resources to win in the future. Strategies differentiate how resources are allocated to win.

Second, the strategy should lead to a shared mindset. As discussed in Chapter 6, a shared mindset represents the firm brand, or identity, to the best customers in the future. Crafting a shared mindset comes when leaders think about what they want their organization to be known for in the future by their best customers. Building unity of mindset helps shape a unique culture inside the organization and a firm brand outside the organization.

Third, articulate desired attributes. These attributes may include what James Kouzes and Barry Posner describe in *The Leadership*

Challenge, the four enduring characteristics of being honest, forward-looking, competent, and inspiring.[4] Other characteristics are important, they found in their research, but they are not as consistent over time: intelligent, fair-minded, broad minded, supportive, straightforward, dependable, cooperative, determined, imaginative, ambitious, courageous, caring, mature, loyal, self-controlled, and independent. Similar lists have shown up in other studies.[5]

Attribute models should be tied to the future, not the past; linked to strategic goals, not be generic; and focused on behaviors, not on ideals. In addition, attribute models should be integrating mechanisms for HR practices. With a clear leadership model, leaders can be hired, promoted, trained, developed, appraised, and compensated against the criteria implied in the model. Attribute models are more likely to be used by leaders who participate in creating them than by those who have the attribute model created for them by a human resource team or outside consulting firm.

Fourth, define desired results. Branded leaders possess attributes and produce results. While most efforts to be better leaders focus on the attributes of leadership, leaders also need to turn their attributes into sustainable results. But because results themselves can be difficult to see on a day-to-day basis, it helps to look for their vital signs, much as a doctor uses selected tests to assess human health.

Clinical experience has shown the medical profession that among the hundreds of available tests, some work best as leading indicators of overall health—pulse rate, blood pressure, blood composition, EKG results, and so on. Likewise, vital signs of leadership results can be specified. Based on recent theory and research on balanced scorecards and our own hands-on experience, we suggest four domains for leadership vital signs that should be defined, assessed, and manifested for every results-based leader: employee, organization, customer, and investor. Leaders generate employee results when they identify specific ways to increase both employee competence and commitment (see Chapter 5). They achieve organizational results by assessing the capabilities needed to win and then creating those capabilities, thereby ensuring that the organization has a unique identity. Leaders generate customer results when they identify target customers, customize their services for these customers, and integrate customers into

HR practices such as staffing and training (see Chapter 3). Finally, they produce investor results by managing their balance sheet through profitable growth, reduced cost, and increasing shareholder value through management equity (see Chapter 3). Branded leaders master and can be measured by vital signs in each result area.

Fifth, link results and attributes into a leadership brand statement. Any leader trying to be more effective must have both the right attributes and the ability to get results. Sometimes leaders start with attributes that then must be turned into results; at other times, leaders start with results that must be accomplished through attributes. By linking attributes and results, leaders create a brand that distinguishes them from leaders in other firms. Part of the brand comes because leaders can choose from the potential result vital signs in each of the four areas and pick those that are most aligned with the goals of their business. With results clearly defined, leaders can then ensure a virtuous cycle that connects attributes and results by starting either with attributes or results but then ensuring the connection of the two. Examples of each follow.

"So That" Statements Link Attributes to Results

Attributes can be turned into results by asking the *so that* query for each attribute. For example, instead of having a goal "to implement total quality management in my division," a more result-oriented goal would be "to implement total quality management in my division *so that* our product quality is measured at the level of 25 (or fewer) defects per thousand." Some *so that* statements show how leadership vital signs can be linked to attributes, thus creating more branded leaders. Leaders in this organization must . . .

- Understand external events *so that* they identify target customers and create unique value propositions for each target customer better than competitors as measured by share of customer revenues.
- Turn vision into operational outcomes *so that* the organization can respond more quickly than competitors as measured by percentage of revenues from new products.

- Build collaborative relationships *so that* talented employees feel more committed to their work team as measured by their retention and a commitment index.
- Possess cognitive ability and personal charm *so that* investors experience credibility with the management team as measured by shareholder value above financial expectations in our industry.

"Because of" Statements Link Results to Attributes

If a leader begins with results, then these results need to be linked to attributes, or the results can be isolated, one-time events. To tie results to attributes, leaders can answer *because of* queries, such as:

- Build long-term customer partnerships with target customers (measured by customer intimacy vital sign) *because of* their ability to create a customer-focused culture.
- Achieve higher employee performance (measured by a productivity vital sign) *because of* deploying high-performing teams and investing in employee development.
- Create a learning organization (measured by ability to generalize ideas) *because of* the investment in technologies that move ideas across units.
- Increase revenue (measured by growth in the top line) *because of* reduced cycle times for new products and clear product-focused strategy.

Again, leaders can start with either attributes or results, but to be branded in a way that distinguishes them, they need to link the two. By so doing, they access vital signs of leadership that enable them to close the gap between their importance and their impact.

Here are some leadership brand statements we have seen from different firms:

- StorageTek leaders act with accountability and speed so that we bring value to every customer interaction. We will become the number one total storage solution provider by effectively delivering high quality products and services resulting in sustainable shareholder value.

- Emmis' leadership brand is built on recruiting, retaining, and challenging a staff of unquestionable integrity so that we can deliver high-quality audiences to advertisers with exceptional levels of service.

- Intel leaders are risk-oriented, results-driven, accountable, and innovative so that we are number 1 on the net, employer of choice, delight our customers, and are able to execute across global markets.

- Pitney Bowes leaders have a global vision, are able to build customer relationships, and are quick and innovative with decisions so that we are first to market with new products and services and we build and retain key customer and employee relationships, all of which lead to increased shareholder return.

These brand statements may be crafted by leaders who have responsibility for an entire organization or by leaders responsible for a specific unit in the organization. The organization-wide leadership brand affects behaviors and results of leaders at all levels of the organization. It offers a unique point of view about leadership within the organization.

Assessing Quality of Leadership against the Leadership Brand

A leadership brand statement adds value only if it is publicized and used. For example, a leadership brand statement should show up in annual reports, talks by senior business leaders, presentations to investors, and communications to employees. The brand should also be woven into the human resources practices of a firm—the competencies used for hiring, the outcomes expected from training, the standards defined for compensation.

We have identified a number of criteria for assessing the results and attributes of a successful leadership brand. Using these criteria, we have found that many leaders have worked well on either attributes or results, but often not on both.

Assessment ensures that leaders throughout the firm are accountable for living the brand. Figure 11.1 provides a matrix for assessing a company's leaders, dividing them into four groups depending on how they stand with regard to attributes and results. The logic of this assessment tool is straightforward: Leaders can be assessed separately on attributes and results. Attributes can be assessed through formal processes such as a 360-degree feedback mechanism or informal processes as executives interview and work with leaders to discern their leadership style. Results can be assessed through a goal-setting, management-by-objectives process where leaders define the outcomes of their unit. Leaders can then be placed into the grid in the figure.

Cells 2 (low, low) and 1 (high, high) are easy to interpret. Leaders who fail on both attributes and results should be removed. Leaders who succeed on both attributes and results should be nurtured and followed because they represent the future. The more demanding choices are in Cell 3 and Cell 4. In Cell 3, leaders have the right intent; their behaviors and attributes are good, but they don't deliver expected results. Leaders in Cell 3 should be given another chance to deliver results. Good intent deserves further investment. The results may be lacking because of timing or circumstances outside the leader's control. Leaders in Cell 4 do produce results, but not through the values or behaviors desired by the firm. Traditionally, Cell 4 leaders who produce results without regard to means get promotions and bonuses ahead of Cell 3 leaders who apply

Delivering the Results

		Low	High
		Low	High
Demonstrating attributes of leadership	High	3 Hard workers who don't deliver	1 Current and future stars
	Low	2 Unlikely to succeed	4 Make it happen, no matter how

Figure 11.1   Assessing the quality of leaders.

the firm's values but don't produce results—and often come in ahead of those in Cell 1 because their results may be more dramatic.

In his 1995 letter to shareholders, Jack Welch, past CEO at General Electric, described GE's version of Figure 11.1:

> Some of our leaders were unwilling, or unable, to abandon big-company, big shot autocracy and embrace the values we were trying to grow. So we defined our management styles, or "types," and how they furthered or blocked our values. And then we acted.
>
> Type I not only deliver on performance commitments but also believes in and furthers GE's small-company values. The trajectory of this group is "onward and upward," and the men and women who comprise it will represent the core of our senior leadership into the next century.
>
> Type II does not meet commitments, nor share our value—nor last long at GE.
>
> Type III believes in the values but sometimes misses commitments. We encourage taking swings, and Type III is typically given another chance.
>
> Type IV. The "calls" on the first two types are easy. Type III takes some judgment; but Type IV is the most difficult. One is always tempted to avoid taking action, because Type IV's deliver short-term results. But Type IV's do so without regard to values and, in fact, often diminish them by grinding people down, squeezing them, stifling them. Some of these learned to change; most couldn't. The decision to begin removing Type IV's was a watershed—the ultimate test of our ability to "walk the talk," but it had to be done if we wanted GE people to be open, to speak up, to share, and to act boldly outside traditional "lines of authority" and "functional boxes" in this new learning, sharing environment.[6]

We recently used this matrix in our work with the CEO of a large retail company. He felt that he had created a new agenda for his firm and that it was being instilled through new leadership actions, and he believed that he was close to meeting the criteria of a leadership brand. When we presented the matrix shown in Figure 11.1, he agreed in principle with the way it could be used to assess how well such a brand was working. But he then posed a specific challenge in his firm. He had a leader who had been assigned one of the lowest performing stores in the system. In a two-year period, she had turned the store around, from the bottom 20 percent to the top 20 percent of financial results, an exceptional performance. However, she did not follow all the values espoused by the firm. She was autocratic, controlling, demanding, and somewhat insensitive to employee needs. She clearly fit into Cell 4 (high results, low attributes). He asked us our recommendation on this leader, adding that he thought it would be naive to suggest that she be fired when she had met financial goals so well. It would also be naive to assume the company could force her to change attributes.

We suggested that he talk with her and ask her for her career aspirations so she could make an informed choice. If she wanted to move into senior management in the company, she would have to learn a new set of behaviors. The company would help her with this personal transformation through training, coaching, mentoring, and development assignments. But the company wasn't imposing this change; it would have to be her choice to learn the new behaviors (remember the Choice-Consequence-Correction cycle of individual learning in Chapter 8). If she did not want to make these changes or if she wanted to remain a store manager, the company would assign her to other turnaround store situations where she could help deliver results. But she would not be able to pick her successors in the stores she rescued, managers who would need to sustain results through the right attributes. This approach made sense to the CEO and he held the conversation with the manager, who opted to give the new behaviors a try because she really wanted a chance to move up in the organization. This solution is less draconian than the one Jack Welch adopted at GE, but it's often more practical in relatively small organizations and those that are just beginning their efforts to develop a modern leadership brand. The gung-ho results orientation has so much tradition behind it that many managers won't believe in the necessity to change until it is presented in some sort of implacable terms, but limited human resources make it worthwhile for the CEOs of such companies to make an extra effort to reclaim Cell 4 managers rather than sending them off to competing firms.

Assessment against the leadership brand requires measuring both the attributes and the results of the leader through a credible process. It then means having honest, blunt conversations between executives and leaders where leaders can make informed choices about their future in the company. If leaders choose to change attributes, they can be supported in that agenda through development experiences. If leaders need to improve on delivering results, they can also be supported through diagnosis of why results are missing and through resources focused on results.

A leadership brand without assessment will not endure. Following the logic in Chapter 9 (accountability), leaders need to have a clear set of standards about what is expected (the leadership brand). They need consequences if they meet or miss those standards, and they need feedback on their performance.

Formal leadership assessments can be part of a larger succession planning process where leaders' attributes and behaviors are measured annually against the future strategies of the organization.

Informal assessment also occurs when leaders send signals about how well other leaders are doing. These signals can be private conversations where the leader shares concerns about behavior or performance. The signals can be requests to attend a training program with clear guidance about the expected outcome of the program, or bringing in a coach to work with the leader on some specific issues, or providing nonverbal feedback by inclusion in key meetings. Informal positive assessment can send especially powerful signals. Calls, notes, or e-mail messages to employees to express appreciation for work well done become valued forms of assessment. Regardless of whether assessment is formal or informal, leaders should know the extent to which they exhibit the brand, on both attributes and results.

Investing in Future Leaders

Leaders have the ultimate responsibility of building leadership bench strength by wisely investing in future leaders. All leaders have predispositions. Some have an easier time with public speaking than others; some listen naturally; others are more comfortable with risk. Investing in future leaders means finding out where people are, then helping them grow into what they can be. No one way to invest in future leaders works all the time because no one way will fit everyone's learning style—and learning styles differ a great deal. To avoid mishandling and losing potential leaders, it is essential to learn and respond to the style of each individual in the leadership pipeline. Table 11.2 provides an overview of the questions to consider in approaching the development of future leaders.

Leadership investment falls broadly into three categories: training, development, and supporting systems. Training comes from the more formal education experiences leaders use to acquire new skills to deliver results. Development represents the cluster of activities to build

Table 11.2   Learning Architecture Worksheet

Question: To what extent do we have . . .	Assessment (1–10)
1. A public commitment to leadership development and learning? (For example: A statement of the importance of leadership.)	
2. A leadership value proposition that shows how better leadership will affect employees, customers, investors, and organization?	
3. A definitive and unique leadership brand?	
4. Assessment tools to diagnose the extent to which the leadership brand exists throughout the organization?	
5. Leaders who model the leadership brand in the demeanor and public dialogues?	
6. Training programs that innovatively deliver the leadership brand?	
7. Offer emerging leaders development experiences through coaching, job assignments, and nonwork experiences?	
8. Measure the impact of leadership investments on business results?	
9. Supporting systems (HR, Finance, IT) aligned to drive the intentions of building leadership brand?	
10. Leaders who make a personal commitment to living the leadership brand?	

leadership outside the classroom. Supporting systems are the management practices that sustain leadership brand.

Training

In Chapter 5, we reviewed key issues related to building talent through training. Here we add to these issues with suggestions for how to use training programs to develop leaders:[7]

- *Who should attend the program (employees, customers, individuals, teams)?* Training has more impact when leaders accompany their work team through the program. Transfer of learning from the workshop to the workplace occurs more readily if people attend the workshop as a team that works together. Ideally, customers of the leader's team also attend the workshop as team members. Customers validate information taught and help build commitment to acting on what was taught.
- *Who should present concepts (faculty, line managers, customers)?* Leaders will be better developed when they present at training forums. When people publicly behave as if they are committed, they become more committed. Leaders should also invite customers, suppliers, investors, or other external stakeholders to present so that emerging leaders who attend workshops see the impact of the leadership brand they are building.
- *Who should design the program (HR professionals, consultants, line managers)?* Leaders should chair workshop design teams, define key issues to be taught, partner with outside presenters, and be active in the workshop design and delivery. Emerging leaders should know that the leadership brand presented during the workshop represents the point of view of the executive. Leaders can use the workshop as significant vehicle for communicating a leadership brand to key players throughout the company.
- *What content should the program present (skills, action planning)?* Leaders should use training workshops to build a leadership brand. The combination of results and attributes should be tied to the strategy of the business, focused on the future, and

linked to specific actions emerging leaders can pursue after the workshop. The leadership brand should become both an academic icon that communicates what is expected of leaders and a behavioral road map leaders can follow to be successful.

- *How will it be delivered (on site or off site, through technology, case studies, or action learning)?* The choice of delivery mode depends on the topic and the audience. Traditional classrooms offer forums for shared discussion, cases, and presentations that communicate ideas and enable face-to-face dialogue about how to adapt and deploy the ideas. Outside the classroom, Web-based learning helps emerging leaders develop through self-paced, individualized, skill-oriented learning modules. In addition, communities of practice can be created where emerging leaders share knowledge and become tutors with each other.

- *How will we tell whether it's working (measures for outcomes, action learning, follow-up)?* Traditional measures of training success come from evaluations—forms participants turn in at the end of a workshop to share their feelings about administrative details of the work, perceived quality of the program, and reaction to faculty. Donald Kirkpatrick suggested that training evaluation include four levels:[8]

  1. *Reaction:* Did participants like the program? (This is the most common form of evaluation.)
  2. *Learning:* What knowledge, skills, and so on did participants gain?
  3. *Behavior:* Do participants behave differently as a result of the program?
  4. *Results:* Did the program affect business results?

When leaders push assessment beyond participant reactions to business results, they ensure that training builds a leadership brand with emerging leaders. A key is follow-up, ensuring that participants in a leadership development program are accountable for acting on insights gained during the program. Edward Trolley and David van Adelsberg have summarized much of the innovative training work in *Running Training Like a Business.*[9] They report that higher performing firms spend 3.4 percent of payroll on training whereas bottom-performing firms spend 1.84 percent of payroll, and that companies investing more in training generated an average of $47,000 more profit per employee.

To answer these questions in ways that instill the leadership brand, we have seen many companies create the position of chief learning officer. This role brings together the requirements of business strategy, principles of training and development, and processes for change. Chief learning officers generally work closely with human resource executives to craft a leadership experience that inculcates the leadership brand into emerging leaders.

Development

Training workshops and forums structure events where learning can occur. But most learning occurs through experiences, not classroom events.[10] Mike Lombardo and Bob Eichinger propose that 70 percent of learning comes from experience, 20 percent from people, and 10 percent from self-development or coursework.[11] Leaders implementing a leadership brand can engage emerging leaders in a host of development experiences that propagate the leadership brand.

Coaching enables emerging leaders to receive personal one-on-one feedback on behaviors and actions. Coaches learn the predispositions of their clients, observe them in action, and offer specific suggestions for behavioral improvement. They also follow up to help emerging leaders work through specific issues. In one company, we coached a senior business leader once every six months for two years. Each visit begins with a stakeholder map where we explore his goals for the stakeholders who affect his business (board of directors, top management, employees, suppliers, customers, investors). We ask how he has done with the stakeholders he was most worried about in the last visit and work with him to lay out priorities, goals, and actions for the future. The stakeholder map has helped the business leader realize that he cannot satisfy all stakeholders all the time. It has also helped him realize that attention to stakeholders may need to evolve over time (e.g., as the renegotiation date for the labor contract approached, he had to allocate more attention to the union and pull back from other stakeholders). As we matched his stakeholder goals with his calendar and time, we were able to help him keep focused on the things that mattered most to him.

Assigning emerging leaders to task forces or project teams allows them to experience new ideas. Emerging leaders can be assigned work assignments that stretch them and expose them to new business opportunities. One firm developed new leaders by assigning them to country strategy teams working on entering new geographic markets. As the team examined the market potential and crafted a plan to do business in the country, the emerging leaders were able to learn how to do business in other markets. Emerging leaders can be assigned to product, process improvement, customer account, or other teams that offer stretch experiences.

Job assignments can be a critical source of leadership development. Leaders can be systematically rotated through jobs that might give them experience in different business settings. Jobs can be classified along a series of dimensions, then emerging leaders given job assignments that familiarize them with diverse work settings: growth versus turnaround, line versus staff, small versus large, capital intensive versus service oriented, consumer focus versus business-to-business focus, start-up versus mature business, and so on.

Development also occurs through experiences outside formal work settings. Emerging leaders can serve on boards of local organizations, take an active role in religious or school settings, or become politically involved.

Through development experiences like these, emerging leaders begin to develop a learning mindset where they constantly go through the choice-consequence-correction cycle we presented in Chapter 7. Learning becomes much less tied to any one experience and more a personal commitment and way of life. Leaders should spend at least as much time thinking about shaping experiences for emerging leaders as they spend designing and delivering training programs, if not more.

Supporting Systems

Investing in training and development must still be coupled to supporting management systems to have full impact. One of the themes throughout this book is that there is no magic bullet or quick fix to make change happen, but that the cumulative effect of many actions builds sustainable impact. Leaders wanting to inculcate a leadership brand have many levers they can use in addition to training and development. Reward systems shape behavior by setting standards and tying consequences to those standards. The attributes and results called for in a leadership brand should be consistent with the standards set in a performance appraisal system. When emerging leaders meet or exceed those standards, positive consequences should follow—and when they miss those standards, negative consequences should follow. This sounds obvious, but all too often when we line up the leadership brand statements and the performance appraisals, there's little overlap. When different people engage in the processes of building a leadership brand and of defining performance standards, it is not surprising that the results differ—but it is a problem.

Communication by senior executives in multiple forums needs to be consistent with the leadership brand. As we discussed in Chapter 2, leaders need to have similar messages repeated redundantly. The themes of leadership brand need to be shared over and over again. An executive once told us his rule of thumb: "The first time I share something, no one will hear me; the second time, someone will say, 'I have heard that somewhere before'; the third time, they will say, 'I like the idea, but have to change to do it'; the fourth time, they will say 'I should do that, someday,' and the fifth time, they may actually try it." While the leadership brand messages may feel old-hat to leaders, emerging leaders still require immersion in the concepts to fully understand them.

Promotions send signals throughout an organization. We have worked with leaders who speak about the new leadership agenda but then promote individuals who clearly do not support it. Such hypocrisy communicates loudly to employees, who observe their leaders' actions more than their words. It is important to promote the right people and to share the reasons behind the promotion so that employees know what counts and what does not. Leaders working to build a new leadership brand may have to change 20 percent to 40 percent of their direct reports because they do not represent the new brand.

Governance focuses on how decisions are made. Leaders can refer to the leadership brand as they approach difficult decisions. They can tie the process for decision making into a broader leadership brand framework to show patterns of how work is governed. Leaders can include periodic discussions of leadership brand as part of their ongoing staff meetings.

Personal interactions between leaders and their subordinates often have the most impact. Sometimes subordinates look for informal more than formal signals. A personal word from a senior leader that says, "I am serious about this" can communicate more than a public speech. We have seen leaders use what we call *relationship equity,* where they draw on their personal relationships with other leaders to support them in shaping a new agenda. In one case, a leader who had a long-term friendship with another senior leader asked the other leader to visibly and publicly support the leadership brand. Of course, if the leadership brand did not support strategy by delivering results in the right way, such favors could have negative consequences. But leaders need both to build and spend relationship equity.

Physical facilities can send signals about how work should be accomplished. The layout of workspaces communicates varying levels of openness, how employees should interact with one another, and what customers experience when visiting the facilities. Leaders may find it useful to periodically observe their work environment and discern what it communicates about leadership style.

Ultimately, what employees see is how leaders spend their time. The most important asset leaders spend is their time. Who do leaders meet with? What information do they pay attention do? Where do leaders focus time (in their office or in others' offices, with employees or customers, with top managers or with

> See a video segment on leadership or complete any tools or assessments online at: www.rbl.net/whythebottomlineisnt.html.

employees inside the company, in meetings or on tours)? What types of decisions do leaders get personally involved with? We have encouraged leaders to have their administrative assistants do periodic time logs on how leaders spend their time. In most cases, the results are surprising to the leaders but not to employees who see the data. Leaders who consciously spend time on the attributes and results of the leadership brand become congruent, have credibility, and make more impact.

As leaders invest in training, development, and supporting systems, they build a development and learning architecture in their organization. The diagnostic in Figure 11.1 offers an assessment of the extent to which these leadership investments deliver leadership brand.

Leadership Implications

Leadership is one of the most visible intangibles. Investors, customers, and employees can identify and observe leaders and ascertain if they add value or not. Leaders wanting to create leadership depth must start with themselves. They must be the kind of leader that they want others to become. Then they must give emerging leaders the opportunity to produce leadership intangibles. When leadership intangibles exist, a leadership brand pervades all levels of the organization. To create a leadership brand, leaders need to clearly articulate strategy, then translate the strategy into a shared mindset, leadership attributes, leadership results, and a brand statement. With a brand statement, leaders can assess and invest in future leaders.

Leaders who generate intangible value:

- Take personal responsibility for being effective leaders. They are willing to model the leadership that they expect others to follow.
- Craft a leadership brand that defines the attributes and results expected of a successful leader.
- Create formal and informal mechanisms to assess leaders against the brand.
- Find ways to invest in emerging leaders through training, development, and support systems.
- Ensure that the leadership brand permeates all levels of the organization.
- Encourage leaders who model the brand to be public and visible to investors, customers, and employees.

12 | Tangible Intangibles: Winning the Game

Intangibles matter—no one doubts or even much debates this premise. Differences in market valuation prove it. What is more difficult is figuring out which intangibles matter most for a firm or work unit and then finding ways to improve them.

Our focus on leadership intangibles proposes a framework to define them and then outlines a host of actions that increase their value. Viewed through this framework, intangibles become tangible—things that leaders can understand and then build and improve with the tools we suggest. It is clear that measurement of intangibles is necessary, but if you don't measure the right things, intangible value will not increase. What makes this task difficult is that the things that are most useful to measure are outside the reach of the traditional financial and accounting approach to intangibles.

Leaders must define and create intangible value as well as track it, and this book helps them do so. For employees, leadership intangibles result in greater commitment, productivity, competence, job security, and personal wealth. For customers, leadership intangibles produce products and services that meet current and future needs. For investors, leadership intangibles ensure sustained market value. Employee value often leads to customer value that leads to shareholder value.

Some have argued that intangibles show up more in new economy, high-tech, or start-up companies than in mature companies. In some ways, this is true. A venture capitalist investing in a new project—one with no corporate track record—weighs the intangibles its leaders bring to the table: a track record of consistent and predictable results in other settings, a business plan or strategy for the future, technical expertise, and the ability to build organization capabilities that will accomplish business results. The dot-com bubble and bust has also shown that intangible value can be both positive and negative. Firms built primarily with rhetoric and ideals crash and burn when they face economic downturns if they don't have definitive and sustainable intangibles as well. The actions we have proposed help avoid such tragedies.

We would also argue that intangibles apply equally to more traditional organizations and across multiple industries. Large, complex firms are inhabited by leaders who commit to doing the things we have covered in this book. By so doing, they help their firms meet goals, pursue growth agendas, have core competencies, and have critical capabilities (talent, learning, shared mindset, speed, accountability, collaboration, and leadership). When leaders identify and implement these capabilities, they create intangible value. Likewise, government agencies exist on political goodwill as the leaders of these agencies build relationships of trust with governing bodies that provide resources to the agency. The intangibles we have discussed become the pillars of political goodwill. Government leaders who learn the concepts and adapt the tools we have proposed will find their agencies not only meeting goals but also exceeding expectations and gaining credibility in the political landscape. Hospitals, schools, charitable agencies, church organizations, and other nonbusiness enterprises also rely on leadership intangibles. When any organization seems to stand out from others, intangible factors are in play. When leaders build these intangibles, they build confidence among their employees, customers, and investors.

The focus on leadership intangibles integrates two distinct and often separate professions: *finance and accounting,* with its focus on the empirical and hard aspects of business, and *organization behavior,* where the emphasis is often on the interpersonal and softer elements of the organization. Forging partnerships between diverse professions brings enormous value. When physics partnered with philosophy, a new paradigm of science emerged. When psychology partnered with statistics, understanding of the human psyche grew rapidly. As finance and accounting partners with organization development and human resources, the result will be a more robust, elegant, and active understanding of the firm and how leaders can add value to it.

Leadership Implications

An overall implication of increasing intangible value is that market value is measured at the corporate level where the company stock is traded while intangibles are developed and built by every team and individual throughout the company. This means that senior leaders must clearly articulate where the company is going and what it stands for and that other leaders at every level must do their part to fulfill that promise to employees, customers, and shareholders. Building value is a job for everyone and success in that job benefits everyone.

This work has additional implications for all the organization's stakeholders, including general managers, finance and accounting personnel, human resource staff, information technology community, and investors.

Implications for General Managers

General managers represent the organization to outside stakeholders, such as investors or customers. Because senior managers represent the organization, they must set direction, articulate company values, and describe how the company will win in the future. They need to create reputations that build confidence. Senior leaders build into their organizations a culture that outlasts any individual leader. Senior leaders focus their intangible work on activities that affect the entire enterprise.

Their zone of influence is broad and the intangibles they create must permeate all corners of an organization. Senior leaders who interact with investors need to create ways of sharing intangibles that go beyond the balance sheet. At times, investors focus on the financial data because it is accessible and relatively easy to interpret. What senior leaders who work with investors need is to find a way to frame their investor conversations around the intangibles we propose.

But leaders throughout the organization must also be sensitive to intangible value. When leaders identify the intangibles that can be created, they create organization units that deliver value. At a plant level, employees may become more committed to the goals of the plant because of the intangibles the leader provides. In managing operations within a country, a leader who delivers intangibles ensures that country operations deliver, as they should. Leadership is a unifying act, not the act of an individual. When a leadership brand focused on intangibles permeates leadership practices throughout an organization, no one leader delivers intangible value, but all do. Shared leadership that produces shared intangibles adds enormous value.

Leaders are responsible both to lead and to build leadership. As we discussed in Chapter 11, to be leaders, they must demonstrate what they demand and become exemplars for others. To build leadership in others, they must define and deliver the leadership brand in their firm.

Implications for Finance and Accounting

Intangibles exist, but until they are defined and measured more accurately, they cannot be fully sustained. This book has not been about measurement—other books do a very good job at laying out principles for that. If you rigorously measure the wrong things, it won't matter how well you measure them. We want to make sure that all of the elements from our architecture for intangibles are measured. The area that has the greatest impact for increasing value and trust are organization capabilities. As these capabilities are specified, measures can then be established to hold leaders accountable and responsible for intangible value.

Since many of the measures that drive intangible value are related to people and organization issues, finance and accounting specialists need to learn more about these areas as they audit and interpret financial results. For example, assessments of a firm's shared mindset might expose underlying weaknesses not currently reflected in financial results, but these weaknesses may be ticking like time bombs about to destroy results in the near term (as happened at Enron). Too often, financial and accounting professionals examine the public and available financial data and fail to explore what lies beneath this data: the leadership intangibles we have proposed. With more collaboration between finance and accounting and human resource professionals, leadership intangibles may be identified, measured, and developed to ensure sustainable value.

In short, rather than avoid the "soft" issues in organization or declare them outside the domain of traditional finance, we advocate that the finance and accounting profession become aware of, help define, improve, and measure the intangible issues.

Implications for Human Resources

The human resource profession has been on a journey toward impact for many decades. When the human resource profession was established in the 1930s, the focus was on labor policies and procedures to help leaders negotiate and contract with labor unions. Over the years, this profession has evolved and shifted to focus on both administrative and strategic issues. In the quest to become a strategic or business partner and a player in the business game, human resource professionals have worked more recently to become coaches, architects, designers, and facilitators of organization capabilities.

The intangible work we posit becomes a playbook for human resource professionals now taking the next step of shaping not only employee but also shareholder value. The intangibles become the deliverables of human resources. Human resource professionals should be able to help define and deliver these intangibles through their collaboration with business leaders. Traditional measures of human resource success (i.e., percentage of managers who received 40 hours of training a year) are replaced with the outcomes of those activities (i.e., delivering one of the leadership intangibles we propose—learning, talent, speed, shared mindset). The human resource-led conversation focuses on intangible value when the capabilities presented become defined and real to the general managers who will use them.

Implications for Information Technology

Like their counterparts in the human resources profession, information technology professionals continue to evolve their role in delivering business value. Evolution has moved information technology focus from improving the performance of individuals to improving the performance of processes and more recently to integrating information across an extended enterprise. In the last decade, CIOs learned to study and understand culture so that they could serve, then educate, and ultimately lead the organization rather than trying to respond to it. The emergence of leadership intangibles as a determining factor in business success presents a new challenge: How to build information management, distribution, and analysis systems that at best enable intangibles and, at worst, support them.

Information technology professionals must look beyond technology features and functions of their systems to examine "fit to desired intangibles." A new list of technology selection questions is necessary, including: To what extent does the technology break down boundaries, enable accountability, help individuals and the enterprise learn? All of the old business capability support requirements still apply, yet a new set of organization capabilities must be woven into system specifications. For example, Jim Dowling and Ben Spencer, then with TechnologyEvaluation.com guided a team lead by Chuck Turner, group director at Milacron Corporation in Cincinnati, Ohio, to select an enterprise resource planning system.

The selection process was not based solely on financial and technical criteria such as total cost of ownership and operation, electronic data interchange, and flexible credit risk management. Culture and firm brand were considered and selection criteria including empowerment, speed of change, collaboration, and learning were added. These intangible criteria were evaluated experientially and in the end carried the decision in favor of the product that best demonstrated the ability to do what Milacron needed and how they wanted to work. It was clear to all members of the decision team that considering technical, financial, and intangible capabilities lead to the solution with the greatest likelihood of implementation success and return on investment.

Information technology performance will soon be measured by the extent to which systems enable (or interfere) with leaders' ability to realize the contribution of intangibles to the company. It has been relatively simple to build measures around layer three of the architecture for intangibles such as operating efficiency, customer intimacy, and distribution. New metrics must include layer four capabilities such as accountability, shared mindset, and learning. Information technology leaders must examine their architectures, infrastructure (people, process, and technology), and business systems under this new light and plan to adapt or replace elements that are incompatible with desired intangible value drivers.

Implications for Investors

Recently, when we presented the intangibles argument to a senior group of executives, one of them said that if we really knew the intangibles that created shareholder value, we should open an investment fund and test our ideas. We agree with his intent. We believe that if leaders are able to create the intangibles we identify in Figure 12.1 (repeated from Chapter 1) by doing the things we suggest in each chapter, the firm will gain more market value than if they do not. The challenge is getting enough information to investors about the extent to which leaders demonstrate leadership skills and initiatives presented in this book and create these capabilities inside their firm. Currently, most publicly required information focuses on financials and the intangibles are left to speculation and investor judgment.

Peter Tanous interviewed a number of people who were considered "investment gurus"[1]—investors who had a long track record of successfully making investment decisions. Some of their quotes highlight the importance of the intangibles we are talking about in their decision making:

Mario Gabelli: We're buying a business and a business has certain attributes. We're not buying a piece of paper and we're not buying soybeans. As surrogate owners, there are certain characteristics with regard to the value of the franchise, the cash generating capabilities of the franchise, and the quality of the management. So, you have quantitative and qualitative measures. (p. 80)

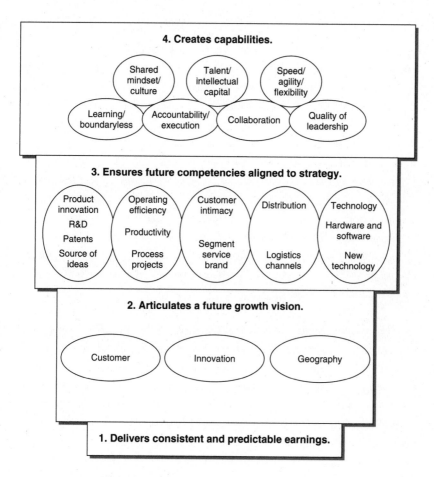

Figure 12.1   Architecture for intangibles.

Focus is the key to success. If you look at most people who have been successful, you find they're focused, very disciplined, about how they conduct business. Therefore, focus is very important. (pp. 139–140)

Laura Sloate: We like managers. Good management is key. We'll buy some companies with secondary managements and great asset values, but we obviously prefer having a good manager. (p. 143)

Scott Sterling Johnston: We rarely buy a company without talking to management. That comes from my audit experience. First, you tap into the great minds at the research firms, who have known the company for years. But by talking to the company, too, you get an undertone. How positive or negative are they? (p. 158)

Foster Friess: [We talk] not only to their competitors; we talk to their customers, their suppliers, and sometimes that's how we come up with an idea. We'll be talking to a company and we'll ask: Of all the companies you're competing with, who do you see the most often? Who do you have the most respect for? (p. 234)

Van Schreiber: I have met the people who run the companies and made judgments about their adequacy. Sometimes those judgments are wrong, but at least we have made a judgment that these people are good, can be trusted, are innovative, have their own money at stake, that they are determined, and that they are not just playing games out there. The process starts with our assessment of management and then moves on to whatever it is that is important for that particular business. (p. 251)

These investment gurus have something in common. They recognize that quality of management is an important factor in their assessment of a firm's value. But—using the tools and language available to them—they've had to talk about leadership quality in general and generic ways. The intangibles we have posited in this book offer specific places for investors to look, and will therefore help them refine their perceptions of leadership quality and its direct effects on firm value.

We anticipate that with the demise of Enron—where the intangible loss of confidence destroyed market value very quickly—and with the continued pressure to discover leading indicators of market value, intangibles will become more than personal judgment and more rigorously woven into market valuations. A privately held firm we work with created phantom stock to motivate its employees. The entire valuation model was based on financials, revenues, costs, and margins or some derivative of these financials. When we suggested adding capabilities and intangibles to this valuation process, the leaders balked because they were not clear about what constituted an intangible, nor how to measure it. This book answers that objection, laying out an argument for what leaders can do to define and deliver intangibles that go beyond platitudes such as quality of management.

Investors need to look behind the numbers. What is the quality of earnings? In our architecture for building intangible value, we proposed some directions to explore that might point to higher or lower quality of earnings. To what extent are the earnings:

- Predictable and consistent?
- Focused on the future?
- Likely to grow from a clearly articulated vision?
- Delivered by the organization's core competence?
- Ensured by a flow of talent?
- Delivered with speed?
- Sustained through the culture, shared mindset, or firm brand?
- Driven by individual, team, and organization learning?
- Linked to clear accountability processes?
- Enhanced through collaboration?
- Tied to a leadership brand that is based on an explicit process to build leaders who will deliver what they promise in the future?

When investors begin to look into these issues, they will begin to discover credible and sustainable intangibles. Currently, investors make their decisions based on judgments about quality of management. We want to bolster that judgment by making leadership intangibles tangible and explicit.

Tips for Creating Intangible Value

The whole process of change is to think big (frame an agenda), act small (experiment, learn by doing), fail fast (adapt and adjust), and learn rapidly (determine what worked and apply it to a new situation). Applied to leadership intangibles, the big, new idea is connecting leadership to market value. The first small action is to experiment and try the ideas we have proposed to see how to make leadership intangibles happen. Some of these ideas will not work, of course, and the failure is part of the process. Learning occurs when the successful ideas are implemented and tried in multiple settings.

Like the early cartographers, we have proposed a map for the world of leadership intangibles. We know the map is not complete. We are in uncharted territory and waters to some extent. However, the map offers a set of actions leaders might take to make intangibles happen. Let us summarize some starting points on this journey:

- *Do an intangibles audit like the one described in Chapter 1.* Figure 12.1 summarizes the leadership intangibles we believe create shareholder value. An intangibles audit brings discipline to the organization improvement process. Organization audits diagnose the extent to which an organization possesses the capabilities, or intangibles, to deliver strategic, product, and financial goals.

- *Lower expectations and deliver more.* In setting goals for future performance, try to moderate expectations to the external community while building confidence among your employees. In public statements, be temperate; in private statements, be convincing. Let results communicate successes—then you won't need rhetoric.

   It is also critical to deliver what is expected. This comes from carefully monitoring progress toward goals and seeking early indicators that may show future problems or lead to future success.

- *Start small.* Find an intangible that is within your control, relatively easy to address, and visible. Succeed with it. Use that success to build other successes and gain credibility by degrees. Build a leadership goodwill account whereby employees, customers, and investors learn to trust you to do what you promise. The tipping point work suggests that small things add up to big things. Momentum may build slowly at first toward a new agenda, but as the cumulative effect of little things adds up, real change begins to happen more quickly. Pick one or two of the ideas in the book and implement them.

- *Simplify your messages, link them to your strategy, and then keep repeating them.* Don't confuse employees or investors with too many initiatives and projects that may obscure your main messages. Cluster different initiatives into common themes; prioritize among many initiatives to find the most important; sequence initiatives that are leading indicators of future success. Find a story line to link old and new messages as the strategy evolves. Use metaphors and illustrations to communicate the same message without becoming redundant. Illustrate the message with charts, experiences, symbols, and icons.

Your message becomes your leadership brand. Make sure that the message you are sharing reflects how you want to be known as a leader. Does it communicate your values? Does it reflect your identity? Is it something you are proud of? Your message and your leadership brand become intertwined.

- *Create a shared direction.* Have a point of view about the future of your industry, your firm, your work unit, or your team that is unique—grounded in customers and exciting to employees. Become a storyteller about your agenda. Ground the story in your history but focus the story on your future. Tell the same story over and over and over again to employees, customers, and investors. Allow them to translate the story to their behaviors. Use symbols, metaphors, and individual cases to personalize and breathe life into your leadership story.

- *Invest in technical excellence.* Identify the core technical competencies where your unit must excel to win. Go out of your way to make sure you are the best of breed in areas that are critical to you because of your strategy. Don't accept anything but a platinum standard for the technical areas that will distinguish you. Disney is aggressive in how it hires creative artists; Microsoft with software designers; Goldman Sachs with risk managers; Pfizer with scientists in its targeted research areas; BP with petroleum and exploration engineers; Unilever with consumer marketing skills—the list could go on indefinitely. Successful firms identify and go after the best of their breed. They build a reputation for technical excellence so that the best want to work for them. Likewise, leaders of teams or divisions make sure that their technical competence meets and exceeds expectations.

- *Surround yourself with talent.* You need to be willing to hire people who are better than you are. Don't be so egocentric as to have to be the best at everything; let others do what they are best at doing. Keep focused on future talent, not the past. Invest in your talent as much as you would any other asset in your organization. Get out of their way; give them a chance to succeed and allow them to fail. Make sure that your best people get rewards that matter to them. Communicate frequently to these talented employees about their value to you and to the firm.

- *Be rigorous and unforgiving of poor performers.* If people consistently miss goals and cannot do the work, move them out, quickly yet fairly. Give poor performers honest and direct feedback and give them opportunities to improve so that if they don't it is their choice to leave the firm, not yours. The most strategic human resource decision you can ever make is to let your worst-performing employees work for your competitor and hope they stay for a long time.

- *Constantly praise and express gratitude to the employees.* Share credit for successes with them and take personal responsibility for failures. Build a community of employees dedicated to delivering value to customers and investors. Don't belittle or deride employees personally in public or private. Find creative ways to show appreciation. Be aware of employees' personal needs.

  Leaders who express gratitude cascade this philosophy throughout their organization. When employees feel understood, accepted, and acknowledged, they develop loyalty to both the leader and the work unit. Within departments and work teams, local leaders need to be seen as both committed and compassionate.

- *See patterns in events.* When something goes wrong, see if the same thing has gone wrong before. Look for patterns. Separate causes from problems and focus on the causes. Look for underlying causes and try to treat them, not just the behavior. Ask five "whys" to expose the cause. If an employee is persistently late, ask *why*. If the answer is that it is because of other pressures, probe further as to *why* this is happening. By the time you are at the fifth *why*, the real underlying problem will probably have emerged. Deal with this problem, not the presenting symptom.

On another level, new leaders to a work team or department should be sensitive to the history and patterns that have gone before. Listen and learn those previous patterns and then decide if they are the right ones for the future. Be willing to confront old patterns by talking about what was done and why it was done; explore why things are different which then should result in new patterns.

■ *Think about your organization from the outside in.* Make your culture your firm brand and make it real to your employees. Identify your target or key customers and see your organization through their eyes. Craft an identity that you would like to have embedded in their minds. Make this identity real to them through all the touch points you have with them. Make this identity real to employees by asking them to change their behavior to be consistent with it.

Experience your organization as a customer. The more you experience the firm from a customer perspective, the more you realize customers' challenges and concerns. Treat target customers exceptionally well, every time. Know who they are and make sure employees can identify them. Make sure that target customers know they are desired and critical to the firm's success. Invite investors to talk to your employees. Let investors ask any employee any question. Let your investors experience directly from employees the extent to which your unit has a shared mindset. Find forums where employees can represent the firm The more employees publicly represent the firm to external stakeholders, the more committed they become to the firm.

Target investors as much as you target customers. Make sure that key investors who are thought leaders in the investment community know your firm not only from an economic point of view but in terms of its leadership intangibles. Include targeted investors in managerial activities such as training, staffing, compensation, and meetings so that they are deeply informed about the how the firm operates. Make sure investors have no surprises when things go wrong, but present solutions along with the problems.

- *Instill personal ownership and responsibility within your organization.* Help people feel accountable for the decisions they make. Become a role model of responsibility. Take personal ownership for the success or failure of the business. Personally contact employees who do things well and let them know you notice and are delighted with their work in public forums, tell stories of exceptional employee service. Create local heroes throughout the organization based on the goals you are trying to accomplish. Share credit widely for successes.

- *Learn constantly by taking risks, experimenting, and reevaluating repeatedly.* Establish a spirit of inquiry throughout the firm. Encourage people to learn about what has been done, avoid mistakes of the past, and think creatively about what could be done to meet future requirements. Move knowledge across units in the company through technology-based and other learning communities.

  As people try new things, codify and share that knowledge. Let experiments proceed, but make sure the word spreads so that they build collective knowledge within the firm. Find people who are innovative and creative. Constantly push creative ideas into commercial ventures. Run many pilot programs with customers to see how they might respond to new ideas, and do after-action reviews of those programs to determine what worked and what did not. Encourage teams to avoid falling into the groupthink pattern where only a few dominant ideas prevail. Periodically, do team audits to assess where the team is working on the right issues and how the team is working together. Keep the team focused on improving and continuing to add value to the customers they serve.

- *Collaborate frequently.* Make the whole more than the sum of the parts by defining standards, sharing information, moving talent, defining processes, and innovating regularly. Encourage local success, but always frame it in terms of global requirements.

  Apply the principles of collaboration to all forms of partnerships or alliances. When doing mergers, be aggressive at gaining efficiencies by consolidation, and then be disciplined in finding ways to use leverage to take advantage of the resources of both partners. When becoming global, create capabilities that engender both local adaptiveness and global scale. When building shared services, turn corporate staff functions into professional service organizations inside the firm.

Demonstrate the leadership behaviors of collaboration by appropriately involving others in decision making, by delegating both accountability and responsibility, and by continuing to focus on the whole as more than the sum of the parts. Create a one-company theme whereby all employees recognize and have pride in the corporation they work for. Help employees see that their unique contributions add value to the entire enterprise.

- *Build leadership brand.* Explicitly define what you expect leaders to know, do, and deliver. Articulate a leadership brand for your organization. Make sure that the leadership brand reflects the strategy of your unit. Tell stories of leaders who live the brand. Use symbols and metaphors to communicate the leadership brand. Create leadership heroes—people throughout the organization who live the brand—and share their stories widely. Assess every leader on the extent to which they live the leadership brand. Invest constantly in the next generation of leadership through multiple actions.

  Be an exemplar of the leadership brand you ask others to apply. Make sure that the leadership brand you articulate coincides with your values and beliefs so that you can live it without hypocrisy. As you live the leadership brand, talk about it with passion and purpose.

Become the leader you hope others will become.

> We would love to hear your experiences about building intangibles and to continue sharing our ideas with you. Keep in touch with us online at our Web site: www.rbl.net.

Notes

Chapter 1: Tangling with Intangibles: Knowing the New Game

1. Baruch Lev, *Intangibles* (Washington, DC: Brookings Institution Press, 2001); Robert G. Eccles, Robert H. Herz, Mary Keegan, and David M. Philips, *Value Reporting Revolution* (New York: Wiley, 2001).

2. Nanette Byrnes and David Henry, "Confused about Earnings?" *Business-Week* (November 26, 2001).

3. See note 1, Lev.

4. See note 1, Eccles et al., pp. 4–5, 6.

5. Ernst & Young, "Measures That Matter." Available from gey.com /research/current_work/valvingintangibles/measures-that-matter.html.

6. Robert S. Kaplan and David P. Norton, *The Balanced Scorecard: Translating Strategy into Action* (Cambridge, MA: Harvard Business School Press, 1996).

7. Brian E. Becker, Mark A. Huselid, and Dave Ulrich, *The HR Scorecard: Linking People, Strategy and Performance* (Cambridge, MA: Harvard Business School Press, 2001).

8. Anthony Rucci, Steven Kirn, and Richard Quinn, "The Employee-Customer-Profit Chain at Sears," *Harvard Business Review* (January/ February 1998), pp. 82–99.

9. Dave Ulrich and Dale Lake, *Organization Capability: Competing from the Inside/Out* (New York: Wiley, 1990).

10. Dave Ulrich, "Organizing around Capabilities," *The Organization of the Future,* eds. Frances Hesselbein, Marshall Goldsmith, and Dick Beckhard (San Francisco: Jossey-Bass, 1996); Dave Ulrich, "Profiling Organizational Competitiveness: Cultivating Capabilities," *Human Resource Planning,* vol. 16, no. 3 (1993): 1–17; Dave Ulrich and Margarethe

Wiersema, "Gaining Strategic and Organizational Capability in a Decade of Turbulence," *Academy of Management Executive,* vol. 3, no. 2 (1989): 115–122.

Chapter 2: Do or Die: Anteing up the Table Stakes

1. Ram Charan, "Stand by Your CEO (Sometimes)," *Fortune* (August 14, 2000).

2. Malcolm Gladwell, *Tipping Point* (New York: Little, Brown, 2000).

3. Jim Collins, *Good to Great: Why Some Companies Make the Leap . . . and Others Don't* (New York: HarperBusiness, 2001).

Chapter 3: Growth: Setting Your Own Odds

1. The work on growth we cite comes from several excellent sources: John Seely Brown, ed., *Seeing Differently: Insights on Innovation* (Boston: Harvard Business School Press, 1997); Ram Charan and Noel Tichy, *Every Business Is a Growth Business* (New York: Times Mirror, 1998); Dwight Gertz and L. Joao Baptista, *Grow to Be Great* (New York: Free Press, 1995); Tony Grundy, *Breakthrough Strategies for Growth* (London: Pitman, 1995); Dave Nadler, Robert B. Shaw, and Elise Walton, eds., *Discontinuous Change: Leading Organizational Transformation* (San Francisco: Jossey-Bass, 1995); Michel Roberts and Alan Weiss, *The Innovation Formula: How Organizations Turn Change into Opportunity* (New York: Harper & Row, 1988); Adrian Slywotzky, *Value Migration: How to Think Several Moves Ahead of the Competition* (Boston: Harvard Business School Press, 1997).

2. George Merck (son of the founder), 1950. The statement is still publicized in internal company communications. Available from http://www.merck.com/careers/.

3. Thomas J. Neff and James Citrin, *Lessons from the Top: The Search for America's Best Business Leaders* (New York: Random House, 1999), p. 82.

4. Parexel's *Pharmaceutical R&D Statistical Sourcebook* (Media, PA: Barnett International, 1997).

5. The shift from international to multinational to global strategies is discussed in detail in Christopher Bartlett and Sumantra Ghoshal, *Managing across Borders: The Transnational Solution,* 2nd ed. (Boston: Harvard Business School Press, 1998); Jay Galbraith, *Designing Organizations: An*

Executive Briefing on Strategy, Structure, and Process (San Francisco: Jossey-Bass, 1995); and Paul Evans, Vladimir Pucik, and Jean-Louis Barsoux, *The Global Challenge: Frameworks for International Human Resource Management* (New York: McGraw-Hill Higher Education, 2002).

6. For more information on the global choices see J. Stewart Black and Dave Ulrich, "The New Frontier of Global HR," *The Global HR Manager: Creating the Seamless Organization,* eds. Pat Joynt and Bob Morton (London: Institute of Personnel Development, 1999), pp. 12–38.

7. The importance of strategic focus was highlighted in Lee Tom Perry, Randall G. Stott, and W. Norman Smallwood, *Real Time Strategy: Improvising Team-Based Planning for a Fast-Changing World* (New York: Wiley, 1993); further advanced in Michael Tracey and Fred Wiersema, *Discipline of Market Leaders: Choose Your Customers, Narrow Your Focus, Dominate Your Market* (Cambridge, MA: Perseus Book Group, 1995).

Chapter 4: Writing the Playbook: Matching Strategy to Skill

1. C. K. Prahalad and Gary Hamel, "The Core Competence of the Corporation," *Harvard Business Review* (May/June 1989): 79–91.

2. Lee Perry, Randy Stott, and Norm Smallwood, *Real Time Strategy* (New York: Wiley, 1993). This work discusses units of competitive analysis (UCA) and how they were required to help a company turn strategy into results.

3. Our review of R&D and performance draws on Zvi Griliches, "R&D and Productivity: Econometric Results and Measurement Issues," *Handbook of the Economics of Innovation and Technological Change,* ed. Paul Stoneman (Oxford, England: Blackwell, 1995), pp. 52–89; Bronwyn Hall, "Industrial Research during the 1980s: Did the Rate of Return Fall?" *BPEA: Microeconomics* (1993): 289–393; Baruch Lev and Theodore Sougiannis, "The Capitalization, Amortization, and Value Relevance of R&D," *Journal of Accounting and Economics,* vol. 21 (1996): 107–138.

4. George Pinches, V. Narayanan, and Kathryn Kelm, "How the Market Values the Different Stages of Corporate R&D . . . Initiation, Progress, and Commercialization," *Journal of Applied Corporate Finance,* vol. 9 (1996): 60–69; Uri Ben Zion, "The Investment Aspect of Nonproduction Expenditures: An Empirical Test," *Journal of Economics and Business,* vol. 30 (1978): 224–229.

5. Keith Chauvin and Mark Hirschey, "Advertising, R&D Expenditures and the Market Value of the Firm," *Financial Management,* vol. 22 (1993): 128–140.

6. Thomas Kinnear's research is reported based on his presentations to the Michigan Executive Programs. For more information, contact Professor Thomas Kinnear at University of Michigan in Ann Arbor, School of Business.

7. Work-Out has been described fully in Dave Ulrich, Ron Ashkenas, and Steve Kerr, *The General Electric Work-Out* (New York: McGraw-Hill, in press).

8. The tools for quality improvement using Six Sigma have been described in Mikel J. Harry and Richard Schroeder, *Six Sigma: The Breakthrough Management Strategy Revolutionizing the World's Top Corporations* (New York: Doubleday, 1999); Peter S. Pande, Robert P. Neuman, and Roland R. Cavanagh, *The Six Sigma Way: How General Electric, Motorola, and Other Top Companies Are Honing Their Performance* (New York: McGraw-Hill, 2000).

9. Jeffrey Pfeffer, "Six Dangerous Myths about Pay," *Harvard Business Review* (May 2001).

10. Much of the excellent work on firm brand can be found in David Aaker's work. For example, see *Managing Brand Equity: Capitalizing on the Value of a Brand Name* (New York: Free Press, 1991); *Building Strong Brands* (New York: Free Press, 1996); *Building Brand Leadership: Building Assets in an Information Economy* (New York: Free Press, 2001). See also David Aaker and Alexander Biel, *Brand Equity and Advertising* (Hillsdale, NJ: Erlbaum, 1993).

11. "The Best Global Brands," *BusinessWeek* (August 6, 2001).

Chapter 5: Boot Camp: Building Your Talent Base

1. For discussions of intellectual capability, see A. Brooking, *Intellectual Capital: Core Asset for the Third Millennium Enterprise* (London: Thomson Business Press, 1996); L. Edvinsson and M. Malone, *Intellectual Capital: Realizing Your Company's True Value by Finding Its Hidden Brainpower* (New York: HarperCollins, 1997); Hubert Saint-Onge, "Tacit Knowledge: The Key to the Strategic Alignment of Intellectual Capital," *Strategy and Leadership* (March/April 1996): 10–14; Ernst & Young, Skandia AFS, "Balanced Annual Report on Intellectual

Capital 1993," working paper (Stockholm, 1993); Thomas Stewart, *Intellectual Capital* (New York: Doubleday, 1997).

2. Thomas Stewart, "Accounting Gets Radical," *Fortune* (April 16, 2001): pp. 184–194.

3. Andrew Osterland, "Knowledge Capital Scorecard: Treasures Revealed," *CFO Magazine* (April 1, 2001): pp. 32–35.

4. We will not attempt to replicate the excellent work by the McKinsey team on the war for talent. Instead, we offer a set of guidelines and tools that complement it, that leaders can use to ensure their supply of talent.

5. Dave Ulrich, "Intellectual capital = Competence × Commitment," *Sloan Management Review,* vol. 39, no. 2 (Winter 1998): 15–26.

6. We have argued this position before; see Dave Ulrich, Jack Zenger, and Norm Smallwood, *Results-Based Leadership* (Boston: Harvard Business School Press, 1999). No one source captures the "competency" movement, but we build on the work of Bob Eichinger and Mike Lombardo, *The Leadership Machine* (Minneapolis, MN: Lominger, 2001). We also draw on one of our articles: Jim Intagliata, Dave Ulrich, and Norm Smallwood, "Leveraging Leadership Competencies to Produce Leadership Brand: Creating Distinctiveness by Focusing on Strategy and Results," *Human Resource Planning Journal* (September/October 2000): 12–23.

7. The focus on turning generic competencies into tailored ones is a major theme of our work on results-based leadership. In this work, specific behaviors link to desired results with the "so that" question (see Chapter 11 on leadership brand). See note 6, Ulrich, Zenger, and Smallwood.

8. In this step, we have used competency models from leading companies (such as General Electric) to stimulate thinking about what social competencies are required for the future. We have also used lists of competencies created by Lominger (conveniently provided in the company's "Career Architect" card deck), which provides a thorough overview of 67 competencies leaders might possess.

9. Work on training for impact comes from David van Adelsberg and Edward Trolley, *Running Training Like a Business: Delivering Unmistakable Value* (San Francisco: Berrett-Koehler, 1999); Jill Casner-Lotto, ed., *Successful Training Strategies* (San Francisco: Jossey-Bass, 1988); and Al Vicere, ed., *Peterson's Executive Education* (Princeton, NJ: Peterson's Guides, 1989).

10. For experience in globalization, see Stewart Black, Hal Gregerson, Mark Mendenhall, and Linda Stroh, *Globalizing People through International Assignments* (Reading, MA: Addison Wesley, 1999). For general adaptability, see Michael Lombardo and Robert Eichinger, *The Leadership Machine* (Minneapolis, MN: Lominger, 2001).

11. Rodger Griffeth and Peter Hom, *Retaining Valued Employees* (Thousand Oaks, CA: Sage, 2001).

12. Many of the ideas on employee commitment come from conversations with Anthony Rucci, executive vice president at Cardinal Health. He has made a number of presentations on commitment versus loyalty versus satisfaction and we draw on his ideas for this discussion. See Anthony Rucci, Steven P. Kirn, and Richard T. Quinn, "Employee Customer Profit Chain at Sears," *Harvard Business Review* (April 15, 2000): 16–32.

13. Work on environmental effects has come from Robert Levering, *A Great Place to Work: What Makes Some Employers So Good . . . and Most So Bad* (New York: Random House, 1988).

14. The employee-customer relationship comes from work by Dave Ulrich, Richard Halbrook, Dave Meder, and Mark Stuchlik, "Employee and Customer Attachment: Synergies for Competitive Advantage," *Human Resource Planning,* vol. 14, no. 2 (1991): 89–102; B. Schneider and D. E. Bowen, "Employee and Customer Perceptions of Service in Banks: Replication and Extension," *Journal of Applied Psychology,* vol. 70 (1985): 423–433; and Benjamin Schneider and David E. Bowen, *Winning the Service Game* (Cambridge, MA: Harvard University Press, 1995).

15. Charles Fombrun, *Reputation: Realizing the Value of Corporate Image* (Boston: Harvard Business School Press, 1996).

16. A number of authors have proposed commitment or engagement indices. Here are some examples: Marcus Buckingham and Curt Coffman, *First Break All the Rules* (New York: Simon & Schuster, 2000); Marcus Buckingham and Donald Clifton, *Now, Discover Your Strengths* (New York: Free Press, 2001). Aon Consulting firm offers a United States@work-2000 study that offers commitment indices for managing commitment, available from http://www.aon.com/about/publications/work/atwork_us2001.asp and Mercer Consulting firm also has a commitment index available from http://www.wmmercer.com/search/index_sitesrch.asp.

17. A large body of academic research and popular press perspectives discuss the antecedents of commitment. For example, see Michael Malley,

Creating Commitment: How to Attract and Retain Talented Employees by Building Relationships That Last (New York: Wiley, 2000); Charles O'Reilly, "Culture as Social Control: Corporations, Cults, and Commitment," *Research in Organizational Behavior,* vol. 18 (1996): 13–17; Denise Rousseau, *Psychological Contracts in Organizations: Understanding Written and Unwritten Rules* (Thousand Oaks, CA: Sage, 1995); Jon Katzenbach, *Peak Performance: Aligning the Hearts and Minds of Your Employees* (Boston: Harvard Business School Press, 2000); Charles O'Reilly and Jeffrey Pfeffer, *Hidden Value: How Great Companies Achieve Extraordinary Results with Ordinary People* (Boston: Harvard Business School Press, 2001); John Meyer and Natalie Jean Allen, *Commitment in the Workplace: Theory, Research, and Application* (Thousand Oaks, CA: Sage, 2000).

18. Our work on commitment comes from collaboration with Anthony Rucci. He was instrumental in defining the concept, terms, and managerial actions. We are indebted to him for his contribution and hope we represent his ideas accurately.

19. Lynda Gratton, *Living Strategy: Putting People at the Heart of Corporate Purpose* (London: Financial Times, 2000).

Chapter 6: Shared Mindset: Creating Unity from the Outside In

1. For more on many of the ideas in this chapter, see Dave Ulrich, Ron Ashkenas, and Steve Kerr, *The General Electric Work-Out* (New York: McGraw-Hill, 2002); and Dave Ulrich, "Culture Change: Will We Recognize It When We See It?" *Managing Strategic and Cultural Change in Organizations,* ed. Craig Schneier (New York: Human Resource Planning Society, 1995).

2. Gordon Bethune and Scott Huler, *From Worst to First: Behind the Scenes of Continental's Remarkable Comeback* (New York: Wiley, 1999).

3. J. Willard Marriott, Jim Collins, Kathi Ann Brown, and Adrian Zackheim, *The Spirit to Serve Marriott's Way* (New York: HarperCollins, 2001).

4. Hugh De Pree, *Business as Unusual: The People and Principles at Herman Miller* (Holland, MI: Herman Miller, 1986); Max De Pree and James O'Toole, *Leadership Is an Art* (New York: Doubleday, 1989).

5. Michael Dell and Catherine Fredman, *Direct from Dell: Strategies That Revolutionized an Industry* (New York: HarperCollins, 2000).

6. Kevin Freiberg, Jackie Freiberg, and Tom Peters, *Nuts! Southwest Airlines' Crazy Recipe for Business and Personal Success* (New York: Doubleday, 1998).

7. See work on culture as shared mindset from John Kotter and James Heskett, *Corporate Culture and Performance* (New York: Free Press, 1992); Kwok On Yeung, "Cognitive Consensuality and Organizational Performance: A Systematic Assessment" (Ph.D. dissertation, University of Michigan, Ann Arbor, 1990).

8. Dave Ulrich, "Blurring the Inside Out and Outside In," *Leading Beyond Walls: Effective Partnerships, Practices, and Perspectives,* eds. Frances Hesselbein, Marshall Goldsmith, and Iain Somerville (San Francisco: Jossey-Bass, 1999).

9. Joseph Wayne Brockbank and Dave Ulrich, "Avoiding SPOTS: Creating Strategic Unity," *Handbook of Business Strategy 1990,* ed. H. Glass (New York: Gorham, Lambert, 1991).

10. We use the phrase *touch points* for what others might call "moments of truth," as in Jans Carlzon and Tom Peters, *Moments of Truth* (New York: HarperCollins, 1989), or "customer experience," as in Joseph Pine, James Gillmore, and Joseph Pine II, *The Experience Economy* (Boston: Harvard Business School Press, 1999).

11. For more on this work on culture change and making it real to every employee, see note 1.

12. We appreciate work by Gordon Hewitt on this framework and hope our use complements his creative thinking.

13. See note 2, pp. 25–27.

14. R. L. Daft and R. H. Lengel, "Information Richness: A New Approach to Managerial Behavior and Organization Design," *Research in Organizational Behavior,* eds. Larry Cummings and Barry Staw, vol. 6 (New York: JAI Press, 1984), pp. 191–233; and R. L. Daft and G. P. Huber, "How Organizations Learn: A Communication Framework," *Research in the Sociology of Organizations,* vol. 5 (1987): 1–36.

15. Alexandra Reed Lajoux and Charles Elson, *The Art of M&A Due Diligence* (New York: McGraw-Hill, 2000).

Chapter 7: Speed: First Beats Best

1. The "new business" world and its realities are captured in many articles and books. James Gleick, *Faster: The Acceleration of Just about*

Everything (New York: Random House, 1999), provides a good introduction to the topic.

2. Stanley Davis and Christopher Meyer, *Blur: The Speed of Change in the Connected Economy* (Reading, MA: Addison Wesley, 1998); Richard Pascale, Mark Millemann, and Linda Gioja, *Surfing on the Edge of Chaos: The Laws of Nature and the New Laws of Business* (New York: Random House, 2000).

3. Work on bureaucracy definition comes from Dave Ulrich, Ron Ashkenas, and Steve Kerr, *The General Electric Work-Out* (New York: McGraw-Hill, 2002).

4. Many were involved in the GoFast! design and delivery. AT Kearney was represented by partners Bram Bluestein and Laura Sue D'Annunzio. The program also included a number of external consultants—Dave Ulrich, Dick Beatty, Jon Biel, Wayne Brockbank, Pan Dennis, Laurie Dodd, Ron Gager, Duke Hernandez, Bill Joyce, Aviva Kleinbaum, Dale Lake, Don Parker, and Craig Schneier—as well as internal GM employees Nancy Bennett and Katy Barclay.

5. For a review of the General Electric program, see Dave Ulrich, Ron Ashkenas, and Steve Kerr, *The General Electric Work-Out* (New York: McGraw-Hill, 2002).

6. The General Electric Change Acceleration Model (CAP) was crafted with input from those inside General Electric (Jacquie Vierling, Amy Howard, Jim Baughman) and external consultants (Steve Kerr, Jon Biel, Ron Gager, Ron Ashkenas, and Dave Ulrich). It has been described and applied in Dave Ulrich, *Human Resource Champions* (Boston: Harvard Business School Press, 1997); and Brian Becker, Mark Huselid, and Dave Ulrich, *The HR Scorecard* (Boston: Harvard Business School Press, 2001).

7. The information in this paragraph and the following list comes from conversations with Steve Kerr, who was chief learning officer at General Electric and the primary architect of the CAP and change processes.

8. Craig Schneier, Dick Beatty, Ron Gager, and Jon Biel were instrumental in adapting the work from General Electric to General Motors.

9. The know-do transition has been discussed elegantly in Jeffrey Pfeffer and Robert Sutton, *The Knowing-Doing Gap* (Boston: Harvard Business School Press, 2000).

10. The GM ChangeFast tool kit was crafted by Craig Schneier with help from many of his colleagues.

Chapter 8: Learning: Changing the Game

1. Many of the ideas presented here on organization learning capability come from work synthesized in Arthur Yeung, Dave Ulrich, Stephen Nason, and Mary Ann Von Glinow, *Organization Learning Capability: Generating and Generalizing Ideas with Impact* (Oxford, England: Oxford University Press, 1999).

2. Ikujiro Nonaka, Hirotaka Tekeuchi, and Hiro Tekeuchi, *The Knowledge-Creating Company* (New York: Oxford University Press, 1995).

3. For more detail, see note 1.

4. Now at Goldman Sachs.

Chapter 9: Accountability: Making Teamwork Work

1. Steve Kerr, "On the Folly of Hoping for A While Rewarding B," *Academy of Management Journal,* vol 18 (1995): 769–783.

2. We draw heavily on work by Steve Kerr throughout this chapter. Much of this from personal correspondence with Steve Kerr, but other insights are "Some Characteristics and Consequences of Organization Reward," *Facilitating Work Effectiveness,* eds. David Schoorman and Benjamin Schneider (Boston: Lexington Press, 1989); "Risky Business: The New Pay Game," *Fortune* (June 22, 1996): 94–98; *Ultimate Rewards: What Really Motivates People to Achieve* (Boston: Harvard Business Press, 1997).

3. Ironically, we discovered that both authors have daughters who have the same challenge with room cleaning. This case is clearly not directed at any one child, but might apply to many. And, as our children point out so insightfully, even we as parents may have cleaning disabilities from time to time.

4. We have drawn the phrase *strategic clarity* and associated ideas from many sources, including Eliyahu Goldratt and Jeff Cox, *The Goal: A Process of On-Going Improvement* (New Haven, CT: North River Press, 1986); Eliyahu Goldratt, *It's Not Luck* (New Haven, CT: North River Press, 1994); and James Ritchie and Hal Robbino, *Managing from Clarity: Identifying, Aligning, and Leveraging Strategic Resources* (New York: Wiley, 2001).

5. Gary Hamel and C. K. Prahalad, *Competing for the Future* (Boston: Harvard Business School Press, 1996).

6. Work at Sears is described in Anthony Rucci, Steven Kirn, and Richard Quinn, "The Employee-Customer-Profit Chain at Sears," *Harvard Business Review* (January/February, 1998): 82–99; and James O'Shea and Charles Madigan, *Dangerous Company: Management Consultants and the Businesses They Save and Ruin* (New York: Penguin, 1998).

7. The work on measurement comes a great deal from the performance management literature. We have drawn on work from Edward Lawler and John Rhode, *Information and Control in Organizations* (Pacific Palisades, CA: Goodyear, 1976); John Bernardin and Richard Beatty, *Performance Appraisal: Assessing Human Behavior at Work* (Boston: Kent, 1984); Erwin Rausch, *Win-Win Performance Management Appraisal: A Problem-Solving Approach* (New York: Wiley Interscience, 1985); Allan Mohrman, Susan Resnick-West, and Edward Lawler, *Designing Performance Appraisal Systems* (San Francisco: Jossey-Bass, 1989); Geary Rummler and Alan Brache, *Improving Performance: How to Management the White Space on the Organization Chart* (San Francisco: Jossey-Bass, 1990); Howard Risher and Charles Fay, eds., *The Performance Imperative: Strategies for Enhancing Workforce Effectiveness* (San Francisco: Jossey-Bass, 1995); Richard Beatty, Lloyd Baird, and Craig Schneier, eds., *Performance Management, Measurement, and Appraisal Sourcebook* (Amherst, MA: Human Resource Development Press, 1995); and James Smither, ed., *Performance Appraisal: The State of the Art in Practice* (San Francisco: Jossey-Bass, 1998).

8. There are many excellent sources for better understanding compensation. Some we rely on include George Milkovich and Jerry Newman, *Compensation* (New York: McGraw-Hill, 1998)—probably the classic text on compensation theory and practice, now in its sixth edition—as well as Thomas B. Wilson, *Innovative Reward Systems for the Changing Workplace* (New York: McGraw-Hill, 1995); Thomas B. Wilson, *Rewards That Drive High Performance* (New York: AMACOM, 1999); Jay R. Schuster and Patricia Zingheim, *The New Pay: Linking Employee and Organizational Performance* (San Francisco: Jossey-Bass, 1992); and Patricia Zingheim and Jay Schuster, *Pay People Right: Breakthrough Strategies to Create Great Companies* (San Francisco: Jossey-Bass, 2000).

9. Lyle Spencer has consistently made the argument that the standard deviations on employee contribution show that high performers deliver significantly more value to the firm than average performers. See Lyle M.

Spencer Jr., *Calculating Human Resource Costs and Benefits* (New York: Wiley, 1986); and Lyle M. Spencer Jr., *Competence at Work: Models for Superior Performance* (New York: Wiley, 1995).

10. The work on what job content drives employee motivation has a long history:

1890s: Frederick Taylor's development of scientific management.

1900s: Max Weber's concept of bureaucracy and the Protestant ethic.

1910s: Walter Cannon's discovery of the "emergency (stress) response."

1920s: Elton Mayo's illumination studies in the textile industry; The Hawthorne studies at Western Electric Company.

1930s: Kurt Lewin's, Ronald Lippitt's, and Ralph White's early leadership studies.

1940s: Abraham Maslow's need hierarchy motivation theory; B. F. Skinner's formulation of the behavioral approach; Charles Walker's and Robert Guest's studies of routine work.

1950s: Ralph Stogdill's Ohio State leadership studies; Douglas McGregor's examination of the human side of enterprise; Frederick Herzberg's two-factor theory of motivation and job enrichment.

1960s: Arthur Turner's and Paul Lawrence's studies of diverse industrial jobs; Robert Blake's and Jane Mouton's managerial grid; Patricia Cain Smith's studies of satisfaction in work and retirement; Fred Fiedler's contingency theory of leadership.

1970s: J. Richard Hackman's and Greg Oldham's job characteristics theory; Edward Lawler's approach to pay and organizational effectiveness; Robert House's path–goal and charismatic theories of leadership.

1980s: Peter Block's political skills for empowered managers; Charles Manz's approach to self-managed work teams; Edgar Schein's approach to leadership and organizational culture.

This history is found at http://www.swcollege.com/management /nelson-quick/uob1e/AppendixA.doc. For an elegant discussion of the work up to its own time, see Richard Hackman and Greg Oldham, *Work Redesign* (Reading, MA: Addison-Wesley, 1980).

11. Alfie Kohn, *Punished by Rewards: The Trouble with Gold Stars, Incentive Plans, A's, Praise, and Other Bribes* (New York: Houghton Mifflin, 1999).

12. Bob Nelson, *1001 Ways to Reward Employees* (New York: Workman, 1994); Bob Nelson, *1001 Ways to Energize Employees* (New York: Workman, 1997).

13. The *Reward Diagnostic* is a product of Global Consulting Alliance. It is created and designed by Steve Kerr, Warren Wilhelm, and Toni Pristo. It is available from http://www.globalconsultalliance.com/.

14. The concept of focusing on what people do rather than what they don't is close to work by Kenneth Blanchard, *The One Minute Manager* (New York: Morrow, 1982).

15. Some excellent work on feedback for change is in James Prochaska, John Norcross, and Carlo Diclemente, *Changing for Good: A Revolutionary Six Stage Program for Overcoming Bad Habits and Moving Your Life Forward Positively* (New York: Avon Books, 1995).

16. Peter Drucker, *The Principles of Management* (New York: Harper-Collins, 1954).

17. We credit Marshall Goldsmith with teaching us much about feedback through personal conversations, lectures, and writing. He alerted us to the importance of focusing forward, not backward. See Marshall Goldsmith, Laurence Lyons, Alyssa Freas, and Robert Witherspoon, eds., *Coaching for Greatness: How the World's Greatest Coaches Help Leaders Learn* (San Francisco: Jossey-Bass, 2000).

18. Marshall Goldsmith quote cited online. Available from http://www.ccl.org/connected/enews/articles/0401goldsmith.htm.

19. Our personal conversations with Marshall Goldsmith have informed us a great deal about how to think about feedback. He does one exercise that is marvelous. He asks people to rate themselves in the top 2 percent, 5 percent, 10 percent, 20 percent, 30 percent, or 50 percent of their profession. Inevitably, people rate themselves high. And the less immediate feedback the profession provides, the more its successful members over-rate themselves—medical doctors who receive no formal feedback routinely regard themselves as being at the top of their field, whereas baseball players whose statistics are public domain generally know quite realistically where they stand.

20. The 360-degree feedback instrument has been used extensively. Some references include Jack Zenger and Joe Folkman, *The Extraordinary Leader* (New York: McGraw-Hill, 2002); Michelle Leduff Collins, *The Thin Book of 360-Degree Feedback: A Managers Guide* (New York:

AMACOM, 2001); Warren Shaver, *Info-Line: How to Build and Use a 360-Degree Feedback System* (Alexandria, VA: ASTD, 1995); and Mark Edwards and Ann Ewen, *360-Degree Feedback: The Powerful New Model for Employee Assessment and Performance Improvement* (New York: AMACOM, 1996).

Chapter 10: Collaboration: It Takes More than Two to Intangible

1. Paul Lawrence and Jay Lorsch, *Organization and Environment: Managing Differentiation and Integration* (Homewood, IL: Richard D. Irwin, 1973).

2. A. D. Chandler, *Strategy and Structure: Chapters in the History of the American Industrial Enterprise* (Cambridge, MA: MIT Press, 1962); A. D. Chandler, *The Visible Hand: The Managerial Revolution in American Business* (Cambridge, MA: Harvard University Press, 1977).

3. *Optimize Magazine* has only had a few issues, but each has carried at least one article on strategic collaboration: See C. K. Prahalad and Venkatram Ramaswamy, "The Collaboration Continuum," no. 1 (November 2001); Michael Treacy and David Dobrin, "Make Progress in Small Steps," no. 2 (December 2001); and Robert Carter, "Trusted Partners at Fed Ex," no. 3 (January 2002). (Note: This entire issue is dedicated to "collaborative business" with a focus on IT solutions to collaboration.)

4. Marianne Kolbasuk McGee and Chris Murphy, "Innovators in Collaboration," *Information Week* (December 10, 2001): 16–19.

5. Much has been written on mergers and acquisitions, including Donald DePamphilis, *Mergers, Acquisitions, and Other Restructuring Activities: An Integrated Approach to Process, Tools, Cases and Solutions* (New York: Academic Press, 2001); Fred Weston and Samuel Weaver, *Mergers and Acquisitions* (New York: McGraw-Hill, 2001); and Michael Hitt, Jeffrey Harrison, and Duane Ireland, *Mergers and Acquisitions: A Guide to Creating Value for Stakeholders* (New York: Oxford University Press, 2001).

6. Mark Sirower, *The Synergy Trap: How Companies Lose the Acquisition Game* (New York: Free Press, 1997).

7. Cited in Toby Tetenbaum, "Beating the Odds of Merger and Acquisition Failure: Seven Key Practices That Improve the Chance for Expected Integration and Synergies," *Organizational Dynamics* (August 1999): 22–28. Merger information is also found in Ronald Ashkenas, Lawrence

DeMonaco, and Suzanne Francis, "Making the Deal Real: How General Electric Capital Integrates Acquisitions," *Harvard Business Review* (January/February 1998): 165–178; and Debra Sparks, "Partners," *BusinessWeek* (October 25, 1999): 106–112.

8. News release from the Conference Board (October 3, 2000). Available from http://www.conference-board.org/search/dpress.cfm?pressid=4591.

9. Gary Hamel and C. K. Prahalad, *Competing for the Future* (Boston: Harvard Business School Press, 1996).

10. See Thomas Freidman, *The Lexus and the Olive Tree: Understanding Globalization* (New York: Anchor Books, 2000); and Patrick O'Meara, Howard Mehlinger, and Matthew Krain, eds., *Globalization and the Challenges of the New Century: A Reader* (Bloomington: Indiana University Press, 2000).

11. We draw extensively on J. Stewart Black and Dave Ulrich, "The New Frontier of Global HR," *The Global HR Manager: Creating the Seamless Organization,* eds. Pat Joynt and Bob Morton (London: Institute of Personnel Development, 1999), pp. 12–38.

12. J. Stewart Black, Allen Morrison, and Hal Gregerson, *Global Explorers: The Next Generation of Leaders* (New York: Routledge, 1999).

13. Richard Branson, *Losing My Virginity: How I've Survived, Had Fun and Made a Fortune Doing Business My Way* (New York: Time Books, 1999).

14. For some of the extensive literature that's begun to emerge on the topic, see Donniel Schulman, Martin Harmer, John Dunleavy, and James Lusk, *Shared Services: Adding Value to the Business Units* (New York: Wiley, 1999); Barbara Quinn, Andrew Kris, and Robert Cooke, *Shared Services: Mining for Corporate Gold* (London: Financial Times, 2000); and Dave Ulrich, "Shared Services: Reengineering the HR Function," *Human Resource Planning Journal,* vol. 18, no. 3 (1995): 12–24.

Chapter 11: Collaboration: It Takes More than Two to Intangible

1. *BusinessWeek* has written for the last decade about sources of future talent, identifying McKinsey and General Electric as two of the most productive seedbeds. See John Byrne, "The McKinsey Mystique," *BusinessWeek* (September 20, 1993); John Byrne and Jennifer Reingold, "Wanted: A Few Good CEOs," *BusinessWeek* (August 11, 1997); and Anthony Bianco, "The New Leadership," *BusinessWeek* (August 28, 2000).

2. We have made the argument for a new definition of leadership in Dave Ulrich, Jack Zenger, and Norm Smallwood, *Results-Based Leadership* (Boston: Harvard Business School Press, 1999).

3. See note 2.

4. James Kouzes and Barry Posner, *The Leadership Challenge,* 3rd ed. (San Francisco: Jossey-Bass, 2002).

5. Some of the most interesting recent work on leadership attributes comes from James Collins, *Good to Great: Why Some Companies Make the Leap and Others Don't* (New York: HarperCollins, 2001); Susan Gebelein, Lisa Stevens, Carol Skube, and David Lee, *Successful Manager's Handbook* (Minneapolis, MN: Personnel Decisions, 2000); and Michael Lombardo and Robert Eichinger, *The Leadership Machine* (Minneapolis, MN: Lominger, 2001).

6. From letter to Share Owners by John F. Welch, Jr., Paolo Fresco, and John D. Opie, General Electric annual report for 1995.

7. To answer these questions, we draw on work from James Bolt, *Executive Development: A Strategy for Corporate Competitiveness* (New York: Ballinger, 1989); Albert Vicere, ed., *Executive Education: Process, Practice, and Evaluation* (Princeton, NJ: Peterson's Guides, 1989); and Robert Fulmer and Marshall Goldsmith, *The Leadership Investment: How the World's Best Organizations Gain Strategic Advantage through Leadership Development* (New York: American Management Association, 2001).

8. Donald Kirkpatrick, *Evaluating Training Programs: The Four Levels* (San Francisco: Berrett-Koehler, 1998).

9. David van Adelsberg and Edward Trolley, *Running Training Like a Business: Delivering Unmistakable Value* (San Francisco: Berrett-Koehler, 1999).

10. Cynthia McCauley, Russ Moxley, and Ellen Van Velsor, eds., *The Center for Creative Leadership Handbook of Leadership Development* (San Francisco: Jossey-Bass, 1998).

11. Bob Eichinger and Mike Lombardo, *The Leadership Machine* (Minneapolis, MN: Lominger Associates, 2001).

Chapter 12: Tangible Intangibles: Winning the Game

1. Peter Tanous, *Investment Gurus: A Road Map to Wealth from the World's Best Money Managers* (New York: New York Institute of Finance, 1997).

Index